of Best

Practice in Clinical Audit

New Principles of Best Practice in Clinical Audit

SECOND EDITION

Edited by

ROBIN BURGESS

Chief Executive
Healthcare Quality Improvement Partnership

Healthcare Quality
Improvement Partnership

Radcliffe Publishing
London • New York

Radcliffe Publishing Ltd
St Mark's House
Shepherdess Walk
London N1 7BQ
United Kingdom

www.radcliffehealth.com
Electronic catalogue and worldwide online ordering facility.

First Edition 2002

Robin Burgess has asserted his right under the Copyright, Designs and Patents Act 1998 to be identified as the author of this work.

British Library Cataloguing in Publication Data

A catalogue record for this book is available from the British Library.

ISBN-13: 978 184619 221 0

The paper used for the text pages of this book is FSC® certified. FSC (The Forest Stewardship Council®) is an international network to promote responsible management of the world's forests.

Typeset by Pindar NZ, Auckland, New Zealand
Printed and bound by TJI Digital, Padstow, Cornwall, UK

Contents

About the editor

Robin Burgess BD (Hons), AKC, CQSW
Chief Executive, HQIP

Robin Burgess joined the Healthcare Quality Improvement Partnership (HQIP) when it was set up in 2008. He has worked for over 20 years in managing public sector health and social care, and in governmental policy roles in the UK. He has written or edited over 20 guidance manuals on various aspects of public sector delivery, mostly in the area of management of addiction problems.

List of contributors

Chapters 2 to 5

Stephen Ashmore BA (Hons)
CASC Director

Tracy Ruthven MSc Managing Quality in Healthcare
CASC Director

Louise Hazelwood Advanced Diploma in Therapeutic Counselling
CASC Associate

The Clinical Audit Support Centre (CASC) was established in 2006. The centre is based in Leicester, although CASC works across the UK and internationally to help healthcare professionals to deliver best practice in clinical audit and quality assurance. Since its inception, CASC has extended its work programme and the centre now supports patient surveys, specialises in risk management techniques, facilitates educational events for clinicians and delivers accredited training courses. CASC has a track record of instigating and supporting projects that raise standards and improve the delivery of patient care.

Appendices

Nancy Dixon Fellow, National Association for Healthcare Quality (USA), FCQI (UK), Certified Professional in Healthcare Quality (USA), MA, BSC
Managing Director, Healthcare Quality Quest Ltd
Nancy Dixon is a specialist in measuring and improving the quality and safety of healthcare services. She regularly teaches clinicians and others how to undertake clinical audit, quality improvement, risk assessment, root cause analysis and governance properly. She designs and manages complex or large clinical audits and quality improvement projects. Nancy develops evidence-based policies in this field and serves as a consultant to healthcare organisations on quality and patient safety improvement. She has written articles, books and manuals on quality-related subjects, managed large-scale quality assurance programmes for large health organisations, and served as a board member for healthcare quality professional organisations.

Dr Christopher Loughlan PhD, MEd, BSc, Cert Ed, Dip Ed
Executive Director, Cambridge Institute of Research, Education and Management
Chris is the founding member and executive director of the Cambridge Institute of
Research, Education and Management (CIREM), a leading independent research
and evaluation consultancy in the UK. He has held senior positions in the NHS
both in Scotland and in England, and latterly was Head of Research and Labour
Market Intelligence for the UK Health Sector Skills Council. He is a Visiting Fellow
in Enterprise and Entrepreneurship at Anglia Ruskin University, and a Fellow of the
National Council for Graduate Entrepreneurship. His current role includes Interim
Project Director for the NHS Health Innovation and Education Collaboration in the
East of England.

Kate Godfrey MSc
National Lead for Local Quality Improvement, Healthcare Quality Improvement
Partnership
Kate is the National Lead for Local Quality Improvement at the Healthcare Quality
Improvement Partnership (HQIP). She has worked in healthcare regulation both as
an area manager for the Healthcare Commission and as a Commission for Health
Improvement (CHI) clinical governance review manager. Prior to that Kate was an
assistant director for clinical governance at an acute trust. She has a background in
nursing, and an MSc in the Evaluation of Clinical Practice.

Dr John Bullivant FCQI, PhD
Director, Good Governance Institute
John Bullivant is the founding director of the Good Governance Institute (GGI). He
is a visiting fellow at the Open University Business School and the Welsh Institute
for Health and Social Care. John has worked in the NHS, central and local government, criminal justice, and for the Audit Commission and a number of consultancy,
research, legal and audit organisations. He has undertaken a number of formal governance reviews, and has co-authored the *Integrated Governance Handbook* (Department
of Health, 2006), *Governance Between Organisations* (Good Governance Institute,
2008), *Integrated Governance* (Healthcare Financial Management Association, 2008),
Clinical Audit: a guide for NHS boards and partners (Healthcare Quality Improvement
Partnership, 2010) and *Governing the New NHS: issues and tensions in health service
policy, governance and management* (Routledge, 2010).

Andrew Corbett-Nolan CQP, BA (Hons) Ebor, MHSM, FSoc Purch, FCQI
Director, Good Governance Institute
Andrew has worked in healthcare for 25 years at local, regional and national levels
in the NHS, not-for-profit and commercial sectors. He has worked for US corporate
organisations and in public hospitals in South Africa. Andrew has interests in quality, risk and governance, and has held various executive and non-executive posts,
including being on the board of a London NHS Foundation Trust and Vice Chair of
the AIDS charity, the Terrence Higgins Trust. He is a Fellow of the Open University
Business School and is widely published in the field of healthcare management.

How to use this book

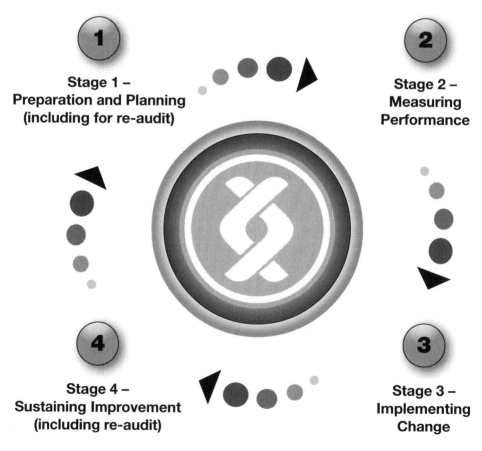

FIGURE A The clinical audit cycle. (Reproduced with permission from HQIP.)

WHAT IS CLINICAL AUDIT?

Clinical audit is a quality improvement cycle that involves measurement of the effectiveness of healthcare against agreed and proven standards for high quality, and taking action to bring practice in line with these standards so as to improve the quality of care and health outcomes.

By following the cycle, any clinician or team should be able to see where their practice can be improved against given benchmarks, to take action, and then to re-measure and make further improvements. Whether conducted by an individual on their own clinical work, for a whole clinical team or unit, or nationally by comparing providers in different organisations against each other, it is the same process. Its purpose is to drive up standards of quality and to achieve better outcomes.

Clinical audit is a systematic process with stages that need to be worked through in order to ensure that it improves care. Chapters 2 to 5 explain this process, offering detailed guidance for each stage.

Although the term 'clinical audit' is not used in all countries (notably the USA, where it is normally referred to as 'chart audit'), the process that is described here as being clinical audit, namely the assessment of clinical practice against standards, is followed universally, and this book provides a manual of best practice for this activity.

WHY SHOULD YOU READ THIS BOOK?

Clinical audit is a process designed to improve quality in healthcare. This book provides a manual on how to undertake clinical audit, either as an individual or as part of a larger team or organisation.

Every healthcare professional and healthcare team, in every country, as well as patients, prospective patients, managers and commissioners, should want to ensure that they provide or receive the best possible care. They should want to ensure that the service offered is in line with best practice standards which are likely to have the most impact on the healthcare problem involved.

In some health jurisdictions, clinical audit is a mandatory requirement, either for an organisation or for an individual clinician. Clinical audit offers a proven and reliable method of demonstrating that treatment and care provided are in line with best practice and are likely to, or do, lead to better outcomes. Clinical audit can help to improve patient safety, reduce infection rates, and identify and prevent errors. By improving the effectiveness and efficiency of care, clinical audit can contribute to saving money and simplifying procedures.

In the UK, participating in clinical audit is a requirement for any doctor, as set out in the General Medical Council guidance, *Good Medical Practice*.[1]

THE PURPOSE OF THIS BOOK

This book makes extensive use of work led by the Healthcare Quality Improvement Partnership (HQIP) in England. HQIP has been given responsibility for reinvigorating clinical audit by the Department of Health in England, but the views contained in this book represent the views of HQIP or individual authors, and not the Department of Health.

This book is a revision and a reinterpretation of the classic text on clinical audit, *Principles of Best Practice in Clinical Audit*,[2] which was first published in 2002 under the aegis of the UK's National Institute for Health and Clinical Excellence (NICE), which at that time had responsibility for clinical audit in England. Since then this book has come to be regarded as the key text that describes best practice in clinical audit.

This new edition, which is written for **both** a UK **and** an international audience, sets out:

➤ the purpose of clinical audit
➤ the continuing value of clinical audit in a changing world of healthcare
➤ some key issues of context for audit practice and how audit relates to these
➤ the core practical methodology of clinical audit, making clear how to conduct an audit project
➤ the key principles of audit practice.

WHO THE BOOK IS FOR

This book is aimed at anyone who uses clinical audit or who is interested in it as a quality improvement methodology.

This can include:

➤ specialists in clinical audit and related quality improvement processes
➤ clinicians (by which we mean **all** healthcare professionals, as clinical audit, although it developed from within medicine, is applicable to all healthcare disciplines) carrying out clinical audit
➤ researchers, commissioners, regulators and managers, both of services as a whole and of quality improvement activity in particular. It is applicable to both national and local clinical audit, although it is of most value to the latter
➤ patients who are interested in audit or who participate in some way, who will find it a useful guide.

This book is designed for use both by individuals and by healthcare teams, perhaps containing several professional disciplines. Much of what is written sets out necessary processes that should be followed both by an individual carrying out a solo clinical audit and by a team in a larger organisation. Some sections are written primarily for the latter, in recognition that clinical audit is very often a team process within larger organisations.

There are some clinicians who cannot always take part in organisational or team audits – locums, for example, or sole general practitioners or family doctors. This does not mean that individual clinical audit is not possible, and this book's methods are still applicable to solo workers. Individual clinicians who want to conduct clinical audit should not feel that without the support of large teams and specialist audit staff they cannot carry out excellent clinical audits. Following the recommended processes set out here, and making use of the various resources available from HQIP, professional bodies or other organisations, individual clinicians can undertake good clinical audits that will improve their practice.

However, in general, individual clinicians should try to conduct audits that are linked to the organisation in which they practise, wherever this is possible. This is particularly true of junior doctors, who are often required by their qualification body to undertake clinical audit as a required part of their training, to learn the relevance of clinical audit to their future professional role. Any audit that is conducted in these circumstances should be discussed with their host organisation. It need not be undertaken without help or entirely independently. There are resources available on the HQIP website and, in the UK, from the Royal College of Physicians, to support junior doctor audit so that it is much more than an individual effort, and has much more value.

Although it will be of particular value to those working in the UK, this new volume is designed to be applicable for use worldwide, and it seeks to present views, discussion and definitive guidance on processes and issues that are international and integral to clinical audit practice and thinking everywhere. We have used references to the UK or English system of healthcare where these are illustrative of wider issues or are specifically relevant, but wherever possible we have strived to make this book usable in any healthcare setting. This includes healthcare in developing countries where a supporting infrastructure for clinical audit activity, that is available, for example, in the UK or the USA, may not be present.

WHY CONDUCT A CLINICAL AUDIT INSTEAD OF AN ALTERNATIVE PROCESS?

Although clinical audit is very often the single best method of ensuring that the care which is provided is in line with best practice, it is not the only method of quality improvement and measurement available. Clinical audit is most appropriate when the intention is to assess the degree to which the **clinical** services offered comply with the highest expected standards. Other processes may have utility for other aspects of healthcare service delivery.

Clinical audit is not simply a measurement process, although sometimes, due to failure to adhere to good practice, this is what it becomes. Some other quality improvement processes rely less on the collection of data, instead focusing on changing hearts and minds without a significant data element, and other processes simply collect data without any related change programme.

Clinical audit is a **complete** cycle that uses evidence-based research, expressed in standards, as the base for its process, but after measuring compliance with those standards, good clinical audit should **always** involve a programme of improvement to drive change.

Routine data on take-up of services, and then throughput analyses, often show a great deal about the way patients are being treated, how quickly they were seen, how many progressed through various stages of care, and a degree of information about outcomes. Analysis of routine data can reveal a lot about how effective a service area is, depending on the quality of the recording and the completeness of the record systems.

Regular review of such data is essential, but it is not **clinical** audit, because the crucial element that is missing is the comparison of what is being done against a standard. Where audit exceeds the value of these other methods is where there is a need to uncover the detail behind the basic process data, and to get to an item-by-item analysis of where care falls down against recommended standards. The most sophisticated analyses conducted through national audits permit further re-examination of the variance in healthcare delivery between units and the sometimes unrecognised reasons why treatment in some settings fails to deliver against a recommended norm.

Clinical audit is an applicable process in all areas of healthcare, but it should be used to complement other processes. Audit may be needed because those other processes point to areas of concern that require more detailed investigation. Clinical audits may be triggered by critical incidents, patient complaints, the publication of new guidelines, or awareness of poor outcomes. However, clinical audit should **mostly** be driven by awareness of the need to keep reviewing practice regardless of whether any concerns have been highlighted, because this is part of good clinical discipline, and perhaps because of awareness that it is too easy to become complacent. Such ongoing review is a part of professional clinical practice.

WHAT THIS BOOK IS NOT

This book is not a guide to the organisation of clinical audit activity at local level, nor to how it should be funded, managed and regulated within a healthcare system as a whole. Chapter 2 goes into some detail about how a specific clinical audit project can be supported and organised within a larger healthcare setting, such as a hospital, but does not discuss continuing arrangements for support of the clinical audit function within a healthcare system or organisation. The book is not about widespread organisational structures for clinical audit or national strategies, nor does it offer or review policy on healthcare improvement generally. Although Chapter 1 includes discussion of how policy provides a context for practice of clinical audit, this book is essentially a practical guide to the methodology, for people who want to conduct clinical audits. It is designed to drive the practice of clinical audit, and to make it more effective in improving healthcare.

There is extensive material on organising a clinical audit programme at the level of a local hospital, for example, on the HQIP website (www.hqip.org.uk), to which extensive reference will be made in this book.

THE STRUCTURE OF THIS BOOK

This new handbook on clinical audit has been entirely rewritten, but is derived from and follows the same basic structure as the previous edition.

There is an introductory chapter, which in this volume summarises the history of clinical audit and the current policy context and then discusses in more detail what this means for audit practice, together with consideration of issues within audit.

The core methodology of clinical audit is set out in Chapters 2 to 5, by Stephen Ashmore, Tracy Ruthven and Louise Hazelwood, and edited by HQIP.

These chapters describe the key stages of audit, and set out how to plan, structure and support the audit process at each stage. The chapters include detailed references to additional sources of material available, often online.

The Appendices support the main chapters, providing detail on key issues, namely ethical issues in clinical audit (Appendix 1, by Nancy Dixon), a discussion of the evidence for the effectiveness of clinical audit (Appendix 2, by Christopher Loughlan), change management to drive the implementation of audit results (Appendix 3, by Kate Godfrey), the criteria and indicators for best practice in clinical audit (Appendix 4, by HQIP), a summarised guide to clinical audit for managing boards of health organisations (Appendix 5, by John Bullivant and Andrew Corbett-Nolan), patient and public engagement (Appendix 6, by HQIP), further sources of guidance available to support clinical audit (Appendix 7), and a list of abbreviations (Appendix 8).

The last edition contained various appendices (and a CD) which consisted mainly of lists of contact details and checklists that were mostly relevant to the UK environment, and nearly all of which, given the pace of change in health policy and structures, rapidly became outdated. Since the emergence, in 2008 in the UK, of HQIP as the body responsible for clinical audit, working on behalf of the Department of Health in England, and the availability of such data in an easily accessible form via the Internet, a large volume of such material has already been placed on the HQIP website (www.hqip.org.uk), where it is not only more accessible, but also more easily updated.

REFERENCES

1 General Medical Council (GMC). *Good Medical Practice*. London: GMC; 2006. www.gmcuk.org/guidance/good_medical_practice/maintaining_good_medical_practice_performance.asp (accessed 2 August 2010).

2 National Institute for Health and Clinical Excellence (NICE). *Principles for Best Practice in Clinical Audit*. London: NICE; 2002.

Editor's note

In the UK, healthcare policy was devolved to governments covering Northern Ireland, Scotland and Wales in 1998. Prior to this, the Department of Health made policy for the whole of the UK. When this book refers to 'national' studies in the context of the four nations that comprise the UK, the term 'national' refers to England only for healthcare policy after 1998, and to the UK as a whole before that time.

Acknowledgements

Many people contributed to the drafting of this book and commented on the text during production. They are too many to name here, but special acknowledgement should be made of the role of HQIP staff, who contributed extensively, notably Kate Godfrey, Liz Smith, Mandy Smith and Eleanor Thomas.

CHAPTER 1

Introduction: Foundations, tradition and new directions – the future of clinical audit in a new decade

Robin Burgess

The purposes of this chapter:
- To put clinical audit into a historical and policy context.
- To discuss the key issues in clinical audit at the present time.

THE HISTORICAL POLICY CONTEXT

Clinical audit has a relatively recent history. Although the practice of comparing clinical practice against standards may go back to the nineteenth century, early steps in medical audit, as it was then known, mainly took place in the USA and in the UK from the 1970s onwards (*see*, for example, for the UK context, articles published in the *British Medical Journal* from 1980[1]). Subsequently it is in the UK that clinical audit has perhaps become most widely recognised as a distinct form of clinical quality measurement and improvement, partly as a result of being actively supported centrally within the National Health Service (NHS) system. However, it is important to emphasise that clinical audit is a quality improvement methodology that is applicable anywhere, within any healthcare system, and the revision of this book is designed to offer an impetus to the conduct of clinical audit by healthcare professionals worldwide.

Clinical audit is extensively used in the USA, albeit often not clearly identified with this title, where the term usually used is **chart audit**. It is compulsory for doctors in France,[2] is practised widely across Europe, and is established practice in Commonwealth countries (especially Australia), and now worldwide to a greater or lesser degree (as, for example, in the developing world).[3-6]

In the UK, the 1990s saw a surge in activity to evaluate and promote clinical audit, led by the Department of Health. That activity was captured in reviews of the time,[7] and was followed by a spate of introspection about the role and value of the process.[8-12] This period led directly to the first edition of this book and other activity around 2000 to make clinical audit more effective.

The publication of the inquiry into the failings at the Bristol Royal Infirmary (BRI) in the UK played a major role in highlighting the potential value of clinical audit.[13] The publication in 2002 of the first edition of *Principles of Best Practice in Clinical Audit* captured the findings of the inquiry, and was the culmination of that period of 'energising' audit, but it also marked the point when clinical audit began to be regarded as not just the activity of clinicians (as hitherto), but also a valuable tool in management. Up until that time, the idea of external scrutiny of clinical practice had not been fully accepted, so clinical audit had been regarded as largely a professional practice for and by doctors, with limited use of the results by managers and even less use of it by patients.

In 2002, when this book was first published, a wider concept termed **clinical governance** had emerged in the UK as the touchstone of the period, expressing the need to ensure that clinical processes were managed and overseen by the organisations within which care took place in an effective, integrated way with other matters. This was a managerial viewpoint on what needed to be done, namely that service delivery would be effective if it was 'managed.' It did not emphasise quality per se, as this was assumed. Although initially it was felt by some that this overarching concept would give clinical audit a new impetus,[11,14] in practice it had the effect of marginalising audit.

This is because during this period the focus moved from 'clinical audit' as a separate theme, as this was seen as just one process within clinical governance as a whole. National resources went into supporting effective clinical governance at management level, which in turn involved clinical audit. As a consequence of the emergence of the broader concept of governance, clinical audit staff at local level were moved into other areas; there was limited national support for audit, and the responsibility for national audits moved sequentially between a variety of UK health organisations, from the National Institute for Health and Clinical Excellence (NICE) to the Commission for Healthcare Audit and Improvement (CHI), and to the Healthcare Commission, like a relay baton. Interest in clinical audit, as measured by studies published in academic journals, declined sharply.

By 2007 it was clear that clinical audit in the UK was in the doldrums. Internationally clinical audit was being overtaken and overlooked as a leading quality improvement (QI) method by the focus on patient engagement, prevention of mistakes, untoward events, and improvement of safety. Newer types of quality improvement were emerging, with whole new organisations promoting these but not promoting clinical audit. There were new ideas about how to collect data and measure change against it, such as clinical dashboards.

However, clinical audit was still happening. In the UK it was still a requirement in professional codes and on academic syllabuses. There were still over 20 national audits funded by the Department of Health in England, a system not replicated outside the UK, where national audit is often unfunded and often occurs only in single cycles. As well as this programme there were still keen individuals who were developing and refining audit practice in centres such as the Royal College of Psychiatrists and the Royal College of Physicians. Luckily for clinical audit, the belief that it was central to the NHS as part of the drive for 'quality' had also not been lost in the Department of Health in England.

In the UK, from around 2007 there began a new fashioning of what mattered in running health services, which was also taking place worldwide. The current driving principle is **quality**, best expressed in England by the Next Stage review *High Quality Care for All*.[15] This movement has several elements and systems to improve quality, of which clinical audit is one strand.

The Healthcare Quality Improvement Partnership (HQIP) now manages the revitalisation of clinical audit in England for the Department of Health. HQIP is a consortium that reflects a partnership between patient interest groups and professional bodies, including those for medicine and nursing. This new book is the expression of this renewed energy about clinical audit. However, the views in the book reflect the views of HQIP and the authors, not those of the Department of Health.

KEY ISSUES AND CONTEXTS FOR CLINICAL AUDIT IN THE 'TWENTY-TENS'

Why do we need a new handbook on clinical audit? Reviewing the first edition of this book in 2002, Walshe wrote:

> The continuing failure of *clinical audit* in many NHS organisations is not a failure of knowledge, which this book might help to address. It is primarily a failure of leadership and organisational culture, something which this book cannot really help to solve.[16]

At one level, this statement is correct. Many people working in healthcare know the basics of clinical audit methodology. However, it is dangerous to assume that there is a firm link between knowing and doing. Audit practice still suffers from the same methodological faults and practice errors as it always has done, and best practice, and encouragement to follow it, need to be set out clearly over and over again. Adherence to proper methodology is the cornerstone of effective audit.

In addition, it is not possible to pretend that clinical audit has not changed, that new ideas do not need to be embraced, that new issues have not emerged, or that the context of healthcare has not altered. All of these things are true. Since 2002, new quality approaches have emerged, and there is a need to both refine and re-state the importance and value of the audit method in this wider context. We shall return to this throughout this chapter.

Nonetheless, the broader point made by Walshe in 2002, namely that audit requires leadership and managerial commitment, remains valid today. There is only so much that an individual clinician or team can do to make the full spread of changes that audit has recommended. In a sense this is what the introduction of clinical governance sought to achieve, but in practice it did not manage to make the link between management and clinical practice adequately. This new edition seeks to reinforce the need to ensure engagement of senior management, especially senior clinicians, in the processes for oversight of audit, and the need for managerial oversight of any programme, as recommended by Bullivant and Corbett-Nolan (*see* HQIP's website,[17] and summary in Appendix 5 of this volume). If healthcare governing bodies, at least in England, as part of the requirements of central government are expected to maintain oversight of clinical audit, in recognition of its value, Walshe's concerns may well be addressed by centrally determined requirements. However, to make practice of clinical audit amongst clinicians and audit professionals effective, guidance is essential, and a manual of best practice is needed more than ever.

Other factors in healthcare policy, most of which are global issues, under the broad heading of 'quality', form a backdrop to and influence the renewed focus on clinical audit. In this chapter we shall review some of these issues, along with others that are specific to clinical audit, as a means of stimulating debate about the future of audit within this context.

There has been continuing convergence and emphasis on the role of **guidelines and standards** and, in the UK, NICE has been central to this. NICE guidelines are widely recognised as being among the very best in the world, and they form the basis for many standards that are used in clinical audit. The role of NICE, and its expertise in producing definitive standards, has enabled clinical audit to be based on a body of evidence that can easily be agreed upon to audit. This has meant that increasingly those who design audits have been able to draw on existing standards rather than seeking to draft these themselves. As a result, the subsidiary activity adopted by some national audits in defining standards for care as part of what they do may become less prominent. This is important in the context of the discussion about what audit is for (which is dealt with in detail below).

The second major issue has been the continuing rise of processes variously referred to as **regulation, inspection, registration** or **accreditation**, depending on their unique aspects. Each of these processes seeks to examine an area of clinical care, or an entire provider, such as a hospital, for the purposes of some kind of recognition or award. This can be from central government, or from an insuring body, or from some international accreditation body to deliver assurance to an insurer. In the UK, this work has expanded hugely since the publication of the first edition of this book, with a new regulator emerging in 2009 which has quality explicit in its title – the Care Quality Commission.

Discussion of this area would need a chapter or more in itself, but the purpose of introducing it here is simply to emphasise that clinical audit has a relationship to these processes. Audit data is a useful source of evidence in measuring compliance with the standards they use. However, clinical audit can examine complex issues in detail, and the level at which the standards are set for these regulatory processes, although they vary enormously, may well be much lower than the standards against

which clinical audit seeks to assess care, and much less detailed. None
of such processes establishes how important audit is as a source of
tors. In an earlier era, audit data were not used for this purpose. W
what this means for practice below.

The role of **patients** as partners in healthcare was already extens...
it now has even greater force. The impact of this for audit is obvious and considerable, and is reflected in this volume extensively.

The **boundaries between secondary and primary care** have shifted, and in some
jurisdictions there is a drive to move specialties out of secondary care to a local setting. Historically, clinical audit has been most effective in secondary care settings,
at least in the UK, and its extensive application within primary care has yet to be
achieved. However, there is no reason why clinical audit should not be useful in
these settings.

The last contextual point is about the rising concern with **safety and prevention
of accidents and errors**. This has emerged as a major paradigm of healthcare worldwide in the last decade. As awareness of this area has grown, it has spawned new
processes of notification and prevention that resemble and relate to audit. Above all,
it has helped to galvanise a wider movement in 'healthcare quality', within which
clinical audit must continually shout in order to have its voice heard.

Another key point that should be made at this stage, given this context, is that
clinical audit perhaps cannot simply be defined in one simple form. Healthcare is
not static, and clinical audit cannot be either.

This book, which is primarily aimed at those at the local level of care delivery
who want to audit their own practice, either as individuals or in teams, will focus
on the core methodologies of clinical audit as they are normally understood. Yet it
should be acknowledged that in some settings, perhaps most obviously in national
clinical audit, there are variant approaches. In an earlier period, clinical audit could
be described as a set of mechanical processes that followed a strict methodology. The
rise of additional methods of quality improvement, and the wider issues in healthcare policy described above, as well as the increasing diversity of healthcare practice
and settings, all mean that audit has often been fitted and adjusted by process and
intent to the setting within which it is being applied, by the specific individuals who
are conducting the study.

Audits that are conducted at national level, certainly within the UK, can sometimes resemble standards-based research, or even simply research itself, where there
is no process of measurement against previously agreed standards. Clinical audit of
this type helps to refine or define new standards, perhaps to be used in subsequent
audits, but whilst very often it measures against **some** existing standards, without
any measurement against existing standards the process has moved from measurement of compliance with the known to identifying the unknown, which **is** research.
To clinical audit purists, this is not clinical audit at all.

Similarly, some clinical audit in primary care, especially when the process is
primarily a review of significant events, may be much more akin to a confidential
enquiry or a case-by-case informal peer review process, without externally defined

standards always being available. For some, this is not clinical audit either.

It is also worth mentioning at this point that the concept of rapid-cycle meas-urement/improvement, at least in methodological terms, does not always fit some purists' view of clinical audit. There is also a variance in view about the necessity of re-audit and what this means.

Without spending much time on these variants of the processes that are collec-tively referred to as 'clinical audit', but recognising that they exist, this book accepts that this diversity of thinking is present. However, our main concern is about reaf-firming what the **core** of clinical audit should be about – that is, driving change and improvement in healthcare through a cycle that uses standards as the basis for meas-urement and action – and setting out as clearly as possible how this can be done.

It may therefore be helpful to think of clinical audit in this decade as a related set of processes, which need to be appropriate to their setting and purpose, and built around a central core, which this book will argue is its nature as a measurement/ quality improvement cycle. The core procedures of the most commonly practised form of audit are described in the main chapters of this book. We recognise that these will need to be adapted to fit the setting within which they are being applied, but without changing the basic nature of what audit is about.

The very term 'clinical audit' may itself be ripe for review, as the process may be helpfully extended to social care, where the term may not fit perfectly. For some, the word 'audit' has unwelcome connotations, and the term 'clinical' is perhaps not appropriate. This is an issue which may well emerge more prominently in the future.

The next section explores some of the main issues in clinical audit practice in more detail.

WHAT IS CLINICAL AUDIT DESIGNED TO DO?

Clinical audit is:

> A quality improvement process that seeks to improve patient care and outcomes through systematic review of care against explicit criteria and the implementa-tion of change. Put more simply, clinical audit is all about measuring the quality of care and services against agreed standards and making improvements where necessary.[18]

The above quotation comes from the first edition of this book, and made it clear that clinical audit is a cycle in which definition of standards, measurement, action and then re-measurement all form one integrated process. This new edition reaffirms that model as the core form of clinical audit. However, it is worth mentioning that in recent years this definition has been the subject of debate, with some (both inside and outside of audit) arguing that clinical audit is not a quality improvement process at all, but simply a measurement process, that the act of improvement is a separate activity, and that in general clinical audit may need re-thinking.[19]

In both perspectives there is still a cycle taking place, namely deciding what to measure, measuring, acting on the findings, and then re-measuring. The question of defining whether the whole process is called clinical audit or arguing that clinical audit is only a part within a cycle, fails to reflect the fact that, almost without exception, the business of the whole cycle is what counts.

At the national level of clinical audit, the separation of measurement from enacting change may seem self-evident, because different people carry out the different parts of the cycle. Local clinicians act on findings identified by central teams who collect the data from them. However, at the level of service delivery, the desire to rename parts of the whole cycle can be seen as irrelevant to everyday practice. This is because the best local practitioners, both audit staff and clinicians, are carrying out the whole cycle which they own and enact throughout. Renaming the cycle's separate parts will not stop it happening as one complete cycle because local professionals know that this is how it works. There is an innate recognition of the fact that where audit has failed it has not been a complete cycle.

The real impact of such potential re-thinking lies in the risk of strangling of the supporting enablers of the drive to reinvigorate clinical audit. One risk is that funding, central support, commitment and much more will fade if the link between measurement and action is broken, and these are seen as being different things. If a board of a healthcare provider has a choice between funding a post that just measures and a post that improves patient care through measurement **and** action, what will it support? If a government body is asked to choose between continuing to support a drive to maintain the number of staff who measure throughput, or supporting a programme which is about improving quality, what will it favour?

The touchstone is surely **improving** quality. Measuring quality is not enough to justify the funding and resourcing of local audit teams, or the time of local clinicians. Continuing to justify their time on audit demands that clinical audit remains conceptualised as what clinicians and local audit staff already know it to be, namely a complete cycle of improvement.

There is also the risk that underselling clinical audit will starve it of willing participants. Understanding that audit is both measurement and improvement is probably the overwhelming reason why most audit staff and clinicians get involved in audit in the first place.

This is as true for national audits as it is for local clinical audit. There are now around 50 ongoing national clinical audits in the UK in which local clinicians supply data, which are then analysed by a central national body, before being reported back to the local level to enable providers to see how they compare with their peers, and act on the findings. The people who analyse data for a national clinical audit in a specialised setting such as a university department or a clinical professional body do not **themselves** carry out action to improve services at a local level, but this does not mean that the process as a whole is not a clinical audit. Someone at a local level acts on the analysed data that they supply. There is still a cycle of deciding, measuring, acting and re-measuring going on. And, in practice, the very best national teams involved in conducting the data collection and analysis part of the cycle as part of a national clinical audit are increasingly involved in helping to drive the action/ change part of the cycle at local level through effective guidance and engagement with local teams.[20]

The last remaining argument for re-thinking audit in this way would be that the action part of the cycle is functionally different from the measuring part, and that by definition action and measurement are often undertaken by different people, as they require different skills. It is sometimes argued that the action stage involves a diversity of processes, whereas the measurement process has a distinct methodology of its own.

If you are a working clinician who combines management, patient care, research and audit into one busy life, this separation of required skills does not hold water. With regard to the cycle, you decide what to measure, measure it, act and re-measure every day. You also enact the process of change and may manage this. You have to do a bit of everything, or it would not get done.

This is true nationally as well as locally. A clinician, as opposed to a researcher, who leads a national audit knows that it is one cycle in which they play one role alongside others who play theirs. If it is not that clinician personally who leads the changes in a local healthcare provider body (although it often is, if their time spent on national audit is limited to one or two days a week, and they spend the rest of their time involved in direct patient care and local management), it is someone like them – one of their professional peers and colleagues. Making decisions about change is something that a managing clinician or a manager does every day. They may get special advice or help with regard to some aspects, but only as part of a whole project that they manage and steer.

Finally, it is also worth mentioning that clinical audit is an international discipline. This book, in addressing an international audience, retains the existing concept of audit that appeared in the initial edition of this book, and which remains the universally accepted definition.

PROVING THAT CLINICAL AUDIT LEADS TO CHANGE IN HEALTHCARE PRACTICE

The international drive to improve quality in healthcare, of which clinical audit forms a part, continues to analyse the degree to which various methods have any impact. These issues apply as much to regulation and accreditation or any other method as they do to clinical audit. Every intervention needs to be able to demonstrate that it makes a difference and is worth the investment.

We have argued above that clinical audit is a cycle which must include both measurement and taking action to improve the quality of care to meet standards, and that measurement on its own is not enough. Yet perhaps the overwhelming charge that has been laid at the door of clinical audit is that, even if the intention is for audit to improve patient care, very often that change to improve practice does not happen – the cycle is not completed. This point was made strongly by the Bristol Royal Infirmary (BRI) inquiry,[13] and in the only Cochrane review on clinical audit to date,[21] and it remains a serious charge today.[22-24] Too many audits are conducted that identify areas where change is needed, make recommendations, **but no significant change ever occurs.** If there is a re-audit, no further change follows. The whole cycle, if it does happen, takes a long time, but no significant benefit from the audit is identified in that the same problems are highlighted over and over again.

The easy way to escape this dilemma is the one discussed above – to suggest that the 'action' or 'improvement' part of the cycle is nothing to do with clinical audit. We have dealt with that already. Although too many audits fail to show much resulting change in practice, the reasons for this are nothing to do with the utility of the audit method per se, but rather they are to do with the way that the audit has been carried out, and the will of clinicians and managers to act on the findings. The literature on how well-conducted clinical audits have been shown to lead to change is extensive, and this introduction cannot do justice to it. I offer here a very few good published examples of national and local audits which have led to real improvements in patient care within the UK[14,25-27] and internationally.[3,28-31]

Much of the reason for lack of effect is simply down to not following best practice, and this book is most centrally a description of how audit methodology should be applied in such a way as to address these issues. Without a full cycle, which usually involves continuing cycles of measurement, it is no wonder that no changes are discerned. There must be a set of useful recommendations and a plan to bring these changes into practice.

This action plan may (but does not always) need additional funding or other organisational changes that require the support of management. Ensuring that managers 'own' clinical audit and are prepared to act on the findings is crucial. Some of the energy that seeps out of clinicians in relation to audit is due to repeatedly conducting technically first-class audits and then seeing nothing done by peers and managers to support changes. Again, this is not a fault of the modality, but rather it is due to failure to act on the findings – the point made by Walshe.[16]

Good technical audits that are undertaken with management support and preparedness for action will lead to measurable changes in patient care. Determining the relationship between change and clinical audit is difficult, given the level of variables and other processes that are also employed every day that may affect practice. At the simplest level there may be intervening variables in relation to how feedback of results from clinical audit, if undertaken in a particular way, may affect subsequent implementation of changes.[21] This is an area that requires further research.

This edition of the book emphasises how change programmes can be carried out. The principles of change management are described in Appendix 3.

AUDIT OF PROCESS VERSUS OUTCOME

Related to the above, but going further, one of the longest-running issues in clinical audit is whether it should focus on process or outcome, and to what extent audit can show that it leads to better healthcare outcomes. Historically, of course, much clinical audit has been solely about process, because the core of audit **is** the assessment of whether practice (i.e. process) meets the standards of recommended process and practice set out in guidelines based on the available research evidence. As mentioned above, assessment of the degree to which change in healthcare practice results from clinical audit is too infrequently built into the audit design (*see* Appendix 2).

Even less often is it assessed whether better healthcare outcomes resulted, and even more rarely are these gains evidenced. Yet clinical audit should surely be able to establish (or at least suggest) the relationship between compliance with best practice and improvements in health outcomes. It should also be alert to broader service impacts that result, on a more routine basis, and which relate to greater effectiveness of services, efficiencies, economies, and better patient experience of care. And because clinical audit often collects data about outcomes in order to demonstrate compliance and improvement, and achievement of an outcome is very often the precise thing that is being measured by some audits, especially national ones, some audits can already demonstrate what outcomes have been achieved.

It is likely that pressure to focus clinical audit on the measurement of both outcomes **and** process will become greater as the need to apply the process to drive quality **and** save money **and** avoid waste becomes more pressing. It is in the interest of clinical audit to actively measure outcomes and other effects arising from change processes, and to become more rigorous in doing so.

A discussion of the evidence that clinical audit can be shown to lead to healthcare 'impacts', in the sense of both patient healthcare outcomes and other system changes, can be found in Appendix 2. It should be noted that the evidence that **any** quality improvement programmes in healthcare can show such changes is limited.[32-35] These recent reviews of different improvement methods have tended not to focus on clinical audit specifically when reviewing the effects of a range of methodologies. However, in any case perhaps the basic approach of such work is flawed, as Walshe has persuasively argued elsewhere.[36]

OTHER CONTEXTUAL ISSUES
Clinical audit as a mark of professional practice
There is a further set of issues that are closely related. Put simply, there is evidence that clinician perceptions of audit, alongside the level of understanding of methodology and basic competence in the method, are important in engaging them to participate and ensuring that they conduct effective audit.[37] There are many who functionally accept the need to undertake audit, and its validity and purpose, but who do not get enthusiastic about it, or make time or opportunity to learn about it. Audit is seen by some as a chore, akin to housework. You know you have to do it and you do it under sufferance, or in some cases leave it to others to do.

Clinical audit has always suffered in this regard by comparison with research. Because audit dwells in the known and the established, rather than exploring the unknown and the innovative, it is sometimes seen as secondary, or even dull. This perception has not been aided by the paucity of adequate training in clinical audit among clinicians.

It is certain that re-conceptualising audit by reference solely to its least interesting aspects, as discussed above (e.g. simply counting data about the 'known') is a likely way of accelerating this negative vision. However, it is also reductive of the power of clinical audit, of where its grace and authority is rooted. Audit is fundamentally a **professional discipline** – an expression of how well a clinician conducts their art. It should be at the core of a true professional's professional identity that they should feel confident that what they do is as good as it could be, as good as it ought to be, and that it makes a difference to patients. In this territory, it is far from research. Many clinicians are modest in their research ambitions and aptitude, but they care passionately about how well their work is received, and that it achieves benefit. Clinical audit, however tiresome some aspects of its methodology may be, is quite simply the best way of knowing that you are good at what you do. Research does not necessarily achieve this.

We have to recapture this as a virtue, bottle it, and sell it to practitioners. It is perhaps an old-fashioned craftsman's virtue or attribute – the sense of satisfaction in one's work. This may need to be taught with more attention during practitioners' training today than it was in the past. We should not dismiss how crucial the appeal to values is to achieving reinvigoration in clinical audit practice. This basic concept of the role of audit is accepted by the various professional bodies in the UK, for whom participation in clinical audit is usually a requirement to practise. However, this requirement needs to be supported with enthusiasm and a sense of value that precedes the instruction.

The application of good practice in audit will also enable the problems that are identified to be overcome, and those who become engaged in audit to feel more enthusiastic about the discipline.

The dual role of audit for managers/regulators and clinicians

This issue reflects the fact that although audit is very much the discipline of professional clinicians, it is also about supplying data on clinical performance to those in management, and to regulators.

Clinical audit needs to look both ways, and this issue is a complex one that warrants discussion. In systems of healthcare where there is concern about targets, management, and burdens of bureaucracy, any sense that audit is a top-down process that is imposed on clinicians will not help take-up, or enthusiasm. Yet, taking the most extreme examples first, the lessons of the Bristol Royal Infirmary, the Mid Staffordshire NHS Foundation Trust and the general practitioner Harold Shipman in the UK demonstrated that it is not enough to leave clinicians alone to get on with collecting data and analysing their own practice. The task also belongs to regulators and management, who have ultimate responsibility for clinical as well as financial oversight.[13,38]

Some critics argue that this risks the takeover of the discipline by management on the basis of extreme examples, when in practice nearly all healthcare professionals are committed to excellence. However, it should be recognised by all that clinical audit has a utility for clinicians, managers and regulators alike. Good clinical audit is a mechanism to drive improvements in clinical practice which sometimes only the board of an organisation has the power to make happen. Engaging managers in the process of audit and acting on the findings is essential not just in order to identify rogue and unsafe practitioners, or to spy. Although it is first and foremost a professional responsibility, within the culture of a good relationship between the clinician and the manager, clinical audit is a shared engine for change. To achieve this it is necessary to ensure that the governing board of a healthcare provider has adequate clinical representation, and that managing bodies, suitably advised by clinicians, use audit data to improve patient care. A detailed guide to how this can be achieved can be found in *Clinical Audit: a simple guide for NHS boards and partners*, which is available on the HQIP website.[17] This contains a wealth of information about the principles of governance that can be applied to any healthcare environment. A summary of this work, the 'top 10 rules for boards', can be found in Appendix 5 of this book.

Clinical audit across different disciplines

Clinical audit is a discipline that is applicable to any profession. However, notwithstanding the British nurse Florence Nightingale's pioneering role in its definition, its main application to date has been largely in medical practice, dentistry and pharmacy. Some disciplines, notably nursing, sometimes struggle to apply clinical audit in the context of the routine patient **care** that they provide, as opposed to **treatment**, where as members of multi-disciplinary clinical teams, nurses and other disciplines fully participate in audit. This is despite efforts to promote audit in nursing, for example, in the UK, over a period of some time, such as the setting up of nursing audit committees as early as 1990,[39] which in evaluation had a measure of success.[7,40]

In practice, there are other methods, related to clinical audit, that also effectively measure the basics of nursing care, such as 'clinical-dashboard'-style continuous recording that care has been provided in line with expectations against a minimum set of standards,[41] and 'care pathways.'[42] However, once again, to investigate more deeply, there is no substitute for good clinical audit to complement these approaches. In addition, as nurses continue to play an ever more significant role in the administration of treatment (e.g. as nurse prescribers), the application of traditional clinical audit methodology will be ever more relevant to the work of increasing numbers of nurses.[43] Nonetheless, it is important that as clinical audit develops, its ability to be applied to all disciplines is tested by new approaches that are more tailored to their specific clinical practice. It is likely that this will be a major theme over the next few years; and although we have cited nursing here, it applies to other professions as well.

Clinical audit as a science

Clinical audit has been called a science,[44] and to clinicians and others whose trade is scientific, we should not falter in striving to ensure that audit is methodologically credible. One of the consistent failures of clinical audit, as we argue throughout this book, and as others have rightly pointed out, has been the failure to conduct audit with methodological rigour.[45-48]

Again in this regard clinical audit has suffered by comparison with the principles of research. Although some will fear that the last thing audit needs is to be bound by the hamstrings of research governance, there is still merit in ensuring that clinical audit is covered by **good** governance. This means not just its methodology but also its ethics. Addressing the ethical issues associated with audit (*see* Appendix 1) definitely does not mean that every audit project needs to be approved by an ethics committee, but the issues concerned still require attention.

Rigour in data collection and management is also crucial. Greater attention to data quality is a vital strand of the current drive to reinvigorate clinical audit. It is not enough to keep conducting audits that do not prove the point which they are striving to make, or that can be brought down by charges of poor methodology, or case-mix issues, or because they take too long to report, or they report the results inconclusively so that no one can act on the findings. All of these failings have been used to argue against the usefulness of audit. Overcoming these challenges is the mark of high-quality audit, and the chapters that follow spend some time on these issues.

Patient or customer engagement in clinical audit

HQIP, from which this publication flows, is owned and run by a consortium of professional and patient organisations. This reflects a desire among the founders of HQIP, from its very inception, to place patient involvement and engagement at the centre of audit. In 2002, although patient involvement was actively discussed, it did not have the dynamism that it has in 2010 in the UK and worldwide. This new edition is quite explicit in setting out the importance of patient engagement throughout the practice of clinical audit. There can be no room for tokenism in this. At one time, patient participation was conceived in terms of communicating effectively to patients. The model espoused in this volume is one of full engagement and co-ownership of the process, wherever this is possible or practical.

However, this principle is not without difficulties. There may be tension between the aims of the clinician and the views of patients about desirable outcomes, and the standards that are used in audits are very often clinical standards rather than standards related to outcomes that a patient may choose. Many audits are more about process than about outcome, and there is nothing wrong with this per se, but the patient interest in process may be different from that of the clinician.

Although clinical audit is functionally 'owned' by audit practitioners, clinicians and managers, in that only they can really collect **all** of the necessary data, its actual ownership as a process needs to be in the hands of a governing group which represents patients as much as the other stakeholders. The ideas for audit, in the form of the precise audit questions, standards and outcomes that are being used, need to reflect patient views about primacy of topics and outcomes as well as the views of clinicians and managers. The collection of data should involve patients, and the dissemination and communication of reports should be **to** and **by** patients, along with their involvement in ideas for service improvement. In the past, even as recently as 2002, the primary audience for the clinical audit report was the individual clinical unit that conducted the audit. At the time of writing, in 2010, it is the patient group who should lead and receive the report just as much as the healthcare provider staff and management.

In the future, a patient ought to ask, at consultation, or when deciding whether to have a procedure completed, or when they have it completed, 'Do you audit your work?' and 'What are your results?' The clinical unit needs to anticipate and be prepared for these questions, confident that they conduct audit and that the results tell a good story which is relevant and understandable to the patient. This means that it is not obscured by technical jargon, delay, or other blurring of accountability. The clinical unit should not just have to answer these questions, but want to do so. This guide includes material throughout which restates how patient engagement should be maximised, but it is covered specifically in Appendix 6. There is further material on presenting audit data to the general public on the HQIP website.[49,50] Increasingly, providers and clinicians may be required to do so.[51]

Clinical audit in the primary care setting

As the role of the primary, general practice or family doctor level of medicine continues to be viewed by healthcare policy makers worldwide as an increasingly important part of future healthcare provision, it is essential that clinical audit is applicable to level of practice. The application of good clinical audit at this level has been highly variable,[52] and audit has been more extensively applied in secondary care, from where the majority of the international literature has emerged, although excellent audit work has of course been undertaken in family doctor settings worldwide.[31] In turn, within the UK, related processes such as significant event auditing (SEA),[53] and systems of recording that trigger payment for carrying out various tasks (the Quality and Outcomes Framework, or QOF, a method of paying GPs to carry out recommended activities),[54] have also occupied some of the space that clinical audit, as defined in its most traditional form, should fill. There should be room for all of these processes to be applied where each is most appropriate.

Once again it can be argued that valuable as these other processes may be (and they are also subject to many of the same issues as described here),[53] they are complementary to, not a substitute for, the kind of detail that is provided by a full clinical audit. As more clinical care moves to a primary care setting, there is a real need to ensure that the methodologies outlined in this book are applied with rigour at this level. In the UK, the barriers to carrying these out are perhaps mostly related to time, available support, appropriate standards, attitude and training, rather than to suitability of process.

The relationship to other methods of quality improvement

One of the reasons why audit has perhaps lost ground in recent years is because of the growth of newer 'kids' on the quality improvement block. Some of these new methodologies have been imported from industry, some focus on safety and prevention of harm first and foremost, and some trade on the emphasis of speed of return of analysis or presentation of data for action. This book is not written to discourage the use of new methodologies, or to criticise them. They play an essential role in healthcare today, and clinical audit can certainly learn from some of them, notably the need to speed up the cycle. However, the view of this book would be that clinical audit offers virtues that go beyond some of the complementary modalities of quality improvement that have emerged since 2002, and by comparison with other methods it presents very favourably as a quality improvement mechanism,[55] especially as these other methodologies cannot point to a significantly better evidence base of effectiveness.[32–35]

The criticism that clinical audit is slow, laboured and confirms what is already known, at a time when people are at risk of dying from preventable harm that rapid reporting cycles and checklists identify, mistakes the complementary nature of the different approaches. Audit can be a short, punchy review, perhaps on a daily basis, of real-time performance against standards (*see* Chapter 5, for example). However, if what is needed is a systematic, ongoing analysis of complex factors in care, then only clinical audit can offer this process. Other shorter and simpler methodologies often identify the need for a proper, detailed clinical audit, which identifies the more complex reasons **why** care is failing, rather than simply telling healthcare professionals and managers that it **is** failing. Clinical audit is a simple methodology that is applied to tackle complex and detailed issues. The richness and detail of what it can say about care far outweigh some simpler methods of identifying failings and measuring compliance. Clinical audit demands a longer attention span and attention to detail. This is a virtue, not a failing.

The issue of patient safety is interesting, because it reflects a tendency in some expressions of healthcare quality improvement by which various processes are lumped together under the banner of 'quality'. It is arguable whether performing routine procedures safely so that the patient does not die is properly categorised as being 'quality' practice. Yet much of the international language of 'quality' seems to be restricted to describing **minimum** levels of performance. The elision of the term 'minimum' into 'quality' as meaning the same thing is expressive of an acceptance that 'minimum' is that to which we aspire. There is no aspiration to quality in seeking only to achieve the minimum, and we should not call it so. Again, although clinical audit **can** be used simply to measure safety and compliance with minimum standards,[56] and to address infection issues, or medication errors, for example,[57,58] it is also the best way of showing that care is in line with the **best** standards. Conducting reviews against the highest level of standards conveys that clinical audit does not settle simply for measurement of prevention of harm, but marks practice that aspires to excellence. For once, it is a quality improvement process that is genuinely about quality. This is another reason why it appeals to clinicians who do not want to settle for the minimum standard that some quality improvement (and regulatory) approaches measure.

The cost benefits of clinical audit

The issue of costs needs to be considered in this context. In older versions of clinical audit practice, the awareness of the cost–benefit analyses was minimal, despite calls for this as early as 1995.[8,59,60]

The demand that audit should be assessed for its cost benefit has become more crucial. The global financial turmoil of 2009 has ensured that all funding systems, both private and public, now demand better assessment of the cost benefits of health-care interventions of different types.

However, the analysis is not straightforward, and it is not just a case of asking 'Do the costs of an audit outweigh the benefits to patient care?' In practice, the costs of carrying out most clinical audits, per single healthcare setting, are relatively minor (the costs of specialist clinical audit staff, and the time of clinicians).

The real costs are incurred by the cost of any new healthcare provision, or adjusted procedures that are introduced as a result of the audit. Coupled with the cost of carrying out the audit, does this equal the gains in patient care?

In practice this is also not straightforward to estimate.[61] Should it be measured in terms of patient satisfaction, or better long-term outcomes, or costs of legal cases avoided or negligence prevented? How are these assessed and defined? In straight financial terms, compliance with best standards of care may sometimes involve more expense. Often, however, new practices can be introduced that save money, and which in addition make 'savings' (through healthcare gains measured in terms of better outcomes and avoided admissions and interventions) that, although difficult to assess financially, are very real indeed.

In all jurisdictions there is a need to find a way of showing that quality improvement will pay for itself, and that it will possibly save money in the long term. In England, the pressure to do this is very great indeed, as described in the Quality, Innovation, Prevention and Productivity (QIPP) agenda,[62] which suggests that by using these methods and improving performance with these factors, economies can be made without sacrificing quality, and indeed with an improvement in quality. Health professionals will have to utilise economic models to support their practice if it is to maintain the same level of funding.

The literature on this area is very scarce, and that which is available is summarised in the evaluation study by Loughlan in Appendix 2 of this book. This is an area where practice will need to grow.

Criteria for high-quality clinical audit

This book is about best practice in carrying out the audit cycle as a complete improvement process. Appendix 4 provides a definitive statement of what leading clinicians and experts from the UK agreed in 2009 marked the criteria for best practice in clinical audit. These principles summarise what a good audit is, what it is about, and by what standards it can be judged.

This book seeks to extend the principles given there into a longer and expanded manual of best practice following those guidelines. The richness and granular detail of the methodology of clinical audit is set out in Chapters 2 to 5, which are adapted from the text of the 2002 edition, and presented here by Stephen Ashmore, Tracy Ruthven and Louise Hazelwood of the Clinical Audit Support Centre (CASC), and edited by HQIP. If these guidelines are followed, many of the typical problems with audit that have been mentioned in this introduction will largely be addressed, and audits will then be able to meet the criteria that are described in Appendix 4.

CONCLUSIONS

Clinical audit is a part of modern healthcare, with all of its complexity. In England, at least at present, clinical audit is regarded as an essential element of driving up quality within a national system,[51] and we hope that this becomes increasingly the case in other jurisdictions, and that this book will support this development. No single volume can do full justice to the web of issues that provide the context for international quality improvement, and clinical audit practice today, as these wax and wane. We have tried to identify issues here that are universal.

The balance between management interest in audit results, the role of regulators, and the exact level that is assessed for accreditation or registration processes will be determined variously at different times and at different places, but these are universal issues. Similarly, in any healthcare system, issues of finance, infrastructure and training will continue to influence the way in which clinical audit is practised, as very often it is issues of capacity that undermine willingness to practise audit, regardless of the attitudes expressed towards it, or the perceptions of its utility.[43,46]

Clinical audit is affected by these factors, but it is also an adaptable discipline, which in some respects can stand outside of the ebb and flow of health politics and fashions, and even lack of specific funding. Clinicians will always seek to measure what they do against a standard, and to act to improve their work if they are shown not to be equal to it. Whether governments, regulators and other healthcare quality bodies show interest in this process will not ultimately determine whether clinical audit occurs. It will, hopefully, always go on, even if the time for it is personal, and the only resources are an off-the-shelf database, measuring standards downloaded from a website in another country. Within the contemporary context this book attempts to guide and improve audit practice in such a way that it effectively fulfils its core process of measuring a clinician's commitment to achieving the highest possible quality of care.

REFERENCES

1 Shaw C. Aspects of audit. *British Medical Journal* 1980; **280** (6226–9).

2 Chevreul K. Evaluation of professionals' practice. *Health Policy Monitor* 2005. http://hpm.org/en/Surveys/IRDES_-_France/05/Evaluation_of_professionals__practice.html;jsessionid=E698856EB65E15D51C6524F89A86220D?content_id=251&sortBy=sortCountry&sortOrder=sortAsc&a=st&lastSortBy=sortCountry&lastSortOrder=sortAsc&p_t=1871&language=en&pageOffset=3 (accessed 16 May 2010).

3 Wagaarachchi P, Graham W, Penney G *et al*. Holding up a mirror: changing obstetric practice through criterion-based clinical audit in developing countries: *International Journal of Gynaecology and Obstetrics* 2001; **74**: 119–30.

4 Graham W. Criterion-based clinical audit in obstetrics: bridging the quality gap? *Best Practice Research in Clinical Obstetrics and Gynaecology* 2009; **23**: 375–88.

5 Koh W, Ren W, Mukherjee R *et al.* Internal audit of a comprehensive IMRT program for prostate cancer: a model for centers in developing countries? *International Journal of Radiation Oncology, Biology, Physics* 2009; **74**: 1447–54.

6 Siddiqi K, Volz A, Armas L *et al.* Could clinical audit improve the diagnosis of pulmonary tuberculosis in Cuba, Peru and Bolivia? *Tropical Medicine and International Health* 2008; **13**: 566–78.

7 Willmot M, Foster J, Walshe K *et al. Evaluating Audit: a review of audit activity in the nursing and therapy professions: findings of a national survey.* London: CASPE Research; 1995.

8 Barton A, Thomson R, Bhopal R. Clinical audit: more research is required. *Journal of Epidemiology and Community Health* 1995; **49**: 445–7.

9 Berger A. Why doesn't audit work? (editorial). *British Medical Journal* 1998; **316**: 875–6.

10 Babu E, Khan A, Khashaba A *et al.* Clinical audit: can we improve further? *Journal of the Royal College of Surgeons of Edinburgh* 2001; **46**: 171–2.

11 Johnston G, Crombie I, Davies H *et al.* Reviewing audit: barriers and facilitating factors for effective clinical audit. *Quality in Health Care* 2000; **9**: 23–36.

12 Walshe K. Opportunities for improving the practice of clinical audit. *Quality in Health Care* 1995; **4**: 231–2.

13 Bristol Royal Infirmary Inquiry. *Learning from Bristol: the report of the public inquiry into children's heart surgery at the Bristol Royal Infirmary 1984–1995.* Command Paper: CM 5207. 1999. www.bristol-inquiry.org.uk/final_report/index.htm (accessed 4 August 2010).

14 Palmer C. Clinical governance: breathing new life into clinical audit. *Advances in Psychiatric Treatment* 2002; **8**: 470–6.

15 Department of Health. *High Quality Care for All: NHS Next Stage Review final report.* London: Department of Health; 2008.

16 Walshe K. *Review of Principles of Best Practice*, first edition. *Quality and Safety in Health Care* 2002; **4**: 392. Copyright © 2002 by Kieran Walshe. Reprinted with permission of the *British Medical Journal*.

17 Bullivant J, Corbett-Nolan A. *Clinical Audit: a simple guide for NHS boards and partners.* London: Healthcare Quality Improvement Partnership (HQIP); 2010.

18 National Institute for Health and Clinical Excellence (NICE). *Principles for Best Practice in Clinical Audit.* London: NICE; 2002 (reproduced with permission).

19 Bowie P, Bradley N, Rushmer R *et al. Clinical Audit and Quality Improvement in NHS Scotland: time for a rethink?* Edinburgh: NHS Education for Scotland; 2008.

20 Irwin P, Hoffman A, Lowe D *et al.* Improving clinical practice in stroke through audit: results of three rounds of National Stroke Audit. *Journal of Evaluation in Clinical Practice* 2005; **11**: 306–14.

21 Jamtvedt G, Young J, Kristoffersen D *et al.* Audit and feedback: effects on professional practice and health care outcomes. *Cochrane Database of Systematic Reviews* 2006; **2**: CD000259.

22 Prasad K, Reddy K. Auditing the audit cycle: an open-ended evaluation. *Clinical Governance* 2004; **9**: 110–14.

23 Lewis R, Collins R, Flynn A *et al*. A systematic review of cancer waiting time audits. *Quality and Safety in Health Care* 2005: **14**: 62–6.

24 Cai A, Greenall J, Ding DC. UK junior doctors' experience of clinical audit in the Foundation Programme. *British Journal of Medical Practitioners* 2009; **2**: 42–5.

25 Hysong S. Meta-analysis: audit and feedback features impact effectiveness on care quality. *Medical Care* 2009; **47**: 356–63.

26 Husk J. Achieving changes in practice from national audit: national audit of the organization of services for falls and bone health in older people. *Journal of Evaluation in Clinical Practice* 2008; **14**: 974–8.

27 Chate RA, White S, Hale LR *et al*. The impact of clinical audit on antibiotic prescribing in general dental practice. *British Dental Journal* 2006; **201**: 635–41.

28 Berk M, Callaly T, Hyland M. The evolution of clinical audit as a tool for quality improvement. *Journal of Evaluation in Clinical Practice* 2003; **9**: 251–7.

29 Lai C, Fan C, Liao P *et al*. Impact of an audit program and other factors on door-to-balloon times in acute ST-elevation myocardial infarction patients destined for primary coronary intervention. *Academic Emergency Medicine* 2009; **16**: 333–42.

30 Ostini R, Hegney D, Jackson C *et al*. Systematic review of interventions to improve prescribing. *Annals of Pharmacotherapy* 2009; **43**: 502–13.

31 Kirby C, Piterman L, Nelson MR *et al*. Gastro-oesophageal reflux disease: impact of guidelines on GP management. *Australian Family Physician* 2008; **37**: 73–7.

32 Øvretveit J. *Does Improving Quality Save Money?* London: Health Foundation; 2006.

33 Sutherland K, Leatherman S. *Regulation and Quality Improvement: a review of the evidence*. London: Health Foundation; 2006.

34 Christianson J, Leatherman S, Sutherland K. *Financial Incentives, Healthcare Providers and Quality Improvements*. London: Health Foundation; 2009.

35 Powell A, Rushmer R, Davies H. *A Systematic Narrative Review of Quality Improvement Models in Health Care*. Edinburgh: NHS Quality Improvement Scotland; 2009. www.nhshealth quality.org/nhsqis/5658.html (accessed 2 July 2010).

36 Walshe K. Understanding what works and why in quality improvement: the need for theory-driven evaluation. *International Journal of Quality in Health Care* 2007; **19**: 57–9.

37 Bowie P, McKay J, Murray L *et al*. Judging the quality of clinical audit by general practitioners: a pilot study comparing the educational assessments of medical peers and NHS audit specialists. *Journal of Evaluation in Clinical Practice* 2008; **14**: 1038–43.

38 Thorne DC. *Mid Staffordshire NHS Foundation Trust Report: commissioning for outcomes supported by excellent use of appropriate data and information*. London: Department of Health; 2009.

39 NHS Management Executive. *Clinical Audit in the Nursing and Therapy Professions*. Leeds: Department of Health NHS Management Executive; 1994.

40 Walshe K, Coles J. *Evaluating Audit: a review of initiatives*. London: CASPE Research; 1993.

41 Allen D, Gillen E, Rixson L. Systematic review of the effectiveness of integrated care pathways: what works, for whom, in which circumstances? *International Journal of Evidence-based Healthcare* 2009; **7**: 61–74.

42 Getgood S. *Clinical Dashboards: the national picture*. NHS Connecting for Health. www.connectingforhealth.nhs.uk/systemsandservices/clindash/publications/Sally%20Getgood%20Clinical%20Dashboards%20CS%204pp%20-%20web.pdf (accessed 9 June 2010).

43 Collis S. A review of the literature on the nurse role in clinical audit. *Nursing Times* 2006; **102**: 38–40.

44 Russell I, Wilson B. Audit: the third clinical science? *Quality and Safety in Health Care* 1992; **1**: 51–5.

45 Hearnshaw H, Harter R, Cheater F *et al*. Are audits wasting resources by measuring the wrong things? A survey of methods used to select audit review criteria. *Quality and Safety in Health Care* 2003; **12**: 24–8.

46 Sealey S. Two common pitfalls in clinical audit: failing to complete the audit cycle and confusing audit with research. *British Journal of Occupational Therapy* 1999; **62**: 238–43.

47 Walshe K. The traits of success in clinical audit. In: Walshe K, ed. *Evaluating Clinical Audit: past lessons, future directions*. London: Royal Society of Medicine Press; 1995.

48 Bowie P, McKay J, Murray L *et al*. Judging the quality of clinical audit by general practitioners: a pilot study comparing the educational assessments of medical peers and NHS audit specialists. *Journal of Evaluation in Clinical Practice* 2008; **14**: 1038–43.

49 Healthcare Quality Improvement Partnership (HQIP). *Guide for Patients in Understanding Clinical Audit Reports*. London: HQIP; 2010. www.hqip.org.uk/assets/Uploads/2-HQIP-CA-PD-024-Guide-for-patients-in-understanding-clinical-audit-reports-19-April-2010.pdf (accessed 9 June 2010).

50 Pearce M. *Guide on How to Present Clinical Audits for the Public*. London: HQIP; 2010. www.hqip.org.uk/assets/3-HQIP-CA-PD-025-Guide-on-how-to-present-clinical-audits-for-the-public-19-April-2010.pdf (accessed 9 June 2010).

51 Department of Health. *Equity and Excellence: liberating the NHS*. London: Department of Health; 2010.

52 National Patient Safety Agency. *Significant Event Audit: a guide for primary care teams*. London: National Patient Safety Agency; 2008.

53 McKay J, Bradley N, Lough M *et al*. A review of significant events analysed in general practice: implications for the quality and safety of patient care. *BMC Family Practice* 2009; **10**: 61. www.biomedcentral.com/1471-2296/10/61 (accessed 9 June 2010).

54 Statutory Instrument 2004 No. 291. *The National Health Service (General Medical Services Contracts) Regulations 2004*. London: HMSO; 2004.

55 Scott I. What are the most effective strategies for improving quality and safety of health care? *Internal Medicine Journal* 2009; **39**: 389–400.

56 Ursprung R, Gray J, Edwards W *et al*. Real time patient safety audits: improving safety every day. *Quality and Safety in Health Care* 2005; **14**: 284–9.

57 Bucior H, Cochrane J. Lifting the lid: a clinical audit on commode cleaning. *Journal of Infection Prevention* 2010; **11**: 73–80.

58 Jainer AK, Noushad F, Coupe T *et al*. Mind the gap – using clinical audit to minimise medication information errors at hospital discharge. *The Psychiatrist* 2010; **34**: 248–50.

59 Payne B. Clinical audit: is it value for money? In: Walshe K, ed. *Evaluating Clinical Audit: past lessons, future directions*. London: Royal Society of Medicine Press; 1995.

60 Lord J, Littlejohns P. Evaluating healthcare policies: the case of clinical audit. *British Medical Journal* 1997; **315**: 668.

61 Robinson M, Thompson E, Black N. Why is evaluation of the cost-effectiveness of audit so difficult? The example of thrombolysis for suspected acute myocardial infarction. *Quality and Safety in Health Care* 1998; **7**: 9–26.

62 Department of Health. *Implementing the Next Stage Review Visions: the quality and productivity challenge.* London: Department of Health; 2009.

CHAPTER 2

Stage 1: Preparation, planning and organisation of clinical audit

Stephen Ashmore, Tracy Ruthven and Louise Hazelwood

Key points

- Clinical audit is a continuous quality improvement process that is used to drive up standards of healthcare and service provision.
- Topic choice will be determined by a number of factors, but the focus should be one of identifying opportunities for improving care. Clinical audit involves looking at one's own practice, not that of others.
- Clinical audits are best conducted within a structured programme, with clearly defined roles, effective leadership to drive the process, participation by all relevant staff, and an emphasis on team working and support. A timetable to maintain momentum is also essential.
- Clinical audit needs to be adequately funded. This includes factoring in the possible increased costs of improving care as a result of the audit findings.
- Stakeholders need to be involved in the process at all stages, appropriately utilising their skills in and knowledge of the audit topic.
- The priorities of those receiving care can differ quite markedly from the priorities of those giving care. User involvement is therefore fundamental to successful, meaningful audit, and there are a number of legitimate and practical approaches to involving users. (For the purpose of this book, the terms 'users' and 'service users' include patients, carers, others who use a service, and members of groups and organisations that represent their interests.)
- All those involved in audit need access to training and/or advice in conducting audit projects to develop their skills and to ensure the effectiveness of projects undertaken.
- Protected time needs to be made available to those involved in audit work if it is to achieve its aim of improving quality in healthcare.

- Audit criteria are clearly defined, measurable, explicit statements of what should be happening for patients, and where possible should be based on up-to-date evidence.
- Performance levels, expressed as a percentage, should be agreed at the outset of the audit for each audit criterion. They are a compromise between clinical importance, practicability and acceptability.
- Audit standards are an amalgamation of each audit criterion with its performance level. These should be valid, reliable measures that are used to determine current practice as well as desirable practice.

The purposes of this chapter:

- To set out the key stage of preparing and planning for an audit, and review some key issues, namely topic selection, definition of standards and criteria. This first section is applicable to clinical audit in almost any setting.
- To look at the organisational issues involved in planning an audit, as a reflection of the importance of getting these right. This second section is most relevant to those working in larger healthcare settings.

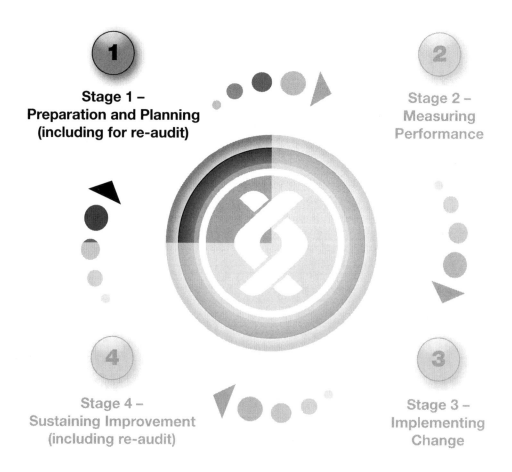

**Stage 1 –
Preparation and Planning
(including for re-audit)**

Stage 2 –
Measuring
Performance

Stage 4 –
Sustaining Improvement
(including re-audit)

Stage 3 –
Implementing
Change

WHY PLANNING IS ESSENTIAL

It can be argued that the preparation and planning stage of any clinical audit project is the most important of all the stages to get right and to do well. As the old adage goes, 'To fail to prepare is to prepare to fail.' Despite this, audit projects are too often put together quickly in order to meet a deadline or requirement without the careful preparation that is needed to achieve success. The result is that these rushed audits often fall at the first hurdle, or limp across the finishing line but without much to show for the effort. It is little wonder then that clinical audit has come under criticism over the years for failing to meet its true potential, a particular point made in England by the Chief Medical Officer in his report *Good Doctors, Safer Patients.*[1] Healthcare professionals and managers are bound to be sceptical about the value of audit if all they see are poorly planned, incomplete audits taking place. This chapter sets out to demonstrate that careful planning and preparation are worth their weight in gold and that, if the steps that follow are practised, audits will be built on a firm foundation from which robust projects will grow to achieve the desired quality improvements.

As noted above, the organisational arrangements for audit that are described in the second part of this chapter are largely geared towards a multi-disciplinary team working together on an audit – for example, in a hospital or community setting. For those individuals who are working independently to accomplish an audit task, the text should be read and applied in the context of the resources available to complete their audit work. For example, a single-handed general practitioner, a nurse practitioner, a medical trainee (undertaking an audit as part of a training programme assessment) or an individual completing an audit project in order to gain a qualification may all be working pretty much alone on their chosen audit. There is an important place for such audit work – it allows for personal reflection and professional development, and growth of a pool of knowledge and skills, in addition to improved care and service delivery for those patients whose management is being evaluated. The book offers ideas and general principles that can be adapted to the individual practitioner's circumstances, acknowledging that the organisation of an audit has to be balanced against the resources available.

GETTING STARTED

There is little doubt that if clinical audit is to be performed well and make a difference to quality, **it requires effective planning and adequate preparation.** However, this need not be the huge and onerous undertaking that is sometimes sold as being necessary to achieve success. In fact the opposite generally applies, because if a team or an individual gets too bogged down with the audit preparation and takes too long to implement data collection, the audit can quickly become out of date and enthusiasm will wane. It is also worth remembering that the process gets easier and often quicker with experience of undertaking audits. Later in this chapter there is a section entitled 'Identifying and developing skills for audit projects', which discusses what roles and skills are needed to facilitate successful audit.

TOPIC SELECTION

Having decided that clinical audit is the best process to use, what topic should be audited? Topics for audit are selected for a variety of reasons, and there are many potential topics from which to choose. Keane *et al.*[2] discuss in some detail the 'triggers' that will prompt the need for an audit. Sometimes there is no choice about undertaking the audit, as it is a requirement for the healthcare organisation concerned, perhaps to satisfy the terms of a contract for the provision of a particular service, or perhaps because it forms part of an annual healthcare inspection that specifies participation in pre-determined audits. In recent times, in England at least, involvement in clinical audit has become less optional, and there are many instances of audit topics being pre-determined externally. A good example of this at a team level would be community pharmacists in England, who are now expected through the terms of their contract to undertake two clinical audit projects per year, the topic for one being determined by the local primary care organisation.[3] At a higher level, NHS trusts in England are increasingly being expected to participate in pre-determined clinical audit projects that relate to NICE guidance, or form part of the National Clinical Audit Patients' Outcome Programme[4] (*see* below), and offer compliance with other regulatory processes operating in England (National Patient Safety Authority compliance), or meet NHS Litigation Authority requirements, Care Quality Commission requirements, etc.

However, a significant number of audit topics should still be selected and initiated at a local healthcare delivery level, where topic choice should be governed by a number of local factors, but primarily that **the topic is a priority to the service concerned.** So how should one topic be prioritised over another?

Useful points to consider when prioritising possible topics

➤ Is the topic concerned with high cost, volume, or risk to staff or users?
➤ Is there evidence of a (serious) quality problem (e.g. patient complaints, high complication rates, adverse outcomes or poor symptom control)?
➤ Is there evidence of wide variation in practice?
➤ Is good evidence available to inform audit standards (e.g. systematic reviews or national clinical guidelines)?
➤ Is the problem measurable against relevant standards?
➤ Is auditing the problem likely to improve healthcare outcomes as well as process improvements?
➤ Is auditing the problem likely to have economic and efficiency benefits?
➤ Is the topic a key professional or clinical interest?
➤ Are reliable sources of data readily available for data collection purposes?
➤ Can data be collected within a reasonable time period?
➤ Is the problem concerned amenable to change?
➤ Is the topic pertinent to national or local initiatives or priorities?
➤ Does the topic lend itself to the process of audit, or is a different process more appropriate (e.g. root cause analysis, activity or workload analysis)?

➤ How much scope is there for improvement, and what are the potential benefits of undertaking this audit?

CHOOSING AUDIT TOPICS

Participation in centrally organised or national audits

Most clinicians will be able to identify their own local priorities for audit topics. However, increasingly there is a need to examine how the audit fits into wider requirements as well as individual clinical interests. There is also the potential to take part in audits designed or implemented by others (e.g. by national research bodies, professional bodies or, more typically, by government and other statutory or regulatory bodies). Sometimes participation in these may be mandatory, either because of government or regulatory requirements, or for accreditation schemes.

These national audits can meet many of the audit needs of local teams, but they do not remove the need for local audit, although they may reduce the time available for local audit in those settings where they are mandatory. From a local team, or healthcare organisation, down to single-handed GP practices, the question of who determines the priorities for audit will depend upon the driving forces for the audit and the level at which the audit is to be undertaken. As well as national priorities, topics will be determined by both clinical priorities and requirements of the organisation's senior management team. Every healthcare organisation, however large or small, will have its own priorities for audit, and these will usually be discussed and selected by a committee, group or team with a remit for managing a programme of clinical audit. This might be the board of the healthcare organisation. At the very least they should ensure that the programmes devised by specific departments fit their strategic needs as well (*see* Appendix 5). It is vital that both the senior clinical team for the specialty and the management team are aware of the local audit programme.

Topics may become important because of a need for public accountability or because of specific events (e.g. in the UK, audits of controlled drugs following the Shipman inquiry, and in England, audits of safety alerts published by the National Patient Safety Agency).

An individual clinician who is considering audit should ensure that whatever they want to do fits into this bigger picture. Any individual audit ought to complement the work of the clinician's department, and may need to fit with national priorities as described above. The clinician needs to be mindful of their organisation's needs in order to ensure that their audit work, which includes the audit work of an individual within it, contributes to the overall work of the organisation as well as that of the individual.

A healthcare provider organisation, whether large or small, needs a balance of locally designed and driven audits with national audit initiatives in its audit programme. This demonstrates that the organisation is aware of and responsive to the needs of its local population, utilising such information as public health statistics to focus priorities on areas of greatest need. It also shows that the organisation is aware of the national quality agenda and how this affects its own local population.

'National' audits come in two forms.

➤ The first type of audit is coordinated and run at a national level under a defined national audit programme – for example, for stroke treatment under England's National Clinical Audit and Patient Outcomes Programme (NCAPOP),[4] whereby healthcare provider organisations participate together in (usually) an annual round of audit that allows benchmarking to take place across all of the participant sites. The results are submitted by healthcare providers to a central data-processing centre where reports are produced and disseminated to the participating sites for discussion and implementation of change at a local level before the next round of audit. There is generally a degree of requirement from central government to participate, achieved through some kind of monitoring or regulatory process. This type of audit is very common in the UK, but less so worldwide. (The HQIP website provides a large volume of information about this programme.)[4]

➤ There are also audits that are designed at a national level, but which are largely undertaken at a local level only, in which participation is largely a result of local clinician interest, often within specialties. Audits of this type are found worldwide. They are often led by societies or other professional bodies, such as the Royal Colleges in the UK. For example, the Royal Pharmaceutical Society of Great Britain has a library of audits, with suggested standards, for use by community pharmacists at a local level. In such audits there is sometimes no aggregation of results at a national level, and only the individual healthcare provider uses them for its own purposes. However, in other cases the society reviews and assembles reports on the participants.

What does a national audit offer?

Many national audits are a central government requirement, and a provider may be asked to show whether they have participated, and the impact of the audit on their work. However, nationally driven and organised audits may not always have the same level of commitment that locally chosen and designed audits have. Some people feel that they prevent local audit ideas from being considered because they tend to be seen as a priority that must be addressed, and which takes up a lot of the available time for audit. Yet the reason why these national audits are important is that they focus on high-cost, high-volume and high-risk areas for which variations in care across healthcare providers are evident, and which are important to government and professional bodies. These audits can reduce such variation and ensure that there is greater equity of service provision and improved care and outcomes for patients. In England, the National Service Framework for Coronary Heart Disease and associated national clinical audits designed to support this, such as the Myocardial Infarction National Audit Project (MINAP), one of the NCAPOP audits referred to above, are key examples of the achievements of such audit projects.[5] They also help to focus attention on a topic as a whole, providing local healthcare professionals with an opportunity to measure their performance against the national averages. They may also identify risk areas for the organisation to be aware of and take action, which might otherwise not have come to light. Finally, these national audits may help to identify further pieces of work, such as new opportunities for partnership working and collaboration with service users, or the addition of more locally devised audit standards that complement the core national audit standards.

Individuals should see that participation in national audits can be useful, especially the second type identified above. As members of teams they may be required to participate in certain national audits of the first type.

Collaborating with stakeholders

In considering audit topics for a local programme, or individual audit, it is important that **the views of all stakeholders, including users, clinical staff, support staff and managers, are represented.** The participation of these groups in selecting topics enables concerns about care to be reported and addressed. Crucially, **topic choice should always involve looking at one's own practice.** Audit by one individual on the work of another individual, or by one service on the work of another service, without their collaboration or consent, is without exception a mistake. Not only will it lead to audit being seen as a divisive, threatening process, but also it is unlikely to lead to change and improved patient care, because those who have gathered and presented the audit data will have no power or support to implement any changes. Clinical audit should be about increasing morale and job motivation, higher-quality individual performance and team coherence, not about breaking these down. Abusing the purpose of audit in order to expose another's performance, rather than focusing on one's own, cannot therefore be justified. Furthermore, reports such as *Good Doctors, Safer Patients* have shown that clinical audit is often carried out in secret, and this does not constitute best practice.[1]

Undertaking audit projects will often provide opportunities for collaborative working, and this is to be encouraged, as it reflects the nature of healthcare delivery from the user's perspective. In general the experience of the user will be one of encountering a number of individuals, teams, services and/or organisations when accessing healthcare. Although there are legitimate occasions for undertaking uni-professional audit, many audit projects will involve more than one professional group and therefore be multi-professional in nature. A clinical team works closely together on the care and management of their patients, so it makes sense that they do the same on their audit projects. For example, a stroke care team may include doctors, nurses, physiotherapists, occupational therapists and speech and language therapists, among others. It is commonplace for such teams to collaborate on audit projects. However, audit projects can be more ambitious still in their level of collaborative working. There is potential to look beyond the clinical team or individual services to cross-boundary or interface audit projects. Here two or more services from two or more different organisations will work on an audit together to reflect the care or management of a targeted group of patients. Examples include the following:

➤ primary care medical services, such as general practice in the UK, working with the community district nursing service and social services when undertaking an audit of pressure area care

➤ diabetes nurse specialists working with podiatrists on diabetic foot care
➤ healthcare drug and alcohol services working with the police and probation services to audit the management of substance misuse
➤ community pharmacy working with primary care medical services to audit repeat prescriptions
➤ ambulance services working with an acute hospital trust to audit call to needle time for thrombolysis.

Collaborative audit projects by their very nature require more planning, preparation and overall coordination than smaller-scale in-house audits. The work involved should not be underestimated, nor should it deter efforts to implement such projects. The need to select a number of topics that involve collaborative working is clear, in view of the nature of healthcare delivery from the user's perspective. A well-managed collaborative audit project can lead to real healthcare benefits for users and great improvement in healthcare quality. The reader may find helpful a report (published on the HQIP website)[6] on established practice in care pathways and cross-sector audits.

Priorities for audit can also be determined and agreed at a team or even an individual practitioner level, and the scope for audits at this level should not be discounted and swept aside just because there are other audit agendas at a service or organisational level. Small teams or individuals undertake some of the best audits, because they are committed to the provision of excellent care, familiar with the users for whom they are responsible, and aware of and able to respond to problems as they arise during the course of the provision of care. Ownership of audit and the desire for change and improvement is often greatest at this level of care. Therefore there should be scope in an audit programme for local small audits of this nature to be supported and encouraged.

Scoring potential audit topics in order to prioritise them
When various topics are considered for audit, at whatever level, there may well be a need to prioritise them in a systematic way. A pragmatic and realistic approach at this stage is essential, as it may not be possible to audit all of the topics initially proposed, and in any case there will be a need to prioritise their order of implementation. All stakeholders should have a voice at this stage, to ensure fairness and equity of topic choice. A scoring system could help to rank topics by order of importance, and the organisation or team may have its own system in use (e.g. a grid listing selection criteria and ranking topics). Practical examples of scoring systems for audit are available on the HQIP website.[7]

Factoring in time for re-audit in the audit programme
Remember that in agreeing audit topics for inclusion in a programme, it is important not to forget to include re-audits and maintenance audits. A significant amount of time will need to be set aside to ensure that re-audits are undertaken in order to complete the audit cycle, and that maintenance audits can be conducted at regular

intervals where a need is identified to ensure that standards are maintained over time.

Is the topic suitable for audit?

Finally, the process of agreeing topics for audit will more often than not raise the question of whether the proposed topic is suitable for audit. As mentioned above, clinical audit is not the only quality monitoring or improvement process used in healthcare, and care must be taken to ensure that it is only used where the methodology can be followed with a good degree of rigour. If this is not the case, an alternative process must be chosen that is appropriate for the purpose. **It is therefore important that every topic considered for audit has been deemed suitable for audit methodology.**

DEFINING THE PURPOSE OF THE AUDIT

A project that lacks clear objectives cannot achieve anything, so a clear sense of purpose must be established before appropriate methods for audit can be considered. Therefore once the clinical audit topic has been agreed, the reason(s) for the project must be clearly defined. In team audits this ensures that everyone involved in the audit is working to a common purpose and so a suitable audit method can be chosen. Do not assume that everyone involved clearly understands the reason(s) for undertaking the audit. A discussion of the nature of the problem that highlighted the need for the audit in the first place is beneficial to ensure clarity of purpose.

Agreeing a working title and clear aims

It is important to be as specific as possible when designing an audit, and a working title for the audit project helps to facilitate this. For example, the title 'An audit of type 2 diabetes' is very broad and ambiguous, and could mean any number of things that potentially leave the audit project open to interpretation. Far more helpful would be 'An audit to improve the monitoring of foot problems in the management of type 2 diabetic patients in a primary care setting.' From such a title the aim of the audit can be clearly deduced. The following series of verbs may be useful when defining the aims of an audit:[8]

➤ to improve
➤ to increase
➤ to enhance
➤ to ensure
➤ to change.

Examples of the use of these verbs are as follows:
➤ to *improve* the door to needle time for patients who require thrombolysis
➤ to *increase* the proportion of patients with hypertension whose blood pressure is controlled
➤ to *enhance* the privacy of patients reporting to the reception desk

➤ to *ensure* that patient confidentiality is maintained when handling patient records
➤ to *change* the process of booking in patients to make it more efficient.

Specifying clear objectives for the audit

Audit project aims tend to be overarching statements of intent. Beneath the aim of the audit it is also helpful to list one or more specific objectives to add clarity of purpose, and against which success can be measured upon completion of the audit. Objectives should specify exactly what will be achieved as a result of the audit, and should therefore:

➤ define the aspects that are being addressed in terms of problem resolution
➤ be clear and focused
➤ be user centred.

Example

Overall aim:
➤ to enhance the privacy of patients reporting to the reception desk.

Specific objectives:
➤ to reduce the incidence of complaints received from patients who feel that their privacy has been compromised when reporting to reception
➤ to enable patients to have a better experience with regard to privacy when reporting to reception
➤ to create a more confidential environment for patients at the reception desk by reviewing processes and procedures.

The adoption of a common language is particularly important, as inconsistent terminology can create confusion for staff from different professional or academic backgrounds. For example, the terms 'standard' and 'criterion' are often interpreted differently (these particular terms are discussed below). Taking time at this planning stage to check out these points will build the confidence of those involved and enhance ownership of, interest in and enthusiasm for the audit project.

Defining audit criteria and standards

Over the years in which audit has been playing a role in the measurement and improvement of quality in healthcare, there has been considerable variation with regard to definitions of the terms 'criteria' and 'standards.' Different professional groups have put their own slant on what is meant by the two terms, and some of these are listed below. Although there are no right or wrong definitions, it is unfortunate that this variation in terminology sometimes causes confusion among health professionals that can lead to problems with the effectiveness of audit. For example, audit criteria that are written as broad statements can be open to interpretation and can therefore be measured differently by different people, thus reducing the reliability and validity of the data collected and the results obtained. Furthermore, depending on the definition used, a performance level (or target) that is expressed as a percentage may not be seen as an essential element of the audit, and may be excluded. Without a discussion around, and the inclusion of, a performance level that aims to be achieved through the audit, how is it possible to know at what level current practice lies, let alone at what level it needs to lie? How is it possible to benchmark or to demonstrate continuous improvements in quality without explicitly stated targets or performance levels? This is in essence what audit is all about, so clear use of the terminology is needed to ensure the quality of projects undertaken.

The following definitions of criterion and standards are reproduced from the previous edition of *Principles of Best Practice in Clinical Audit*, with permission.

BOX 2.1 The various definitions of 'criterion' and 'standards'

Definitions of a 'criterion'
- An item or variable that enables the achievement of a standard (broad objective of care) and the evaluation of whether it has been achieved or not.[9]
- A definable and measurable item of healthcare that describes quality and which can be used to assess it.[10]
- A systematically developed statement that can be used to assess the appropriateness of specific healthcare decisions, services and outcomes.[11]

Definitions of a 'standard'
- An objective with guidance for its achievement given in the form of criteria sets that specify required resources, activities and predicted outcomes.[9]
- The level of care to be achieved for any particular criterion.[10]
- The percentage of events that should comply with the criterion.[12]

Rather than becoming too concerned with rigid definitions, it is perhaps more helpful to accept that clinical audits have the greatest chance of success when they include not only measurable statements of what should be happening (i.e. criteria), but also explicit and quantifiable performance levels expressed as percentages (often also referred to as standards or targets). For the purposes of this book, the term 'standard' is defined as an amalgamation of both the criterion and the performance level or target. Thus it is a quantifiable statement made up of two component parts, rather than being described solely as a percentage. However, it is important for the reader to be aware that the terms 'criteria' and 'standards' will be encountered in their different forms depending upon the setting in which the audit is taking place.

Sometimes the terms 'criteria' and 'standards' will be used separately, and an example of how these may be phrased is given below:

➤ criterion: *'Patients with diabetes should have a record of retinal screening in the last 15 months'*
➤ standard: 90%.[13]

Sometimes only the term 'standard' will be used, and an example of how this may be phrased is given below:

> *'Ninety per cent of patients with diabetes should have a record of retinal screening in the last 15 months.'*[13]

The important point here is that the audit team or individual agrees on the definitions of the terms to be used when discussing the audit. This will prevent confusion and possible weaknesses in the phrasing of those aspects of care that are going to be measured in the audit. Crucially, agreeing a performance level or target (expressed as a percentage) should not be overlooked, as this is a key component of the measurable elements of the audit.

Selecting and developing appropriate audit criteria

Most audit topics have the potential to include a number of audit criteria, and it may be tempting to include more than necessary. However, if the audit topic has clearly agreed and understood aims and objectives, with a clear focus, then it will be easier to identify those criteria that need to be measured in the audit in order to determine whether or not the objectives have been achieved.

When considering possible audit criteria, it is helpful to discuss what aspects do need to be measured, as well as those that do not. It is all too easy to include numerous criteria in the belief that this will offer greater potential for change and improvement. However, these over-ambitious projects tend to lose momentum over time because they expect too much of those involved, and are complex to interpret and to identify where changes should be made. On the other hand, audits that are more selective in their chosen criteria provide a better focus on specific aspects of care. They also tend to lend themselves to greater potential for change, because they are realistic in their expectations of those involved and they pinpoint where change is needed. Compliance with audit is more likely to occur where there are attempts at selectivity. The risk that the project will try to collect too much data is particularly high in national audits.

STRUCTURE, PROCESS AND OUTCOME

Avedis Donabedian[14] proposed that the quality of healthcare consisted of three inter-related parts – structure, process and outcome. It is helpful to think of audit criteria in terms of:
➤ structure (what you need)
➤ process (what you do)
➤ outcome (what you expect to happen as a result).

Structure criteria

Criteria that concern the 'structure' of care refer to the physical attributes needed and the resources required to deliver healthcare. They may include audit of the numbers of staff, skill mix, organisational arrangements, the provision of equipment and physical space, as well as the handling of patient records, or even the very existence of particular types of services.

An example of a structure criterion, taken from the record-keeping guidance of the UK's regulatory body for nursing, the Nursing and Midwifery Council (NMC), but which also reflects on quality of care, is given below:

> All entries to records should be signed. In the case of written records, the person's name and job title should be printed alongside the first entry.[15]

Although structure criteria do not always **directly** relate to the care given to patients, they often provide an indication of how well resourced a team or department is in order to function effectively and support care given. Although the presence of a good structure to support care does not necessarily ensure the quality of that care, the absence of a good structure may well reduce the ability to provide the best care possible. Audits of structure have their place in the clinical audit arena when there is a need to demonstrate the efficiency of the environment in which care and service delivery takes place. A good structure provides the cornerstone of good care, offering tangible evidence that potential markers of quality are in place.

Process criteria

Clinical audits nearly always measure process criteria more than the other measures, because these focus directly on the actions and decisions taken by practitioners together with their patients, and the comparison of these with agreed standards is at the core of clinical audit. These actions may include communication, assessment, education, investigations, prescribing, surgical and other therapeutic interventions, evaluation and some aspects of documentation.

An example of a process criterion is given below:

> In the last 9 months patients with hypertension should have had their blood pressure recorded.[13]

It is simplistic to criticise process criteria as being the poor relations of outcome criteria, although this often happens. It can be argued that using process criteria encourages clinical teams to concentrate on the things they do that contribute directly to improved health outcomes, and that the link between them is quite possible to demonstrate (*see* Appendix 2 in this volume for a discussion of these issues). However, process criteria are variable measures of the quality of care, as a poor outcome does not occur every time there is an error or omission in the process of care. Nonetheless, the importance of process criteria is determined by the extent to which compliance with them influences the outcome. The process that is being audited must have been evidenced as valuable in having an impact on the healthcare outcomes that the patient experiences as a result.

Outcome criteria

Donabedian defined 'outcome' as the changes in a patient's current and future health status that can be attributed to antecedent healthcare. Outcome criteria are typically measures of the physical or behavioural response to an intervention, reported health status, and level of knowledge and satisfaction. However, surrogate, proxy or intermediate outcome criteria are often used instead, because suitable outcomes may not be measurable or demonstrable. These surrogates and other outcome criteria relate to aspects of care that are closely linked to eventual outcome, but are more easily measured. For example, measuring blood pressure control in patients with hypertension is a more practical and immediate measure for driving improvements in care, and then better outcomes, than only measuring eventual morbidity due to associated conditions. An example of such a criterion may thus be phrased as follows:

> In the last 9 months patients with hypertension should have a recorded blood pressure reading of 150/90 or less.[13]

Some audits, especially national ones, focus specifically on outcomes and do not include formal criteria, but instead collect data about the outcomes of care. This is a practical possibility when outcomes are easily measurable and occur soon after the delivery of care. If the outcomes are also of major importance to patients (e.g. post-operative complications), the direct measurement of outcomes is not only appropriate, but also expected. However, audit using outcome measures alone sometimes provides insufficient information for developing an action plan for improving practice. This is typically where local audits can supplement national audits, so that local clinicians can understand exactly what are the causes – in the form of actions that should have been undertaken – of the outcomes.

When outcomes are used for comparative audit, adjustments may be needed for case mix, a process known as 'risk adjustment.' Failure to use either a formal or informal method of risk adjustment to account for any variation in patient populations sometimes leads to misinterpretation of the findings. However, it is important to avoid falling into the trap of assuming that poor outcomes are explained by case mix alone, when in fact they are due to failures in the process of care.

Writing clear audit criteria

Crucial to the collection of valid data is the wording of clear, unambiguous audit criteria. Remember that these are explicit statements which define exactly what is being measured. They represent the items of care or aspects of service provision that are relevant to the audit objectives, and which will be measured in order to assess the quality of care that a patient has received. If the wording of the criteria is open to interpretation, there is the potential for data collectors to interpret them differently, which can lead to data being mis-categorised in relation to the criteria. The consequence of this is that the results achieved may not reflect the true level of performance.

This can be illustrated by an example in which three slightly differently worded criteria are given. If we wanted to look at whether patients with hypertension had had a blood pressure recorded within the previous 9 months that was within the range of 150/90 or less, only one of the criteria below would measure this precisely and accurately. The other two would produce inaccurate levels of performance because they would allow different patients to be either included or excluded on the basis of whether they met the criterion, thus affecting the performance level achieved.

1 *Patients with hypertension should have a record of a blood pressure reading within the last 9 months of less than 150/90.*
2 *Patients with hypertension should have their last recorded blood pressure reading of 150/90 or less.*
3 *Patients with hypertension should have a record of a blood pressure reading of 150/90 or less within the last 9 months.*

The first example would exclude those patients with a blood pressure of exactly 150/90 from meeting the criterion, when in fact these patients should be included. The results could therefore reflect a lower performance level than is actually the case.

The second example would include any patient whose last recorded blood pressure measurement was within the stated limits, regardless of when it was recorded, because no time frame is stated. The results here would reflect a higher level of performance than should be the case, because any blood pressure recorded within the target range would be counted, regardless of how long ago it was recorded.

The third example, on the other hand, should produce more valid and accurate results that reflect the true level of performance, because the criterion is not open to interpretation. It tells us exactly what blood pressure we are looking for and within what time frame. Therefore only those patients with a record in the last 9 months of a blood pressure of 150/90 or less will be counted as having met the criterion.

When agreeing criteria for audit projects, it is advisable for them to be compatible with SMART guidance – that is, Specific, Measurable, Achievable, Relevant and Theoretically sound or Timely.

Inclusion/exclusion criteria

In order to review whether the **right people** are receiving the right care, it is vital that the audit sample represents the target group accurately. For example, if you are conducting an audit on treatment for childhood asthma, you may wish to exclude children under the age of 2 and over the age of 16 years. Other criteria may include aspects such as gender, disease type, treatment regime, place of treatment, and so on.

Exceptions

Once a sample group has been identified and data collection has commenced, it may be necessary to discontinue data collection on certain cases – for example, if a patient has been unable to receive the prescribed treatment due to contraindications, or where treatment has had to be stopped due to side-effects or refusal of treatment.

In these cases the reasons for discontinuation must be clearly recorded and marked as non-applicable so that they are not included in the analysis.

Sources of possible audit criteria

Evidence-based guidance

Research suggests that audit criteria are not always based on research evidence.[16] Where possible, audit criteria should be drawn from up-to-date evidence-based guidance, as this will provide objective and explicit statements about what should be happening to patients for specific topic areas. For the majority of clinical audit topics today it is likely that this guidance will be readily available and often in routine use. In the UK, for example, NICE produces evidence-based guidance on a wide range of topics, and these come with suggested audit criteria. The Department of Health in England has produced National Service Frameworks for a number of disease areas. In the UK, various Royal Colleges and societies produce their own evidence-based guidance, such as the Royal College of Physicians (for stroke) and the British Thoracic Society (BTS) (for asthma). Other organisations also produce guidelines on a range of topics, including the Scottish Intercollegiate Guidelines Network (SIGN), whose guidance includes specific aspects of management that could be used as the starting point for developing criteria for different subgroups of patients. The development of guidance by such bodies depends on careful review of the relevant research evidence so that the criteria contained within the guidelines are likely to be valid. National audit programmes will also have a role in defining or refining audit criteria.

Up-to-date literature searches

Where there is no national (or local) guidance available, a literature search of specific journals or good-quality systematic reviews can be undertaken to identify the best and most up-to-date evidence that can be used to generate audit criteria. Hearnshaw's study[16] highlighted problems in gathering and assessing literature upon which to base audit criteria in terms of assessing how recent and valid it is. It is vital that this is done well if the audit is to stand up to scrutiny. Literature searches may be conducted with the help of a librarian or library resource, often available as a resource within the healthcare organisation. Online resources may also be useful when searching for agreed best practice on which to base an audit. In England, for example, clinical audits undertaken in the National Health Service may be supported by accessing sites such as www.evidence.nhs.uk or www.library.nhs.uk.

Professional consensus

Sometimes it may be necessary for a group of professionals to formulate their own criteria where national guidance or evidence-based literature are not available, and here the use of formal consensus methods is preferable. A checklist is useful to ensure that an explicit process is used to identify, select and combine the evidence for the criteria, and that the strength of the evidence is assessed in some way.[17]

Several sets of locally based criteria have been developed by involving clinical experts and consensus panels. For example, in an initiative to transfer outpatient follow-up after cardiac surgery from secondary to primary care, protocols for optimal care in general practice were developed in collaboration with a consultant cardiologist, with criteria and standards being agreed between the cardiologist, general practitioners and nurses.[18] Locally developed criteria have the advantage that it is easier to take into account local factors such as the concerns of local users.

In practice, the most efficient approach is likely to be the use of criteria developed by experts from evidence, together with criteria based on the preferences of users determined locally.

Once a source has been identified, relevant criteria can be selected from this to form the basis of the audit. Provided that the audit has well-defined objectives and a clear focus, it will be relatively straightforward to select and agree these criteria. Although the guidance from which the criteria are drawn will most likely cover management of a broad number of aspects of care, only those aspects that are relevant to the audit objectives should be used. For example, the BTS guidance on asthma covers many aspects of management, and auditing all of these in one audit would be a major undertaking. However, if the objective of an audit was to improve the diagnosis of asthma, the criteria drawn from the guidance would be those that focus specifically on confirming the diagnosis using spirometry or peak flow measurement.

Involving users in developing audit criteria
There are now increasing opportunities for working collaboratively with users when writing appropriate and relevant audit criteria. Users will bring a different perspective to those aspects of the audit that they consider important to measure. With new ways of accessing representative groups of users for developing audits, it is possible to identify the specific needs of people with a particular condition, taking account of age and ethnic or social backgrounds. Audit teams can collaborate with users to establish their experience of the service and the important elements of care from which criteria can be developed. Several qualitative methods are available to help with understanding users' experiences. These include:
➤ the critical incident technique[19]
➤ focus groups[20]
➤ consumer audit.[21]

Working with users to identify criteria might result in different and therefore additional criteria being added to an audit in order to reflect aspects of care and service provision that are important to the users. It might also identify the same aspects of care delivery, but users may have different views about these to health professionals. In such situations a facilitated and open approach is required in order to reach a mutually acceptable consensus. The guidance in Appendix 6 suggests ways of engaging with service users to fulfil the role set out here.

SELECTING AND DEVELOPING APPROPRIATE PERFORMANCE LEVELS

Measuring compliance – in this context, performance – is the core of audit, so getting this right is crucial.

Remember that performance levels are expressed in the form of percentages to represent the proportion of patients or occasions that must fulfil each criterion.

Agreeing and setting performance levels or targets is an area of audit planning that sometimes causes controversy. **It is generally agreed that each audit criterion should have a performance level or target assigned to it.** Indeed, failure to do this can lead to missed opportunities for improvement, even where practice appears to be good. However, the precise level at which performance levels should be set is not always obvious. Open discussion among the audit team members and relevant stakeholders needs to take place in order to agree the most appropriate performance levels. These are necessary to determine to what degree the audit criteria should be achieved, and to identify whether or not change needs to be implemented. Setting performance levels at the outset of the audit helps to generate discussion about where the team believes it should be in terms of delivering a quality service. The team is motivated by having explicit targets to aim for. Such targets also help the team to focus on gauging where current performance levels lie, recognising that there is a shortfall, and thus justifying the need for the chosen audit criteria.

Reviewing performance levels

Deciding on performance levels to measure against is an important part of the planning of an audit. Although it is worth spending some time agreeing reasonable performance levels to aim for, it is not necessary to spend too much time on this part of the process. In team audits with multi-disciplinary participation across care pathways, it is possible that not everyone will agree on all the performance levels for the audit criteria to audit, so compromise may need to be sought when it is felt that all points have been made. It may be helpful to acknowledge that performance levels are not always set in stone. If, after collecting the data, analysing the results and implementing changes, the re-audit shows that some performance levels still have not been reached, it may be appropriate to review these. However, performance levels are designed to be worked towards, so it may be that further change and more time is needed to reach the desired performance levels. In such situations it is helpful for the audit team to be able to compare their performance with that of others who may have undertaken a similar audit. Benchmarking is an effective way of determining whether one's own performance falls short of, matches or exceeds that of others. This is one benefit of participating in national audit programmes where benchmarking is used to compare practice, stimulate debate at a local level and motivate change to drive up quality.

What is a reasonable performance level?

The point at which performance levels are set for each criterion will depend on three key factors:[22]

➤ clinical importance
➤ practicability
➤ acceptability.

A balance between these three factors needs to be sought when agreeing performance levels. In an ideal world, performance levels would always be set at 100%, but in healthcare this is not always a realistic goal. Resources are limited, and competing priorities lead to the need to make compromises based on the factors identified.

Clinical importance

Unless it is critical to the safety of patients that a performance level of 100% is achieved, this target tends to be chosen less often than lower, more realistic targets. The criterion 'Penicillin allergy should be marked on the front of patient records' would justify a performance level of 100% because of the potentially life-threatening consequences of not doing this. On the other hand, the criterion 'Patients with a transient ischaemic attack or stroke should have a record of total cholesterol in the last 15 months' might justify a lower performance level because the consequences of not achieving this for every stroke patient are less significant.

Practicability

In theory there are many audit criteria for which a performance level of 100% is possible. However, the resources that would have to be expended to achieve these ideals are unrealistic. Time and energy spent on achieving 100% on some aspects of care and service provision will inevitably be at the expense of other aspects. Unless it is of critical importance that 100% is achieved, it is more practical to set performance levels that take account of the reality of healthcare provision. The effort that is put into reaching the performance level must be justified by the anticipated quality improvements.

Acceptability

Both those who deliver the care and those who receive it must feel that the performance level is reasonable and attainable. An unrealistically high target will not foster motivation, enthusiasm or support among hardworking health professionals who feel that the expectations of the audit are too high. Equally, a target that is set too low may be received with scepticism on the part of those who give and receive care, because it might appear that little importance is given to that aspect of care, and the motivation to achieve more may be low.

It might also be helpful to think about performance levels in terms of minimum, ideal and optimum levels.[10]

Minimum level

This is the lowest acceptable level of performance. Minimum levels are often set nationally and may be linked to some sort of incentive. This minimum level tends to set the bar below which performance is considered to be unacceptable. Since clinical audit is about continuous quality improvement, it can be said of minimum performance levels that they do not encourage best practice. It may be tempting for busy health professionals to settle for reaching the minimum performance level rather than devoting time to introducing changes that would raise performance even higher, thus benefiting more patients. It is therefore easy to settle for minimum performance levels because these are considered acceptable.

Ideal level

This is the highest possible level of performance. It would be possible to provide this under ideal conditions, without any constraints on resources. Generally, however, this is rarely set or expected in clinical audit for the reasons stated earlier in relation to the three key factors.

Optimum level

This lies somewhere between the minimum and the ideal level. It requires those involved to use their judgement to reach the most appropriate level. It takes account of what is the best that can be provided for patients, given the resources available, under normal conditions of caregiving. It allows healthcare professionals to consider at what level current practice lies, and then to decide on the preferred level to which they could aspire.

In the UK, NICE suggests explicit performance levels in its audit tools that accompany its guidance. These often reflect optimum performance levels that allow for improvement, yet at the same time acknowledge that ideal levels are unrealistic in most circumstances. The quality payment scheme for general practice in England, the Quality and Outcomes Framework (QOF),[13] sets both minimum and optimum performance levels for which there are different payments depending upon the level achieved.

AGREEING EFFECTIVE AUDIT STANDARDS

Remember that, for the purposes of this book, audit standards are made up of both the audit criterion and the associated performance level (or target). Identifying and selecting appropriate audit criteria and agreeing levels of performance to create robust audit standards requires experience as well as a good understanding of the process. The more rigorous this process, the more likely it is that the resulting standards will be valid and reliable, measuring precisely and clearly what they intend to measure in order to determine current practice as well as to move towards desirable practice. In addition to what has been covered under selecting and developing audit criteria and performance levels, the following questions may be helpful when finalising audit standards.

➤ What sources of evidence have been identified and considered?
➤ If national standards are to be used, do they need to be tailored to local circumstances?
➤ Who has been consulted about possible standards?

➤ How have standards been selected and agreed?

➤ Will the chosen standards answer the audit questions?

➤ Are the standards written clearly and understood by all?

➤ Do the standards support the ethos of continuous quality improvement by giving something to aim for over and above current practice?

PLANNING THE AUDIT PROJECT TIMETABLE

Once the audit team is up and running, the stakeholders are on board and the aims and objectives have been agreed, **it is crucial to draw up and follow an audit timetable.** Many an audit will appear to start off well, with everyone clear about their roles and the tasks to be completed. However, problems regularly occur when the team fails to set in place agreed timescales by which each task needs to be completed. A timetable helps to ensure that all team members are aware of the expectations placed on them, as well as maintaining the momentum of the audit. Too many potentially good projects have not been completed because no timetable was formally agreed and the audit tasks dragged on, with those involved eventually giving up. In order to achieve results the audit must be effectively project managed, and a key aspect of this is timetabling.

The audit timetable does not need to be onerous, and can greatly assist a team with scheduling the audit work into the rest of the routine day-to-day workload, taking account of such factors as busy and quiet periods, annual leave of team members, and training commitments. The timetable should include, as a minimum, the following:

➤ the start dates and end dates of each and every task of the audit

➤ what each task involves (i.e. a breakdown of each step of the audit)

➤ who is involved in completing each task

➤ space against each task to sign it off when it has been completed.

The audit project lead should manage the audit timetable to ensure that it stays on track. Team members need to inform the audit lead if the timescale of any task is likely to need to be reviewed and, where adjustments need to be made to the timetable, all those affected must be informed. A timetable also helps to motivate the audit team, and aids the overall planning and scheduling of an audit programme, increasing the potential for success.

ORGANISATIONAL ISSUES

Providing a structure within which audit can take place

This section primarily applies to team audits within organisations.

Identify an audit lead/coordinator

An individual needs to take responsibility for overseeing and project managing the audit. This should be an individual with good audit knowledge and skills to ensure that the process followed is robust and that the right people are involved and that they are deployed in the most effective ways. Equally important is their ability to motivate others, inject enthusiasm into the process and keep the audit running to the agreed timetable. This individual may or may not have a hands-on role in performing the audit work, but will always be instrumental in the progress of the project. Facilitation skills will therefore be necessary to ensure that meetings to plan and manage the audit are effective and action-oriented. In addition, this individual will need to be accessible to all those involved in the audit work, so that queries and problems can be ironed out at any time and without undue delay to the audit process. The audit lead is the driving cog in the audit wheel, and without them audits will often flounder. They ensure that team members complete their tasks by the agreed deadlines, and enable a seamless flow from one stage of the cycle to the next without the communication breakdowns that can lead to delays and even failure of an audit project.

Organise a working group/audit team

The first question to ask is whether a working group or audit team is needed. In the case of individuals working alone on audits, this will not be possible, although the individual is encouraged to seek out and make use of any support that is available. Generally, however, an audit team will be necessary, particularly if standards need to be agreed, a data collection tool needs to be designed and a meaningful amount of data needs to be collected. If this is the case, it is important to get the team members together as soon as possible. Members need to be accessible, available and representative. If they are not, the audit team can take too long to meet because of the unavailability of one or more members. Securing commitment from key individuals and getting the first meeting in their diaries as quickly as possible requires someone to organise this efficiently and without protracted communication. **The audit team should be kept as small as possible**, so that there are fewer people to organise and manage when working on the audit design and methodology. So long as key stakeholders are represented, including service users, the group can be kept as small as possible. Allocating roles to individual members of the team is also a helpful way to get commitment, divide up the audit work fairly, and ensure clarity of direction and purpose. This could even be done prior to the first meeting, in discussion with individual members, so that they feel valued and prepared for their contribution to the audit project.

IDENTIFYING THE STAKEHOLDERS

In addition to the core audit team who will assume responsibility for undertaking the audit, it is helpful in the early planning stages to consider all stakeholders who will be affected by the audit and its anticipated changes. This may happen in a variety of ways, including being asked to identify the important aspects to measure in the audit (i.e. audit standards), collecting audit data, participating in a meeting to discuss the results of the audit and contribute ideas for potential changes, implementing changes, ongoing monitoring, etc.

It is not always immediately apparent who all the stakeholders will be, as their roles in relation to the subject that is being audited will vary. For example, an audit of falls prevention among the elderly in the community may be organised by a community nursing team. They may decide to collaborate with occupational therapy and physiotherapy colleagues, as well as with user representatives and social care services. However, they perhaps do not automatically consider how their audit will affect administrative and support services, such as clinic reception staff and records staff, whereas in fact changes resulting from the audit may well have an impact on these staff. Other wider stakeholders who are not immediately obvious but who could make a potential contribution might include national charities, local voluntary groups, ambulance services, Accident and Emergency departments, residential and nursing homes, and primary care medical services.

One way of assisting in the identification of important stakeholders involves creating a flowchart to illustrate the major steps and activities undertaken within the care process that is being audited. An example is shown in Figure 2.1.

Flowcharting, or workflow analysis as it is sometimes called, helps teams to:

➤ explore the relationships between different activities
➤ identify stakeholders (those who will be affected by the audit)
➤ focus attention on where improvement efforts need to be concentrated
➤ pinpoint weaknesses in processes and systems that contribute to the occurrence of errors.

MAKE USE OF WHAT IS ALREADY AVAILABLE

The planning of any audit project requires the undertaking of background research to find out what is already available that might inform the chosen audit topic. Once the topic is agreed, there may well be established, evidence-based guidelines and/or audit protocols that can be tailored for use in the chosen audit. Sometimes these might be in a template format, which will assist greatly with the design and planning of the audit. In the UK, for example, NICE designs an audit tool for use with each set of its published guidelines.[24] These tools not only set out the audit criteria and standards, but they also supply a data collection tool. Where guidelines are available in relation to the chosen audit topic, these can be used to draw out relevant and appropriate audit standards, although a data collection tool will probably still need to be devised. Making use of what is already available takes care of a lot of the planning and preparation that would otherwise need to be undertaken by the audit team.

Where they are available, staff with a remit for audit should be contacted at the earliest opportunity to secure help, advice and practical assistance wherever necessary. Although the audit team should have some working knowledge of audit, they may not always have an audit expert in their midst. The audit lead may therefore need to access sources of specialist advice early in the process to ensure a robust audit design. Too often an audit team will launch into an audit without the necessary rigour, only to contact audit staff for assistance when the audit encounters difficulties,

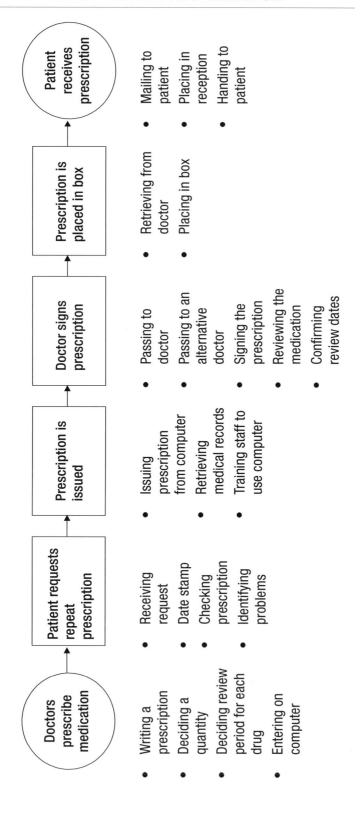

FIGURE 2.1 An example of a top-down flowchart describing the repeat prescribing process at a GP's practice. (Reproduced with permission from Cox et al.)[23]

which are often caused by flaws in the methodology that could have been avoided if advice had been sought at the outset.

Key to the success of any clinical audit project is having a sound structure in place to support the undertaking of the audit. The following factors need to be considered to ensure that the structure is in place:

➤ quality assurance of audits
➤ funding
➤ protected time.

Quality assurance of audits

Healthcare organisations need a mechanism to ensure that clinical audit projects which are being proposed and undertaken meet certain key criteria that reflect their quality. Any audit project must stand up to scrutiny so that the resources expended can be justified. Healthcare organisations often have their own project assessment framework or clinical audit proposal form, which has to be completed for any proposed audit project to assess whether or not it meets the level of rigour required to be effective. This paperwork is therefore a vital part of the process of quality assuring any planned audit activity. The reader can view an example proposal form on the HQIP website,[6] as well as other referral forms and associated paperwork for audit planning purposes.

Walshe and Spurgeon[25] proposed nine elements against which to assess the likely quality of a proposed audit, namely reasons for topic selection, impact, costs, objectives, involvement, use of evidence, project management, methods and evaluation. Ethical issues associated with the audit were not included in this list, but Morrell and Harvey[26] recommend the need to include consent, confidentiality, effectiveness of audit, and accountability. Individuals and teams who are undertaking audits should be familiar with their policies and guidance on consent and confidentiality. It is essential that any audit project upholds the requirements to obtain user consent where necessary, and to maintain data protection and confidentiality of all those individuals whose records are used in the audit. On the HQIP website the reader can access the document *Ethics and Clinical Audit and Quality Improvement (QI) – A Guide for NHS Organisations* for further guidance.[27] An adaptation of this work for an international audience can be found in Appendix 1 of this book.

For anyone who is undertaking an audit, it is good practice to apply a process of quality assessment of the audit to ensure that it meets the minimum requirements necessary to be a robust piece of work.

Funding

Another reason why it is important to justify any proposed audit project and to plan and prepare for this carefully is the cost associated with undertaking the audit. Costs can be measured in terms of a number of variables, including manpower, training, energy and equipment costs. Costs associated with implementing changes to improve practice must also be considered, and if possible predicted and estimated at the outset to determine whether or not the audit is a worthwhile investment. Thus a key part of the planning stage involves making a clear costing for the audit inputs and, as part of the project design, an analysis of how the project will incur costs or save money.

The cost of audits will vary according to their size and subject matter, but it is worth costing even the smallest of projects to assess its value. Generally the larger the project the greater will be the costs associated with it, but the gains from improving healthcare are likely to be greater, too. **There may also be significant savings to be made from the changes implemented as a result of audits**, including improvements in the efficiency of procedures, simplification of processes, etc.

In general, clinical audits that are undertaken on the back of any new evidence-based guidance, such as that produced by NICE for the NHS in the UK, are likely to lead to increased direct healthcare costs, most often from increased prescribing and the need for more regular and consistent patient monitoring and review. However, these costs should be offset against the benefits gained from better patient management, better symptom control, fewer hospital admissions, avoidance of waste and unnecessary systems and procedures, and reduced morbidity and mortality.

It is important that the processes of undertaking clinical audit as well as responding to the findings of audit are supported by adequate resourcing if audit is to realise its full potential to improve quality of healthcare. The cost of adequate clinical audit staff, clinical and support staff, and user involvement in audit should not be underestimated. Clinical staff will struggle to participate in and complete effective clinical audit projects unless they have expert support in terms of project management, knowledge of clinical audit techniques, facilitation, data management, staff training and administration. However, as mentioned above, the costs of this support are likely to be covered many times over by the gains in healthcare quality.

In any organisation it is essential to have support and commitment for audit from the budget holders, not only in terms of resourcing the actual audit work but also, perhaps more importantly, devoting serious consideration to the findings that a service needs further resources in order to improve. It is essential therefore that budget holders are involved in the setting of the organisation's clinical audit programme, so that expected costs can be forecast and accounted for in advance.

Some organisations and services allocate a proportion of their annual budget to fund clinical audit work. It is important to review the size of the allocation in order to ensure that funding meets the required level of audit activity. Increasing demands are being placed on organisations to participate in such initiatives, as national audits are changing each year, and funding needs to reflect this.

Making time

When the first edition of this book was published in 2002, the main barrier to audit reported in the literature was lack of resources, especially time. Both protected time to investigate the audit topic and collect and analyse data, and time to complete an audit cycle were in short supply. Little has changed in the last eight years, and **it remains a challenge for healthcare professionals to find sufficient time for clinical audit work.** However, this is essential in any setting if clinical audit is to realise its potential as a quality improvement process. Commitment to making time for clinical audit work begins with managers, who need to make protected time available on a regular basis to show that they recognise the importance of this activity. **Clinical audit cannot be seen as an optional extra, but must be embedded in the culture of the organisation at all levels.** In both large and small organisations, managers have a responsibility to ensure that this happens.

There are a number of ways in which audit can be 'built into' routine practice, rather than merely being 'bolted on' if and when time allows. These are summarised below.

Standing agenda item

Audit can be made a regular standing item on the agenda of team meetings. This helps to ensure that audit is seen as part of routine practice, keeps it relevant and enables regular discussion about potential topics and progress of current audits. Most crucially, it offers an opportunity to experience the satisfaction of seeing the improvements that result from the team's audit work. This stimulates interest in and ownership of audits by team members, and thus greater commitment to participation in the process.

Change and share audit roles

Sharing the work associated with audit projects can help to manage the time required for carrying them out. Too often members of a team or individuals working for an organisation get typecast into performing the same tasks every time an audit is undertaken. For example, in a primary care general practice setting in the UK, the practice manager will often project manage the audit, design the audit tool, analyse the data and create a presentation for the team to discuss. Nursing staff (often only one individual) will collect the data and may have to analyse these, too. General practitioners or family doctors will usually attend meetings to plan and discuss the audit, but often do not design tools for the audit or undertake data collection or analysis. Therefore a good way to keep an audit on track is to revise team roles for the audit work and ensure equity of labour. This enhances understanding of all stages of the audit cycle, and helps to maintain interest in the different tasks of audit. Often the justification for clinical staff collecting and analysing data is that non-clinical staff will not understand the clinical content of the data sources. However, the use of a well-designed data collection tool, with guidance notes for completion, should be straightforward for both clinical and non-clinical staff. It is important to involve users in the process as well (see later), as they are key stakeholders and, with the right training and support, can make a major contribution to the work associated with an audit.

Use communication mechanisms to keep people informed

Audit can be 'built into' routine practice by making use of as many quick and accessible communication methods as possible to keep people informed of audit activity taking place within the team, service or organisation. Inviting ideas for audit, disseminating results and providing information about changes and improvements in practice as a result of audit work can stimulate interest and promote the purpose of audit as a quality improvement process. For example, asking those who have participated in audits to write short articles for publication in a team or organisation newsletter is an effective means of keeping audit current, real and meaningful. It can also encourage others to participate if they see their colleagues getting involved. In larger organisations, an annual audit study day or conference is an ideal way to share 'good news' stories of audits that have made a real difference and benefited users and staff alike. Commitment to funding such a day and making time for staff to attend will demonstrate the value that is placed on audit by an organisation.

Enlist the help of audit support staff

The clinician should contact any staff within an organisation who have a remit for clinical audit, either as part of their role or as a dedicated specialist. Clinical audit staff may be employed by an organisation or may be available from a local commissioning body or at a regional or national level, for example, for advice and/ or practical support for audit work. This could include private sector consultancy. However, it is not uncommon for teams or individual clinicians to struggle with the design of an audit project, to spend a long time collecting and analysing data, and then to attempt to agree changes without accessing the expert advice and support that audit staff can provide. Even where audit staff are not available, there is merit in identifying key online resources that can be utilised to ensure that audits are well designed and carried out effectively. For example, the HQIP website contains a number of audit resources. The various healthcare professional bodies also often have clinical audit resources available on their websites.

Identifying and developing skills for audit projects

This section applies primarily to larger organisations.

To be successful, a clinical audit project needs to involve the right people with the right skills from the outset. Therefore identifying the skills required and organising the key individuals should be priorities. Certain skills are needed for all audit projects. These include the following:

➤ project leadership, project organisation and project management
➤ clinical, managerial and other service input and leadership
➤ expertise in clinical audit methodology
➤ data collection and analysis skills
➤ change management skills
➤ facilitation skills.

Audit project teams

The audit team, a concept that was introduced earlier in this chapter, will be customised to the specific audit project, with each team member contributing relevant knowledge and/or skills to the audit project. When working as part of a multi-disciplinary team there is a great array of valuable sources of information and advice available when planning an audit, each source contributing different skills and knowledge.[28]

CLINICAL STAFF

Most audits start with clinicians, who very often lead the audit. They will primarily contribute ideas about what aspects of care or service delivery need to be measured, as well as how these can be measured. They will be familiar with the process of clinical care and the recording systems used, so they are ideally placed to develop the audit standards and to identify appropriate data items that will need to be collected. However, they may not have the audit knowledge or skills necessary to ensure precise wording of the audit standards so that these are measurable, or to design the data collection tool. This may need to be the role of another team member, either someone who has attended training in audit methodology or a designated audit professional to whom the team has access.

SUPPORT STAFF

It is also important that the audit team includes members from all of the relevant groups involved in care delivery, not just those with a clinical role. These may include ancillary staff, reception staff and administrative staff. They will be aware of what goes on in the background to support clinical care, and are therefore ideally placed to point out important factors that the audit design will need to take into account if it is to run smoothly, such as how to access the records needed for data collection and other organisational factors that affect the treatment and management of the target population.

MANAGERS

Service management representation on the audit team will also be a valuable addition, particularly where it is likely that there will be significant resource implications as a result of the audit findings. Managers can liaise with budget holders, for example, and ensure that the audit project is realistic and manageable. They may also have skills to contribute in areas such as project and change management, negotiation and motivation. The degree of involvement of managers in clinical audit projects will vary, but a lack of commitment from managers can lead to serious misunderstandings. Therefore it is vital that all managers understand the aims of audit and support those involved.

COMMISSIONERS

Commissioners may suggest audits or require them, and may wish to be involved in the audit team in some circumstances. In any case they should be kept informed and consulted.

SERVICE USERS

It is important to recognise that service users have a crucial role to play in the audit team. Although it is still relatively uncommon to find user representatives on an audit team, there are increasing justifications for including them. **Service users are key players in determining whether their experience of healthcare is of an acceptable quality.** They can certainly contribute to important aspects of care and service delivery to measure in the audit, as they know from experience what works well and what does not work so well.

EXTERNAL BODIES

Some audits are funded by industry or commercial bodies, and they may wish to be involved in audit governance and practice. This needs to be carefully managed, and there is a guide available on the HQIP website which sets out the probity issues involved and the processes required to ensure that the audit is ethically appropriate.[29]

All members of the audit project team have the right to make a contribution to the discussion of results and the identification of changes that can be implemented to improve practice. All too often this is seen as the domain of the clinical team members, because they are regarded as the 'experts' in the aspects of care that are being measured in the audit. However, it is also too often the case that the very people we do not think to ask or include are the ones who come up with the best ideas for improving care. They are more likely to have a fresh approach that enables them to see wider possibilities than the clinical staff, who can become constrained by their clinical training, protocols and model of clinical management. Only by respecting and considering all of the contributions that are made will the audit reach its full potential.

In summary, all of the audit team members should have:

➤ a basic understanding of clinical audit, although not necessarily skills in audit methodology, so long as at least one team member possesses these to advise the team as it works on the audit (see later)

➤ an understanding of and commitment to the plans and objectives of the audit project

➤ an understanding of what is expected of the project team – this needs to be clarified at the outset and may be expressed in a 'terms of reference' document.

If the audit team is to improve the delivery of a clinical service, team members must be able to communicate effectively with their colleagues. Members of the audit team must therefore have the full confidence and support of the staff and organisation and be able to promote the audit and plans for quality improvement. This is greatly assisted by an organisational culture that actively promotes and supports clinical audit as a quality improvement process.

Roles of clinical audit staff in audit projects

In some countries, such as the UK, it is commonplace for healthcare provider and commissioner organisations to employ clinical audit staff. Their roles and remits will vary, as will their number, but this valuable staff resource can assist in many ways with an audit project. A good understanding of and skills in audit methodologies, as well as significant organisational and analytical skills, are needed when carrying out clinical audit work. Some of the key skills of audit staff include the following:

➤ **Information/knowledge support:** in collaboration with colleagues in library and information services, audit staff have access to information technology (IT) facilities to help to gather evidence for standard setting and search for other projects on the same topic.

➤ **Data management:** clinical audit staff have expertise in a range of data collection tool designs, as well as in data entry, analysis and presentation of results.

➤ **Facilitation:** some clinical audit staff have particular training and skills in group dynamics. The role of a facilitator in the context of clinical audit is to help the team to assimilate the evidence, to come to a common understanding of the clinical audit methodology, to guide the project from planning to reporting, and to enable the group to work together effectively.

➤ **Project management:** project management and leadership are an important factor in quality improvement projects. In the words of McCrea,[28] 'Since both healthcare and clinical audit depend on the quality of teamwork, more attention needs to be given to the development of appropriate skills of team leadership.' Achieving improvements in quality through clinical audit often depends on managing relationships and resources across the wider organisation as well as addressing issues within the team immediately involved in the audit.

➤ **Change management:** audit staff are well used to the process of change as part of the audit cycle, and know what sort of changes are likely to work. They can guide the audit team discussion so that an action plan is agreed and implemented.

➤ **Training:** audit staff are often involved in training and support in a wide range of quality improvement skills for clinicians, managers and staff who have a requirement to get involved in clinical audit activities.

Clinical audit staff may include an audit manager or coordinator who performs a central coordinating function and manages audit staff. This individual needs to be visible and accessible so that they are in a position to keep audit high on the organisation's agenda. There may also be one or more audit facilitators and/or project officers, whose role tends to be more 'hands on' in the audit process. They will possess the skills necessary to undertake audit work, and again they need to be accessible in the organisation. There may also be audit assistants who help the facilitators and project officers with such tasks as data access, processing and analysis. The skills of clinical audit staff need to be used appropriately to ensure efficiency and effectiveness in the audit process.

The role of audit staff is greatly assisted by the presence of clinical leads to champion audit in the clinical professions within the healthcare organisation concerned. These individuals should play an active role and have a high profile, commanding authority and respect among their colleagues. This is not a role for audit sceptics, since the aim is to encourage clinical professionals to embrace audit. For any organisation there is a need to define clearly the roles and responsibilities of those with an audit remit, to ensure that this resource is not diverted away from clinical audit functions to other quality assurance or monitoring activities. The clinical audit agenda is likely to be significant, and there is a need to protect the time of those involved in audit work in order to ensure the success of the audit programme.

Developing skills

Lack of training and audit skills is a common barrier to successful audit. One assessment framework states that an ongoing programme of training in clinical audit for clinical professionals should be available to members of clinical staff from different departments/services and different professions.[25] If an organisation has a clinical audit staff resource that offers advice and support, it is important to tap into this and find out what is on offer. Earlier in this chapter the roles of audit staff were considered. They will generally provide advice on such aspects as correct wording of audit standards, selecting an appropriate method, ongoing help with the use of methods, data processing and analysis, presentation techniques, change facilitation and re-audit requirements.

Training provision

Although there will always be a need for advice and support, it is also necessary and desirable to provide clinical and non-clinical staff with their own skills in undertaking clinical audits. The need for training of staff in clinical audit skills, particularly in developing multi-disciplinary audits, was highlighted in a report on the progress made by primary care trusts in implementing clinical governance in primary care in England.[30] A further study highlighted the importance of training provision in literature searching and critical appraisal to assist effective audit criteria development.[16] It is unrealistic to expect that audit staff can support every audit that is taking place in an organisation, so healthcare professionals, as well as non-clinical support staff and managers, really need to develop their own set of core skills to enable them to carry out simple but effective audit projects. This requires the provision of accessible and effective 'in-house' training events that are tailored to the needs of specific target groups within an organisation. This is not easy, since providing cover for staff development and training has budgetary implications, and staff salaries are the major expense involved in audit. Again this is where the commitment of the organisation and managers to clinical audit has to be strong, so that training is made possible for all those who need it. Ideally, a range of training sessions at different levels will be provided by clinical audit staff, and often include some or all of the following:
➤ basic training at staff induction for all new employees, with supporting information
➤ practical workshops and seminars of differing lengths (e.g. a half day or one day)
➤ small group or team sessions (e.g. built into a team meeting or held over a lunch break)

➤ one-to-one sessions to provide intensive training
➤ distance learning courses
➤ e-learning training packages.

Some of the above training can be undertaken by staff in their own time and may lead to a recognised qualification, while other courses will take place during work time and will provide the necessary practical skills, but without a qualification. The greater the range of training options available, the more opportunities there will be for staff to attend training to meet their individual needs. Staff training needs in clinical audit can be supported and recognised in a number of ways, and where possible this should form part of the annual staff development appraisal to support continuing professional development (CPD). Clinical audit does demand a sound practical knowledge base and some practised skills in order to be carried out effectively. Staff should not be expected to undertake audit work without some core training and building it into appraisal, and CPD recognises the importance of this. Doctors in the UK now expect to be asked at their annual appraisal about recent audits in which they have been involved. Furthermore, doctors applying for any job from foundation to consultant level would expect to be able to demonstrate a sound understanding of clinical audit at interview.[2]

INVOLVING USERS

Since the first edition of this book was published there have been significant developments in user involvement in clinical audit. As was stated in the 2002 edition, users can be genuine collaborators, rather than merely sources of data. Efforts have been made in recent years to collaborate more extensively with users where clinical audit is concerned. Although the degree of involvement still varies, progress has been made and this needs to be built on in order to ensure that user involvement becomes part of routine audit practice.

Sources of user information

Traditionally in healthcare settings there have been a number of readily available sources of information from users that can be utilised as a starting point to inform clinical audit. These often relate to users' concerns, and may include any of the following:
➤ letters containing comments or complaints
➤ individual patients' stories, or feedback from focus groups
➤ direct observation of care
➤ direct conversations
➤ critical incident reports.

Methods of user involvement

In the changing and increasingly complex world of healthcare, **it is essential that users are involved at every stage in their care.** Treatment options and procedures available to service users are now more numerous. This leads to greater choice, and users have the right to be involved in these choices. Most audit projects will concern aspects of treatment and caregiving, so there is a real opportunity to work with users to obtain their perspective on what they consider to be the important aspects for inclusion in an audit.[31]

By far the most common method of user involvement to date has been the patient satisfaction survey. Although this has a legitimate place in the measurement and improvement of services from a user's perspective, it can be seen as tokenism when it is used as a method for involving users in audit. Unless users have been involved in the design and content of the survey, and unless they are involved in the discussion of the results and identification and/or implementation of change, it cannot genuinely be regarded as a method of user involvement in audit.

However, in recent years there has been a shift towards higher levels of user involvement in different stages of the audit cycle. In the NHS in the UK it is now not uncommon to have user representatives on groups and committees with a remit for clinical audit. Users now have a voice to contribute directly to the setting of audit topics. In agreeing the aims of an audit and in planning the criteria and standards, representative user groups are being more widely consulted about what aspects of care are important to them, and should be included in the audit. The results of audits are being disseminated to users and ideas invited for changes to services to make improvements.

Ways to involve users in clinical audit projects

➤ Approach a local group, such as a stroke support group, to ask for user input to identify and agree audit criteria and standards, discuss the results and suggest changes to practice.
➤ Set up a focus group for users, such as those accessing mental health outreach services, and discuss with the group topics for audit, standards, audit results and possible changes.
➤ Train service users to ask fellow service users questions for feedback about specific services accessed, such as antenatal services.
➤ Ask service users to read and review the design of surveys to ensure that they are user friendly and relevant to users.
➤ When agreeing audit standards, ask users to prioritise a list of possible audit standards that reflect the level of importance to them.
➤ When identifying a possible topic for audit, ask users (e.g. via a focus group) to identify what works well and what does not work so well for them when accessing and using the service concerned.
➤ Contact regional or national associations or charities that represent specific groups of users, and ask for involvement from the association in the audit.

Access to a guide to involving patients and the public is available on the HQIP website under *Patient and Public Engagement*[32] (and further information can be found in Appendix 6 of this book).

Users are not only increasingly seen working within an audit team at organisational level, but at a national level user representatives are more frequently found in groups with a remit to develop audit protocols and tools. For example, NICE in the UK has user representation on the development group for every piece of guidance, and each of these includes a team tasked with writing an audit protocol to accompany the guidance.

At every level the user's voice needs to be heard and involved, so that the true meaning and potential of clinical audit can be realised. With user involvement we are more likely to measure the right things in the right way, leading to real improvements in caregiving and service delivery that are meaningful to the user and healthcare professional alike.

REFERENCES

1 Department of Health. *Good Doctors, Safer Patients: proposals to strengthen the system to assure and improve the performance of doctors and to protect the safety of patients.* London: Department of Health; 2006.

2 Ghosh R, ed. *Clinical Audit for Doctors.* Nottingham: Developmedica; 2009.

3 Statutory Instrument 461. *The National Health Service (Pharmaceutical Services) Regulations 2005.* London: HMSO; 2005.

4 Further information about the National Clinical Audit and Patient Outcomes Programme (NCAPOP) can be found at www.hqip.org.uk/national-clinical-audit-and-patient-outcomes-programme (accessed 9 June 2010).

5 Boyle R. *Coronary Heart Disease Ten Years On: improving heart care.* London: Department of Health; 2007.

6 Pearce M. *Guide to Carrying Out Clinical Audits on the Implementation of Care Pathways.* London: HQIP; 2010. www.hqip.org.uk/assets/7-HQIP-CA-PD-031-Guide-to-carrying-out-clinical-audits-on-the-implementation-of-care-pathways-19-April.pdf (accessed 1 August 2010).

7 Brain J, Bywaters C. *Clinical Audit Programme Guidance Tools: clinical audit tool to promote quality for better health services.* London: HQIP; 2009. www.hqip.org.uk/assets/Downloads/Clinical-Audit-Program-Guide-and-Guidance-Tools.pdf (accessed 2 August 2010).

8 Buttery Y. Implementing evidence through clinical audit. In: *Evidence-based Healthcare.* Oxford: Butterworth-Heinemann; 1998. pp. 182–207.

9 Royal College of Nursing. *Quality Patient Care: the dynamic standard setting system.* Harrow: Scutari; 1990.

10 Irvine D, Irvine S. *Making Sense of Audit.* Oxford: Radcliffe Medical Press; 1991.

11 Institute of Medicine. *Guidelines for Clinical Practice: from development to use.* Washington, DC: National Academic Press; 1992.

12 Baker R, Fraser RC. Development of audit criteria: linking guidelines and assessment of quality. *British Medical Journal* 1995; **31:** 370–3.

13 Statutory Instrument 291. *The National Health Service (General Medical Services Contracts) Regulations 2004.* London: HMSO; 2004.

14 Donabedian A. Evaluating the quality of medical care. *Millbank Memorial Fund Quarterly: Health and Society* 1966; **44**: 166–204.

15 Nursing and Midwifery Council (NMC). *Record Keeping: guidance for nurses and midwives.* London: NMC; 2009 (quoted with permission of the NMC).

16 Hearnshaw H, Harker R, Cheater F *et al.* A study of the methods used to select review criteria for clinical audit. *Health Technology Assessment* 2002; **6**: 1–78.

17 Naylor CD, Guyatt GH. Users' guide to medical literature. XI. How to use an article about a clinical utilization review. *Journal of the American Medical Association* 1996; **275**: 1435–9.

18 Lyons C, Thomson A, Emmanuel J *et al.* Transferring cardiology out-patient follow-up from secondary to primary care. *Journal of Clinical Governance* 1999; **7**: 52–6.

19 Powell J, Lovelock R, Bray J *et al.* Involving users in assessing service quality: benefits of using a qualitative approach. *Quality in Health Care* 1994; **3**: 199–202.

20 Kelson M, Ford C, Rigge M. *Stroke Rehabilitation: patients' and carers' views.* London: Royal College of Physicians; 1998.

21 Fitzpatrick R, Boulton M. Qualitative methods for assessing healthcare. *Quality in Health Care* 1994; **3**: 107–13.

22 Crombie IK, Davies HT, Abraham SC *et al. The Audit Handbook: improving health care through clinical audit.* Chichester: John Wiley & Sons; 1993.

23 Cox S, Wilcock P, Young J. Improving the repeat prescribing process in a busy general practice: a study using continuous quality improvement methodology. *Quality in Health Care* 1999; **8**: 119–25.

24 Available at www.nice.org.uk/guidance (accessed 25 May 2010).

25 Walshe K, Spurgeon P. *Clinical Audit Assessment Framework.* HSMC Handbook Series 24. Birmingham: University of Birmingham; 1997.

26 Morrell C, Harvey G. *The Clinical Audit Handbook.* London: Bailliere Tindall; 1999.

27 Dixon N. *Ethics and Clinical Audit and Quality Improvement (QI) – A Guide for NHS Organisations.* London: HQIP; 2009. www.hqip.org.uk/assets/Downloads/Ethics-and-Clinical-Audit-and-Quality-Improvement-Guide.pdf (accessed 2 August 2010).

28 McCrea C. Good clinical audit requires teamwork. In: Baker R, Hearnshaw H, Robertson N, eds. *Implementing Change with Clinical Audit.* Chichester: John Wiley & Sons; 1999. pp. 119–32.

29 Healthcare Quality Improvement Partnership and CiREM. *Guidance on Working with Industry on Clinical Audit.* London: HQIP; 2010. www.hqip.org.uk/clinical-audit-resources3/#prof (accessed 3 August 2010).

30 National Audit Office. *Improving Quality and Safety – Progress in Implementing Clinical Governance in Primary Care: lessons for the new primary care trusts.* London: The Stationery Office; 2007.

31 Balogh R, Simpson A, Bond S. Involving clients in clinical audits of mental health services. *International Journal for Quality in Healthcare* 1995; **7**: 343–53.

32 Healthcare Quality Improvement Partnership. *Patient and Public Engagement (PPE): PPE in clinical audit.* London: HQIP; 2010. www.hqip.org.uk/patient-and-public-engagement (accessed 2 August 2010).

CHAPTER 3

Stage 2: Measuring performance

Stephen Ashmore, Tracy Ruthven and Louise Hazelwood

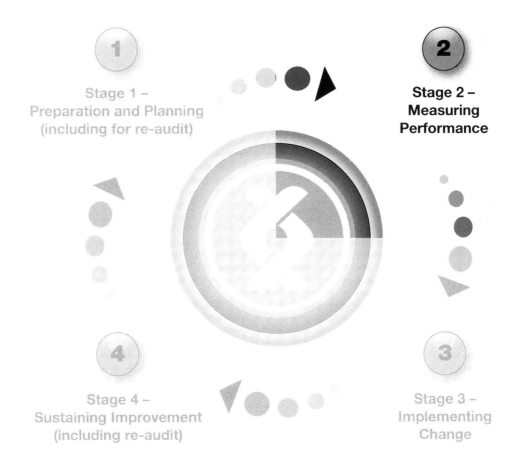

1

Stage 1 –
Preparation and Planning
(including for re-audit)

2

Stage 2 –
Measuring
Performance

4

Stage 4 –
Sustaining Improvement
(including re-audit)

3

Stage 3 –
Implementing
Change

INTRODUCTION

The preceding chapter examined the preparation, planning and organisation necessary for carrying out effective clinical audits. This chapter moves to the second stage, namely the process of measurement.

The methodology associated with conducting clinical audits can be daunting to anyone who has not encountered the process before. Tasks such as calculating sample sizes, locating and counting numerous data items, performing statistical analysis and preparing graphical presentations all come to mind. These tasks are unfamiliar territory for many health professionals, but in fact need not be complex or onerous in the vast majority of clinical audits. Although a high degree of rigour is necessary to ensure that the chosen audit methods are effective, they generally do not require any skills that cannot be easily learned. Where advice and support from staff with experience of audit methodology are available, it is sensible to make use of this to ensure that this part of the audit is set up and implemented effectively. HQIP has also produced a practical guide, *An Introduction to Statistics for Clinical Audit*, which is available on their website.[1]

Collection of any data and the use of data for audit will be subject to the governance rules relating to the handling of clinical data pertaining to the health setting any provider works within. In the UK, for example, there are clear rules for when and how data can be collected and then used for various purposes. Before collecting any data these rules should be consulted carefully.

PLANNING DATA COLLECTION

Many studies have reported the obstacles imposed by lack of expertise in audit methods, including inappropriate and haphazard data collection.[2] To avoid these obstacles, and before data can be collected, the following questions need to be asked in order to ensure that the process is effective.

➤ What type of data do I need to collect (quantitative and/or qualitative)?
➤ What data items will need to be used to show whether or not performance levels have been met for each standard?
➤ What data sources will be used to find the data?
➤ Will a data collection tool need to be designed?
➤ Will I need to collect data prospectively and/or retrospectively?
➤ What size is the target population and will I need to take a sample?
➤ How will data be collected (manually and/or electronically)?
➤ How long will it take to collect the required amount of data?
➤ Who will be collecting the data?

Quantitative or qualitative data

By and large, audit data will be quantitative (i.e. numerical data that can be counted in order to determine whether or not performance levels have been achieved). This is the usual format of audit data, whereby the number of patients or occasions for which each standard is met is counted.

However, a data collection strategy may include descriptive elements, such as additional comments within a questionnaire or transcripts from focus groups or interviews. Qualitative data are concerned with words rather than with numbers, and qualitative methods provide a means of assimilating a rich source of information on people's experiences in relation to a clinical topic. Analysis of transcribed tape-recorded interviews or free-text comments in questionnaires can be a time-consuming but rewarding exercise, which often produces ideas for improvement in healthcare that can be explored further. With increasing user involvement in audit, it is important to be aware of this form of data capture. If data are to be collected qualitatively, it is advantageous to consult appropriate publications,[3,4] and to enlist the support of audit staff or others with skills in designing qualitative data collection tools, where this is available.

Selecting data items

Collect only what you need

Careful identification and selection of only the data items necessary for the audit is important to ensure the efficiency and effectiveness of the data collection. When looking through data records, it is sometimes tempting to gather more data than are really needed to determine whether standards have been met. Sometimes audit team members will use the opportunity to gather additional facts that they think will be interesting or informative, but which actually do not relate directly to measurement of any of the audit standards. This can detract from the audit's objectives, and will certainly make the data collection task longer and more laborious. **Any additional data items need to be justified and a valid reason given for their use in the process of improving healthcare.**

Do you need patient demographics?

Audits will often be complicated by the automatic assumption that it is necessary to gather a lot of extra data on patient demographics, such as patient age and gender. This tends to be done purely to provide a profile of the patient population that is being audited. However, the question of whether this is really necessary has to be asked. It takes time to record this information manually on a data collection form. Unless it is needed to inform the discussion of the audit results and influence change, there is little to justify its collection.

Avoid collecting extra data items out of interest only

One problem in some audits is the temptation to collect additional clinical data items. The audit will have clearly agreed aims and objectives that focus on particular aspects of caregiving, yet somehow the data collection tool becomes overloaded with several extra aspects of clinical care. This may happen for a number of reasons. For example, an over-zealous clinical member of the audit team may decide that they would like to know one or two extra facts about the topic that is being audited, to link into a different piece of work they are doing. Or the organisation may have another agenda to fulfil concerning the topic that is being audited, and may ask for the collection of further data items to gather evidence. One has to be mindful of attempts to 'hijack' the audit for other purposes. Even if this is not the intention, the effect can be that the audit objectives become lost among these additional demands, or the impact of the audit is diminished because the focus is lost, and it may become a research project. In addition, the collection of unnecessary data may breach 'Caldicott' rules about information governance.[5] It also uses additional resources in terms of audit staff, and reduces their capacity to complete other audits. Wherever possible, data collection should remain focused and linked directly to the audit standards.

Data sources

In an ideal world, if an aspect of care is important enough to be audited, all of the necessary data items would have been collected routinely and be readily accessible. In reality, data items are often held in several databases, on paper or electronically, in different departments, even in different organisations, or may not be collected at all. If the required data are not collected routinely, a specific paper or electronic encounter sheet can be devised for healthcare professionals to record additional information during each consultation or patient contact.

Existing record and information systems may already be adequate for clinical audit purposes. For example, management information systems may already collect the data required for clinical audit. The availability of performance indicators that healthcare providers may be required to collect can also be converted into audit standards for audit purposes. Examples of this in England include the Quality and Outcomes Framework (QOF) indicators that have formed part of the General Medical Services contract for general practices since April 2004.[6]

As information systems in health service delivery improve, a greater range of data will be readily available (e.g. in the form of electronic patient records). An opportunity arises to review information requirements whenever services are re-designed or new systems of work are introduced. With such developments in the availability of more valid, up-to-date and complete data sources, clinical audit data collection will become faster and more reliable, making real-time clinical audit far easier and more accessible to healthcare professionals. The need for sampling will decrease, since it will be possible to search for data on complete target populations using computer searches to generate data and perform the analysis in a fraction of the time that it would take to collect clinical audit data manually.

For any audit that is being undertaken, it is helpful to think about which data sources will be used at the time when the audit criteria are selected. It is important to avoid the situation where data collection proves lengthy and incomplete because it was not discovered until the time came to collect the data that the audit criteria could not readily be measured due to a lack of robust data sources. Thinking about data sources early on in the process also helps one to identify and be aware of their limitations so that any gaps in data that are evident from data collection can be factored into analysis of the results to ensure that as accurate a picture as possible is produced.

Data are available from a variety of sources, and often the same information will be recorded in more than one record (e.g. in the patient record as well as in the pathology report). The choice of which source to use will depend on various factors, including accessibility, accuracy and completeness. Each data source will have its own advantages and disadvantages with regard to its use, which need to be appraised before the best source or sources are selected.

Typical data sources include the following:

➤ admission records
➤ coroners' reports
➤ death certificates
➤ direct observation
➤ discharge records
➤ disease registers (e.g. cancer registry)
➤ encounter sheets – to record specific additional data
➤ interviews
➤ laboratory records (e.g. haematology, microbiology, pathology)
➤ mortality data
➤ patient records/case notes – medical as well as paramedical
➤ pharmacy records
➤ prescribing data
➤ surveys/questionnaires
➤ theatre lists.

Designing a data collection tool

Most audits require the design of a specific data collection tool, usually a paper-based form or an electronic database or spreadsheet, in order to record the relevant data items relating to the audit standards. Data for audit are generally collected retrospectively (i.e. some time after the care has been provided), so it should be a fairly straightforward matter to extract the items and transfer them on to a bespoke form. National audits, in which participants send their data to a central location for analysis, will generally provide a pre-designed data collection tool on to which data are recorded.

Data collection forms must specify precisely the information to be extracted from the data source, and allow the data collector to indicate clearly whether or not each audit criterion has been met for each record audited. They should be as easy to use as possible, so there are a number of aspects to consider when designing an effective data collection form, whether it is manual or electronic.

Layout

Forms should be uncluttered and provide enough space for data entry. The data should be entered in a logical order on to the form, with the section relating to each criterion clearly identified. A clear heading should be given to identify the form. Columns and rows should also be clearly headed with totals at the end of these, where appropriate, to allow for easier calculation of performance levels. The date on

Individual user
Audit period: 12 months prior to
date of data collection

Age	
Id No.	

Criterion 1
History and examination
(a) Record of:

Leakage on exertion	y	n	dk
Volume of loss	y	n	dk
Nocturia	y	n	dk
Frequency	y	n	dk
Urgency	y	n	dk
Dysuria	y	n	dk
Dribbling	y	n	dk

(b) Bladder chart

	y	n	dk

(c) Record of examination:

Abdominal	y	n	dk
Pelvic	y	n	dk
Rectal if appropriate	y	n	dk

Criterion 2
Urinalysis

Urine dipstick performed	y	n	dk
or			
MSUS sent (symptoms, ± abnormal dipstick)	y	n	dk

Criterion 3

PVR volume measured	y	n	dk

Criterion 4

Presumed type identified	y	n	dk

If yes:

Stress	y	n	dk
Mixed	y	n	dk
Overflow	y	n	dk

Criterion 5
Risk factors assessed
and documented

Medication review	y	n	dk
Atrophic vaginitis	y	n	dk

Criterion 6
Risk factors assessed/
documented

BMI	y	n	dk
Constipation	y	n	dk
Smoking	y	n	dk

FIGURE 3.1 Audit of the management of urinary incontinence: data collection form for an individual user.[7] (Reproduced with permission.)

which the form was completed should also be recorded to allow for cross-referencing of data in the event of queries. Space for the name of the person completing the form is also useful in the event of queries relating to completed forms, especially where many people are completing the forms.

Confidentiality

A key point that is sometimes overlooked concerns protection of the confidentiality of those service users whose data are being recorded on a data collection form, whether it is computerised or manual. Data collection forms must use an audit number for each record audited, and this should be generated specifically for the audit. This avoids the need for any actual identifiers to be used that could allow service users to be identified. Therefore data items such as **patient names, initials, date of birth, unique identification number, etc. should not be recorded on the audit data collection form**. Instead records are best numbered chronologically from 1 to however many records are being audited, and a separate reference sheet, on which the same audit numbers from 1 upwards are listed with their corresponding service user unique identifiers next to them, is stored in a secure place. This enables service user records to be referred back to in the event of any recording anomalies on the data collection form.

In the UK, sharing of identifiable data about patients within a healthcare provider for clinical audit is permissible without any external permissions. However, sharing such data with national audits, or in regional audits, or in comparison with another provider, needs special permissions. This is a complicated area and advice should be sought (*see* below).

Piloting the form

It is good practice to pilot the data collection form to enable any inherent problems to be detected and corrected before data collection goes live. Different data collectors may interpret some record entries in the same record in different ways. It is important that data collectors undergo training in the use of the data collection form so that any confusing items are identified and a clear policy is established on how data items should be recorded. Pilot testing also enables the validity of the form to be tested in order to check that the form collects what it is designed to collect for performance to be measured against the standards. It is easy to overlook the need for a particular data item to be included on a form that will be needed for analysis. A pilot test ensures that any such omissions are picked up at an early stage.

Guidance notes

These should be provided for data collectors to follow when deciding whether the patient record provides sufficient information to suggest that a criterion has definitely been met. **Data collectors should be able to seek advice if they encounter entries in records that are particularly confusing.** Guidance notes can also take the data collector through the form step by step to ensure that it is completed correctly.

Reliability testing

Before starting an audit, the reliability of data collection should be checked by asking data collectors to independently extract data from the same sample of records and then compare their findings. The percentage of items that are the same, or the

stic, is calculated in order to estimate inter-rater reliability.[8] If reliability
data collection procedures must be reviewed.

..trospective or prospective data collection

Retrospective data collection provides a picture of care during a time period in the
past (e.g. during the previous 6 months). The main advantages of collecting data
in this way are first that the data are already available and can be gathered relatively quickly, and secondly that the data reflect true practice during the time period
audited. However, the main disadvantages are the limitations of the data sources,
with their inability to provide complete and accurate information, and the fact that
the data can quickly become out of date.

Although retrospective data collection provides a baseline of care provision, it has
its limitations, so working with concurrent data (i.e. data collected prospectively) can
be a useful alternative. Prospective data looks forward, so a specific data capture tool
has to be designed to gather the data as the care is given. In contrast to retrospective
data gathering, this has the advantage that there will not be gaps in the data, so a
more complete picture of present practice can be obtained.

Prospective data collection provides feedback on current performance, and can
act as a positive reinforcement to improve or maintain practice. Prospective data can
be gathered and presented on paper or electronically. Appropriately designed and
used electronic records can also provide prospective data that can be used to support
the continuous improvement of practice.

One disadvantage of prospective data collection should be noted. The Hawthorne
effect can come into play when data are collected prospectively. This relates to the
tendency for individuals to change their behaviour to that which they know they
should be practising when they know that they are being monitored or audited. Thus
there may be a temptation for healthcare professionals to comply with the requirements of the audit standards for the duration of the data collection period, and then
to slip back into their usual practice once data collection is complete. Furthermore,
the data gathering tool acts as a reminder of what should be done for patients, so
again the results may portray a picture of care that is better than usual.

Identifying the target population

The first point to establish is the size of the target population. This may not be as
straightforward as one would expect. **The target population needs to be clearly and
precisely defined so that the correct figure is obtained.** This requires the identification of all inclusion as well as all exclusion cases. For example, if a general practice
chose to audit its adult type 2 diabetic patients, it would need to ensure that the target population did not include any children (age limits to be defined) or any type
1 diabetic patients. An accurate disease register would help to identify legitimate
patients in the target population.

A slightly different scenario exists when the target population is not finite or
fixed. For example, an audit of the care of stroke patients in an acute care unit would
need to calculate the size of the target population by a defined time period, say 3 or

6 months, the length of which would depend on the throughput of patients in the stroke unit, to ensure that enough patients are included in the audit. In this case it is still necessary to define the inclusion and exclusion cases in order to obtain an accurate target population size. For example, will the records of all patients who came through the unit in the defined time period be included in the audit, regardless of outcome, or will those patients who died on the unit be excluded from the audit? This may depend on the criteria that are being audited, so it is important that the defined target population links in with the audit criteria.

Sampling

The decision as to whether or not to take a sample from the target population depends upon how much time is available to collect data, and how accurate a picture of care one needs to obtain from the audit. Sampling is a useful way of reducing the work associated with data collection and analysis when the target population is large and it is known that it will not be possible to audit all records. However, in order to be confident that the conclusions drawn from the audit results, based on a sample, accurately reflect the entire target population from which the sample was drawn, a degree of rigour needs to be adopted. Care must be taken not to fall into the trap of simply auditing, say, the first 50 records, or a 10% sample for every audit undertaken. These are common mistakes in audit, and they risk producing results that are not a true reflection of practice, because the sample selected was too small to be representative of the target population. A compromise must be struck between the need for scientific accuracy and the time required for data collection. Remember that the proposed decisions and changes that are made on the basis of an audit are based on the audit results, so it is important to be sure that those results are accurate, valid and reliable. If the sample is too small, there is a risk that the decisions which are made will be based on unrepresentative data that do not give the true picture of care. If the sample is too large, the time-saving benefits are lost and the audit risks losing momentum.

Calculating sample size

Various methods can be used to calculate sample sizes, depending on the type of data. In audit, it is usual to compare the proportion of users whose care is in accordance with the standards before changes in care with the proportion whose care meets the standards after the changes. The calculation of sample size for proportions is relatively simple, but if the data are in a format other than proportions, statistical advice should be sought. For clinical audit purposes, it is generally agreed that a 95% confidence interval ($\pm$ 5%) is acceptable for producing reliable results. The easiest way to calculate the sample size is to consult a sample size calculator, examples of which are given in the references.[9]

Once the sample size has been established, it is necessary to decide how the records will be selected from the target population. Usually it will be necessary to search records from a defined time period (e.g. within the last year or the last 3 months), since users do not form a static population, and the users that make up the population may change during the audit. This is a reasonable approach provided that admission rates and the quality of care are not influenced by major seasonal factors. Where necessary, the sample chosen may need to allow for case-mix adjustment, and if this is the case then statistical advice may need to be sought.

There are a wide range of approaches to sampling for clinical audit, and these will now be discussed briefly.

Random sampling

If the sample is drawn from a defined population, random sampling is preferred, as it avoids introducing bias into the sample. A random numbers table or a mathematical calculator will generate random numbers that can be used to select the corresponding numbered records from the target population until the required amount for the sample has been obtained. An example of such a resource can be found at www. random.org.

Systematic sampling

An alternative and rather simpler way to draw a sample is to do so systematically. This involves selecting every *n*th record from the target population until the required number of records has been obtained. However, caution must be exercised with this method if it is known that the records are grouped in a certain way that could introduce bias into the sample (e.g. patient records sorted by address or by surname).

Two-stage sampling

This method may improve efficiency.[10] A small sample is selected first, and if unequivocal conclusions can be drawn, no more data are collected. If the results are ambiguous, a larger sample is selected.

Rapid-cycle sampling

The traditional clinical audit cycle often involves selecting relatively large amounts of data over a long time period, once before any changes are implemented and again after the changes have been implemented. Although this approach, if correctly applied, provides useful information about performance, it can make the process of change slow. An alternative approach involves the use of small samples, with many repeated data collections to monitor serious fluctuations or changes in care. The cycle is completed quickly, and reliability is improved by the repeated data collections.[11,12]

Manual or electronic data collection

Although it is common for audit data to be analysed electronically, it is still far less common for them to be collected electronically. Generally some type of paper-based data capture tool is used to collect the necessary data, particularly for retrospective data collection. The following key questions need to be asked when determining which method will be used.

➤ How are the data stored?

➤ Where are the data stored?

➤ Who will be collecting the data?
➤ Where will the data be collected?
➤ Are data being collected retrospectively or prospectively?

In general, for retrospective data collection, if the data are predominantly stored on paper-based records, are not stored in one place and are going to be collected by several people, then it is more likely that a paper-based data collection tool will need to be designed. This is because the data collector will most probably have to go to where the notes are held, and in large hospitals this often means going to several different locations to gather all the data. Therefore they will need to be able to take the data collection tool with them if the records cannot be removed to one location. The more data collectors there are, the less easy it becomes to collect data in a single place. On the other hand, when there is only one or possibly two data collectors and the data can be located or taken to a single place where there is access to a computer, there is the potential to extract the data from the records directly on to an electronic data capture tool ready for analysis. Where possible, pre-existing data sets should be used to gather data, so long as they are complete, accurate and accessible. This may be particularly appropriate for audits of process where routine data can provide both a specific intervention and a defined population.[13] Dedicated databases (e.g. to monitor outcomes in surgery) may also be worth developing where regular audits are necessary, and to reduce the amount of time needed to collect data each time an audit is performed. Ugolini *et al.*[14] have described the benefits of such a database. It is also worth stating that there will be opportunities for easier data collection as access to improved data storage and retrieval technology becomes more widely available in healthcare settings, where the use of new data capture methods is already evident, including scanners and hand-held devices.

In situations where the data are already stored electronically, there is the option of performing electronic data collection. This is done by setting up searches on the data using queries that define what data items need to be extracted and counted, which means that data collection and analysis become almost a single process rather than two separate ones. This is possible in situations where there is one individual responsible for data collection (and usually analysis, too), and where the data are stored in one place and can be accessed easily from a computer. Training may be necessary to learn the skills to set up and run accurate queries and manipulate these in a spreadsheet or database. Where there is access to clinical audit staff in an organisation, this training may well be provided to develop the skills to perform such tasks.

Prospective data collection offers more scope to choose either electronic or manual data capture, because the data are not yet stored anywhere and have to be captured specifically for clinical audit purposes. This offers an opportunity to think about the most efficient and effective form of data capture. Again this choice will depend upon such factors as ease of access to an electronic storage medium, the individual(s) who will be collecting the data, and where the data will be captured.

Healthcare professionals often capture prospective data during the course of caregiving and recording. If the health professional is sitting in front of a computer screen as they consult with the patient (e.g. as usually happens in a general practice consultation), it is possible to make use of this tool to record the additional audit data as the computer screen is scrolled and updated with new items of information. Community-based healthcare professionals increasingly also carry portable hand-held electronic data capture devices to record healthcare interventions as they take place. This provides a further opportunity to capture data electronically for audit purposes at the point of delivery.

On the other hand, if there is no ready access to electronic data capture devices, manual data collection tools will need to be designed. For prospective data collection this will generally be facilitated by a form that is attached to the usual paper records that are completed during and after healthcare interventions. It is likely that the form will be completed by a number of individuals and in a number of places before being gathered by the individual(s) responsible for data analysis, who will then undertake further manual extraction of the data in preparation for analysis.

Time period for data collection

There are a few points worth mentioning in relation to determining how long a time period will need to be allocated for collecting the required data. This will have been given some thought in the planning stage, to ensure that the time allocated is reasonable and realistic. Few things are more frustrating for anyone involved in an audit than for the audit timetable to slip because data collection becomes protracted. Of course the factors that influence data collection running over schedule will be different for retrospective data collection and prospective data collection. It is likely to be easier to calculate the time it will take to gather the required amount of data prospectively, so long as the throughput of patients or events is known and is fairly constant and therefore easy to predict. It is also easy to factor in time for data collection if computerised techniques are employed. Here again experience will indicate how long it will take to complete electronic data capture. Setting up, running and verifying queries will not take long at all if the individual is experienced in this skill. However, collection of data retrospectively and manually from records can be fraught with a number of interruptions or delays that are not always predictable.

To avoid problems occurring with timetable slippage, it is advisable to undertake the following three steps.

1 Time how long it takes to search for and record the required data items in five or ten sets of records taken from patients in the target population. Then calculate how long it will take to audit all records according to the number of data collectors who are available.

2 Factor in time taken to locate records from which data will be collected, using knowledge and experience of where the records should be located and available for use, and how often records are not available.

3 Finally, identify how much time each day is available for collecting data, in order to work out how long it will take to complete the data collection. Remember that data collectors will probably have other work to complete, perhaps other audits

going on at the same time, so it is important to be realistic about the daily allocation of time for the audit in question.

In addition to these points, some general principles apply when planning any data
collection.
➤ Avoid holiday periods.
➤ Plan around the workload.
➤ Have a contingency plan in place for unexpected disruptions.

Preparing data collectors

Those with a responsibility for collecting data may or may not have had previous
experience of audit. If clinical audit staff collect the data, they will be experienced in
knowing what to look out for and how to complete the process efficiently. On the
other hand, if the data collectors are healthcare professionals or healthcare support
staff, there is a need to prepare them adequately for this task. **It is good practice to
hold a meeting of all data collectors to explain why they will be collecting data,
what will be involved and how they will achieve the task.** They may have questions that need to be answered, and the best way to deal with these is in a meeting.
It is advisable to demonstrate form completion, whereby each part of the data collection tool is explained in turn in order to clarify its purpose and the format for
entering data items on to the form. **Consistency in form filling is crucial to successful audit.** As was mentioned earlier, piloting the form and issuing guidance notes
will help to ensure good understanding and improve reliability of completion. In
fact, the meeting may serve to raise new points that were not previously identified
in the pilot or in the guidance notes, thereby offering a final opportunity to make
adjustments to the data collection tool or add to the guidance notes before data collection takes place.

DATA ANALYSIS

Preparing the data

Once data collection has been completed, the data need to be gathered together so
that the person responsible for analysis can prepare the data for this task. More often
than not this will involve collecting up all of the completed data collection forms
so that the complete data set is available for interrogation. The data will need to be
organised into a format that lends itself to accurate analysis and correct interpretation. This needs to have been considered during the planning stage so that the data
analyser is clear what needs to happen with the data (e.g. transfer on to a spreadsheet
for computerised analysis, or use of summary sheets to transfer relevant totals from
the data collection forms). Whether computerised or manual analysis is used, the
data can be interrogated effectively and in different ways.

Organising the data

Once the data have been collated, it is important to put them into a logical format when analysis takes place, in order to prepare for presentation. The main requirement is to decide on suitable groupings for the data so that they can be presented appropriately (e.g. grouping time periods such as waiting times into ≤ 10 minutes, 11–20 minutes, 21–30 minutes, and > 30 minutes, or grouping blood pressure ranges, or door to needle times, or lengths of stay in days, etc.). This will help to get a feel for the data, the range and where outliers might fall. Anything that can enhance understanding of the data is helpful at this stage.

Interpreting the data

Correct interpretation of audit data requires familiarity with and a good understanding of the data, as well as a keen eye for noticing anything that stands out as different. Anomalies in the data need to be challenged and cross-referenced or checked against the records from which the data were drawn, as well as from the completed data collection forms. It is possible that errors in transferring data from the patient record to the data collection form, or errors in recording data items correctly on the data collection form may have occurred (e.g. data may have been included on the form that are beyond the stated parameters). Any outliers that fall outside the expected range can be checked for validity. If necessary, anything that looks odd or that stands out as different can be verified by referring back to the completed data collection form or patient record. Finally, it is important to understand and take account of any data limitations (e.g. bias, whether the data are representative, completeness and accuracy of data, missing data, etc.). This will help to ensure that the data are interpreted correctly, taking account of limitations and allowing consideration of all possible explanations for the results. It is good practice to perform a validity check on a small proportion of the data in order to detect any common errors that occurred during data collection.

Maintaining a clear focus

The main aim of audit data analysis is simple, namely to determine whether or not performance levels have been reached, and thus whether or not audit standards have been achieved. Analysis needs to establish whether care was unsatisfactory and, if so, why. It should help to determine whether practice needs to change and, if so, how. Analysis should therefore be closely linked to the audit aims and objectives so that the results focus attention on what, if anything, needs to change in order to achieve the audit's aims. This will provide a clear focus for the analysis. Care is needed to avoid superfluous extra analysis that deflects the focus away from the specific audit standards. It is understandable why one might be tempted to draw out any interesting facts and inferences that become apparent from the data. After all this is probably the most interesting part of the audit so far, because those involved are keen to discover what the audit has revealed about the aspects of care and service delivery that are being measured. However, losing the focus now can impede the process of identifying and implementing changes that are going to improve performance levels in those aspects that are being measured in the audit.

Type of analysis

The type of data analysis that is to be used should be identified at an early stage, as it influences both the type and amount of data collected. The analysis can range from a simple calculation of percentages, through to relatively sophisticated statistical techniques. However, **for the majority of audits simple methods are preferable, and indeed if the results are to stimulate change, the analysis must be simple enough for everyone in the care process to understand it.**[12] Furthermore, so long as samples have not been used, statistical tests are superfluous. If samples have been taken, the most appropriate calculation to perform is confidence intervals.[15] In general, computerised analysis will allow for much quicker analysis and more complex statistical interrogation of the data, but manual analysis is still a relatively straightforward alternative where access to a computer or the relevant skills are not available. Remember that audit does not in general require complex statistical calculations to be performed, and although manual analysis will take longer, the calculations necessary for audit can all be performed easily using pen, paper and a calculator.

Calculating performance levels

Percentage achieved

The minimum calculations required in an audit involve working out the percentage of cases or events that have met each audit criterion in order to establish whether or not performance levels were reached. This means selecting the appropriate total number of applicable cases for an audit criterion, and the total number from within this that met the criterion, and calculating what percentage this represents.

Correct denominator

Calculating a percentage is straightforward enough, but nonetheless errors do occur. The most common error occurs when the wrong denominator is used in a calculation. This happens when the denominator changes for certain criteria, but this is not reflected in the calculation. For example, supposing the records of 200 patients with hypertension were included in an audit looking at blood pressure monitoring and control. Suppose that the audit was measuring whether a blood pressure had been recorded in the last year and, where recorded, whether it was controlled within normal limits. If the results showed that 170 patients had had a blood pressure recorded in the last year, this would equate to a percentage of 85% (170/200). If the results also showed that 100 patients had their blood pressure controlled within normal limits, this would equate to a percentage of 59% (100/170). For the second calculation the denominator changes to 170, rather than 200, because 30 patients had no blood pressure recorded in the last year, so these records should now be excluded from the second calculation for control of blood pressure. The mistake occurs when the percentage is calculated using the original denominator of 200, which would give a falsely low percentage of 50% (100/200). Therefore care should always be taken to check what the correct denominator is for each criterion that is being calculated. This will change according to the number of applicable records that emerge from the calculation of each audit criterion.

Other useful analysis

Other calculations that may be useful, depending on the nature of the audit topic, include the arithmetic mean, the median and the mode. These are of particular value when auditing such factors as waiting times and appointment availability.

Arithmetic mean

Taking the example of an audit of general practice waiting times in surgery, it may be of relevance to know the mean (often known as the average) waiting time, perhaps by day of the week, or by morning or afternoon surgery (or even by doctor). This is calculated by adding all of the observed values and dividing by the total number of values. These figures would establish whether there is higher demand on different days or at different times of day, to help to focus change on areas where demand is greatest and waiting times are longest.

Median

Sometimes the mean can give a misleading result because of a few extreme outliers. An alternative to the mean that helps to give a more accurate reflection of results in this situation is the median or middle number. Here all figures, in the above example all waiting times, perhaps grouped by day of the week and by morning or afternoon surgery, are placed in order from shortest to longest and the middle figure is selected. Where there is an odd total number there will be one middle figure, and where there is an even total number there will be two middle figures, which should be added together and divided by two in order to obtain the median.

Mode

This is the most frequently occurring value in a dataset, and it can also provide useful information. To use the example of the surgery waiting times, the mode would be calculated by counting how many times each waiting time was recorded, perhaps again by day of the week and by morning or afternoon surgery. The waiting time that occurs most frequently would be the mode, and it may help to gauge how long most patients have to wait in surgery.

Further guidance can be obtained from the HQIP guide to statistics, which gives worked examples for calculating the mean, median and mode, as well as other calculations including standard deviation, variance, range, upper and lower quartile and inter-quartile ranges. The reader is also directed to other audit publications that cover statistical analysis in more detail, such as Crombie *et al*.[16]

PRESENTATION OF RESULTS

Just as the analysis should be as simple as possible, the findings should be presented simply and clearly to aid understanding and encourage open discussion among all relevant stakeholders. The important question to consider when preparing the results for presentation is who the target audience will be. Most probably a broad mix of stakeholders will be interested in the results, which therefore need to be presented clearly and effectively to communicate the key points to the audience in order to facilitate discussion. The aim is to maximise the impact of the audit to stimulate and support action planning.

Methods of presentation

Several different presentation methods may need to be used to ensure that the results are communicated in a timely fashion to all stakeholders. One or more verbal presentations are likely to be made at relevant meetings. In addition, a written report may be necessary for committee papers. Finally, opportunities should be sought to present the results visually (e.g. in poster format), to reach as many stakeholders as possible. Posters can be displayed in staff rooms, service user waiting rooms and clinics, to name but a few places where the impact of the audit can be enhanced to encourage feedback and discussion.

Visual representation of the results, depicting the performance levels set and whether they were reached for each audit standard, is the best way to communicate the results. Graphical presentations, such as bar charts, have become the most common format because they provide an accessible way to interpret the results easily. The use of tables alone can be confusing because of the volume of figures that have to be interpreted. However, the numbers should be available in separate tables, in addition to the graphs, so that individual figures can be identified and cross-referenced with the data if necessary. A results summary table, which states the number of applicable cases for each criterion, the number of cases that met each criterion, the performance level set and the performance level achieved, is especially useful.

Such a chart needs to be accompanied by a table showing the data from which the chart is drawn.

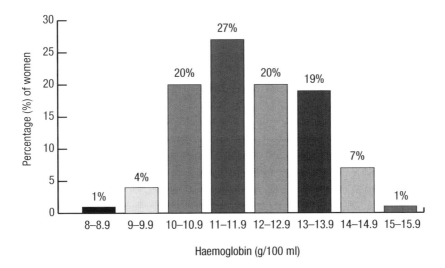

FIGURE 3.2 Example of presentation of data in the form of a histogram. (Reproduced with permission from Moore *et al.*)[1]

Illustration of presentation of data from two years of audit[1]

You carried out an audit of pressure tissue damage in 2008 and repeated the audit in 2009. Now you want to display the data in order to compare the findings between one year and the next. Your results are displayed in the table.

Patients with pressure tissue damage by grade of pressure tissue damage in 2008 and 2009

| Grade of pressure tissue damage | 2008 | | 2009 | |
	Number of patients with pressure tissue damage	Percentage of patients	Number of patients with pressure tissue damage	Percentage of patients
0	6	30%	7	35%
1	4	20%	5	25%
2	3	15%	4	20%
3	5	25%	3	15%
4	2	10%	1	5%
Total	**20**	**100%**	**20**	**100%**

Source: Reproduced from Moore J, Smith M, Barwick M. *An Introduction to Statistics for Clinical Audit.* London: HQIP; 2009, with permission.

Statistical quality control charts can help to develop understanding of process performance and provide longitudinal information that may not otherwise be detected. For example, a control chart of the number of patient falls per month, with non-constant control limits due to the varying number of patients, shows three atypical out-of-control events in an otherwise stable process.

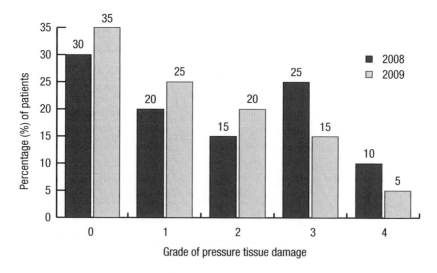

FIGURE 3.3 Example of a chart showing how results changed on re-audit. (Reproduced with permission from Moore *et al.*[1])

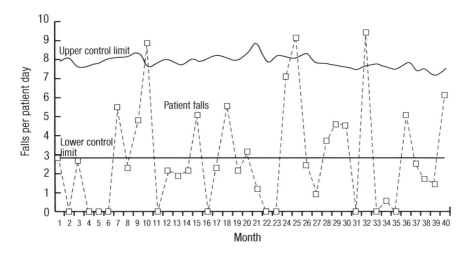

FIGURE 3.4 Example of a statistical control chart used in a clinical audit.[17]
(Reproduced with permission from *Principles of Best Practice in Clinical Audit*.)

Graphs and charts are now easy to reproduce electronically using standard graphics software packages, and there are also a number of specifically designed tools, such as Epi Info (mentioned earlier in this chapter in relation to sample size), that are available to aid the production of graphs and charts.

It is important that the results of each and every audit criterion are presented to the stakeholders, so that each in turn can be discussed in terms of its performance and what if anything needs to change. In summary, the presentation of results needs to cover the following:

➤ data familiarity, including limitations
➤ results summary
➤ performance levels reached for each and every audit criterion
➤ graphical presentation of results against performance levels
➤ tables of detailed figures
➤ trends and patterns emerging
➤ other relevant supporting information
➤ suggested interpretation of the results for discussion
➤ evidence to back up findings.

Remember also to ensure that wherever possible, reports on audit should be designed in such a form that they are understandable to patients, and avoid unnecessary jargon and complication.

DATA PROTECTION, CONFIDENTIALITY AND CONSENT

Data collection has ethical implications for healthcare staff and users. There are a number of helpful guides that can be downloaded from the HQIP website, including

Guide for Clinical Audit, Research and Service Review,[18] *Ethics and Clinical Audit and Quality Improvement*[19] (*see also* Appendix 1) and *Information Governance Guide for Clinical Audit.*[5] Keane *et al.*[20] provide further practical advice. Data protection covers both manual and computerised data, and aims to protect both staff and service users. **Audit data should be stored securely and destroyed once they have served their purpose. Whilst in the UK patients do not need to consent for data about them to be used for clinical audit within a single healthcare setting, they should be informed that audit is happening and what its purpose is. In most cases, audit data should be anonymised and used only for the purpose stated in the audit aims.** Thought should be given to who will need access to the audit data and how consent will be obtained from service users whose data are being used in an audit. These issues of confidentiality and consent are ones that the healthcare organisation should address early in order to provide guidance, ideally in the form of a policy to which individuals or teams can refer. The audit team, or any individual undertaking an audit, should familiarise themselves with the policy in order to comply with the requirements therein.

At the national or regional audit level, where data is being passed to a third party, in the UK specific rules apply to the handling of any identifiable data, and there is a requirement that patient consent is given. However, whilst identifiable data is not always required by these audits, in many cases it is for such audits to work. Local teams contributing to such audits need to ensure the adequate permissions from the relevant governing body are in place for the release of data of this sort, and if consent is needed from patients, this is obtained.

REFERENCES

1 Moore J, Smith M, Barwick M. *An Introduction to Statistics for Clinical Audit.* London: HQIP; 2009. www.hqip.org.uk/assets/1-HQIP-An-Introduction-to-Statistics-for-Clinical-Audit.pdf (accessed 2 August 2010).

2 Johnston G, Crombie IK, Davies HT *et al.* Reviewing audit: barriers and facilitating factors for effective clinical audit. *Quality in Health Care* 2000; **9**: 23–36.

3 Mays N, Pope C. Qualitative research in healthcare. Assessing quality in qualitative research. *British Medical Journal* 2000; **320**: 50–2.

4 Pope C, Ziebland S, Mays N. Qualitative research in healthcare. Analysing qualitative data. *British Medical Journal* 2000; **320**: 114–16.

5 Harrison W, Sharpe H. *Information Governance Guide for Clinical Audit.* London: HQIP; 2009. www.hqip.org.uk/assets/Downloads/Information-Governance-and-Audit-Guide.pdf (accessed 2 August 2010).

6 Statutory Instrument 291. *The National Health Service (General Medical Services Contracts) Regulations 2004.* London: HMSO; 2004.

7 Cheater F, Lakhani M, Cawood C. *Audit Protocol: assessment of patients with urinary tract incontinence.* CT14. Leicester: Eli Lilley National Clinical Audit Centre, University of Leicester; 1998 (reproduced with permission).

8 Altman DG. *Practical Statistics for Medical Research.* London: Chapman and Hall; 1991.

9   For example, the public domain software program Epi Info is produced by the Centers for Disease Control and Prevention in the USA, and may be downloaded (available from www.cdc.gov/epiinfo). A further online resource is available from www.raosoft.com/samplesize (accessed 9 June 2010).

10 Alemi F, Moore S, Headrick L *et al*. Rapid improvement teams. *Joint Commission Journal on Quality Improvement* 1998; **24**: 119–29.

11 Alemi F, Neuhauser D, Ardito S *et al*. Continuous self-improvement: systems thinking in a personal context. *Joint Commission Journal on Quality Improvement* 2000; **26**: 74–86.

12 Plsek PE. Quality improvement methods in clinical medicine. *Paediatrics* 1999; **103**: 203–14.

13 McKee M. Routine data: a resource for clinical audit? *Quality in Health Care* 1993; **2**: 104–11.

14 Ugolini G, Rosati G, Montroni I *et al*. An easy-to-use solution for clinical audit in colorectal cancer surgery. *Surgery* 2009; **145**: 6–92.

15 Gardner MJ, Altman DG. *Statistics with Confidence*. London: BMJ Publishing Group; 1989.

16 Crombie IK, Davies HT, Abraham SC *et al*. *The Audit Handbook: improving health care through clinical audit*. Chichester: John Wiley & Sons; 1993.

17 Benneyan JC. Use and interpretation of statistical quality control charts. *International Journal for Quality in Health Care* 1998; **10**: 69–73 (reproduced with permission).

18 Brain J *et al*. *Guide for Clinical Audit, Research and Service Review*. London: HQIP; 2009. www.hqip.org.uk/assets/Downloads/Audit-Research-Service-Evaluation.pdf (accessed 2 August 2010).

19 Dixon N. *Ethics and Clinical Audit and Quality Improvement (QI): a guide for NHS organisations*. London: HQIP; 2009. www.hqip.org.uk/assets/Downloads/Ethics-and-Clinical-Audit-and-Quality-Improvement-Guide.pdf (accessed 2 August 2010).

20 Ghosh R, ed. *Clinical Audit for Doctors*. Nottingham: Developmedica; 2009.

CHAPTER 4

Stage 3: Implementing change

Stephen Ashmore, Tracy Ruthven and Louise Hazelwood

Key points

- A group of interventions, tailored to the specific needs of the audit, will be more effective than a single intervention in the successful implementation of change.
- Barriers to change, whether perceived or real, need to be identified in the early stages of the process so that solutions can be found to overcome them.
- Effective facilitation from start to finish is necessary to make the process easy for the team to work towards their goal, maintain cohesion of the team and get the most from the team.
- Presentation and discussion of the results should be made to all key stakeholders so that agreement on the need for change, a clear understanding of objectives and a tailored strategy for change can be achieved.
- Involve everyone affected by the changes in the discussion and identification of effective changes that will address the underlying causes of the problem.
- Ensure that those implementing change have the power to act so that any changes which are identified and agreed will be resourced and supported at all levels.
- Design changes that are 'built into' systems and processes so that they work effectively within routine practices, rather than choosing 'bolt-on' changes that are less likely to be sustained over time.
- Prioritise the implementation of changes according to need and whether they are short term or longer term. Identify 'quick wins' that can be implemented speedily and make a difference so that those affected can see the benefits of change.
- Consult widely about the changes proposed, and publicise them.
- Agree and write a detailed action plan for change that includes actions agreed, how they were achieved, reasonable time scales, individuals responsible and outcome measures.
- Throughout implementation provide support, consult with others and modify plans as required.
- Evaluate the outcomes of change to ensure that they have had the desired effect.

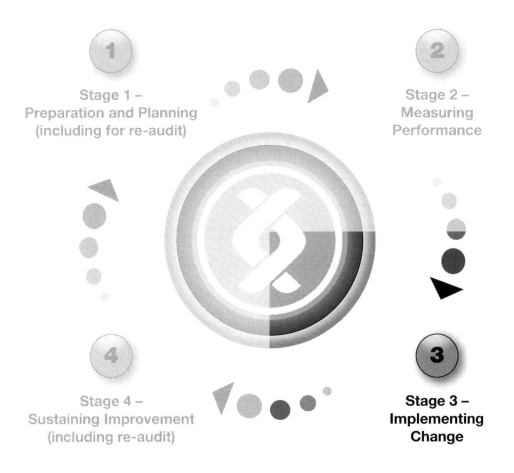

Stage 1 –
Preparation and Planning
(including for re-audit)

Stage 2 –
Measuring
Performance

Stage 4 –
Sustaining Improvement
(including re-audit)

**Stage 3 –
Implementing
Change**

The purpose of this chapter:
- To describe how change programmes can be introduced.

INTRODUCTION

Clinical audit is a change process. As identified throughout this book, audit that simply measures but does not drive change to address problems identified, is not good audit. All audit projects must include a programme of change activity and post-identification of the findings from audit, to ensure necessary changes happen. The starting point for this is detailed analysis of what the data shows, so that there are clear areas identified for change in clinical practice. Having done this, methods for making these changes happen need to be developed.

Change is not always easy, and this chapter (along with Appendix 3) looks at the theory of change as much as how it can be achieved. The first step is the acceptance of where and why deviations from agreed best practice have occurred, and as such how improvement methods can be applied to address the problems identified. The solutions can come in the form of a wide variety of change mechanisms, from new systems and protocols, to training and induction, revised team organisation or procedural checklists. They can also include changed referral systems, different procedures for requesting diagnostic tests, new prescribing regimens, and much more. The expanded literature of quality improvement offers a variety of processes, with their own methodologies, which may be appropriate to ensure change, whatever it may be, happens and is sustained. The first step is to work out clearly what has gone wrong, and some clear ideas for how it can be altered. This is a job for the audit team, working with senior clinicians responsible for the service, to ensure it is worked through carefully.

The extent to which an audit successfully implements change will depend strongly on how well the audit topic was chosen and designed and, most significantly, on how effectively it involved those affected by it throughout the process, from planning to completion. One of the major purposes of planning is to anticipate change, which is made easier if the need for change can be identified. A key function of clinical audit is to identify the need for change.[1]

ACTING ON THE FINDINGS OF CLINICAL AUDIT

Audit projects that reach this stage of the audit process have a good chance of making a difference. Data have been collected, analysed and prepared for presentation by the audit team to key stakeholders, clinical staff and managers. They are in a format ready to discuss at appropriate meetings in order to fulfil the primary aim of clinical audit, namely to improve quality. This is, of course, achieved through the introduction of one or more focused changes designed to bridge the quality gap between current practice and desired practice.

Theories and models of change management may helpfully be applied to assist the process of successful implementation of change. A review of methods for effecting change identified the following features as being frequently present in successful studies:

➤ local development
➤ negotiation leading to general agreement
➤ provision of feedback on quality of care
➤ facilitation of discussion of findings.[2]

No single method is guaranteed to be effective in securing change. The best chance of success may result from utilising several different interventions together. However, interventions do need to be carefully selected. A systematic review of guideline dissemination and implementation strategies[3] indicated that multifaceted interventions did not appear to be more effective than single interventions, and the effects of multifaceted interventions did not appear to increase with the number of component interventions. The authors concluded that decision makers need to select those interventions which are most likely to be effective in any given circumstance, based upon consideration of the feasibility, costs and benefits that potentially effective interventions are likely to yield.

It may be helpful to undertake a diagnostic analysis to identify factors that will influence the likelihood of change (*see* Box 4.1) before selecting the most appropriate strategies and interventions for implementing change.

BOX 4.1 Some methods of identifying barriers to change

- Interviews with key staff and/or users.
- Discussion at a team meeting.
- Observations of patterns of work.
- Identification of the care pathway.
- Facilitated team meetings, with the use of brainstorming or fishbone diagrams.

FACILITATION OF CHANGE

The role of clinical audit staff was discussed in Chapter 2, and this included mention of facilitation skills to guide the team through the different stages of the audit process. When implementing change in audit, the skills of a good facilitator come into their own. The facilitator's role is to:

➤ make it easy for the team to work towards their goal
➤ maintain the cohesion of the team
➤ get the most from the team.

It is therefore important to focus on the process and allow the team to tackle the problem. A good facilitator will keep the team on track, anticipate problems, ensure understanding of the objectives, make sure that everyone participates, and keep the team running to timescales. While doing this, the facilitator must remain neutral in order to maintain the team's trust and respect. This means ensuring that everyone has an equal opportunity to contribute, and the facilitator not expressing his or her own opinion. Impartiality is best achieved when the facilitator is not an active member of the team. Therefore clinical audit staff are ideally placed to fulfil this role in teams involved in audit projects.

The facilitator can give constructive feedback, encourage participation and listen actively to ideas. They can also be of practical assistance to the team by obtaining the resources required (e.g. negotiating protected time for discussion, researching information for which the team identifies a need, etc.). Another aspect of the facilitator's role is to control conflict, which should be used as an opportunity to allow different opinions to be aired and problems to be tackled so that the team can move on – conflict is healthy so long as it does not become personal. A good facilitator will allow the team to own the problem and find its own solutions without leading the process too directly. Open questioning, clarifying points to avoid different interpretations, and suggesting ideas to bring the team back on track when necessary are all key skills, as is the need to occasionally direct the team to find the focus.

The facilitator(s) of the change process will need to give careful thought to how feedback on the audit results will be provided, and this must be guided by pragmatic factors and local circumstances.[4]

THE CHANGE PROCESS

HQIP has produced a guide entitled *How to Implement Local Changes from National Clinical Audit* for NHS organisations in England and Wales that participate in the national audit programme.[5] The ideas and practical suggestions that this offers to audit professionals can be applied to local audit as well as national audit in many respects.

Change is a complex process and involves a number of activities that may or may not occur in a certain order, depending on other variable factors and local circumstances. This makes change management challenging because of the unpredictability of external factors that influence the change process. An adaptable, flexible approach is therefore needed to ensure that the process of change is not hindered by these factors. Gale and Grant designed a model of medical change which identified a set of core activities that needed to take place, not necessarily in a linear order, in order to maximise the chance of success.[6] Drawing from this model and incorporating the activities into the audit's action plan for change (*see* below; *also see* Appendix 3) can help to maximise the likelihood of change being accepted and adopted by those involved. The core activities identified by Gale and Grant are used below as side headings, under which further detail of what needs to take place is then described.

Establish the need for change
Making presentations

Presentations of the results need to be scheduled into key meetings in the organisation. For audit feedback to be effective it needs to be timely.[7] Meeting attendees should be sent a concise report of the results prior to the meeting, committing them to listing the issues and points that they wish to raise at the meeting. It is important to present the results of the audit to relevant audiences with whom involvement about potential change is needed. This includes service users, and to assist with this HQIP has produced a *Guide on How to Present Clinical Audits for the Public*.[8] The main objective of the presentations is to obtain agreement on the need to implement change, and so receive support and backing from those who need to give this for change to succeed. Involving as many potential stakeholders as possible will increase the ownership of any changes that are proposed, which will in turn increase the likelihood of these being embraced and implemented. Some organisations run clinical audit events, which vary in frequency from monthly to yearly, and it may be possible to tap into such a meeting as a forum for presenting the results to interested parties.[9] Bear in mind that interactive workshops are more effective in changing behaviour than passive lectures, and that combining feedback with educational materials and meetings that raise awareness of the desired change is also known to be effective.[7]

During presentation of the results and the discussion that ensues, the first point to establish is whether there is actually a need for change. This may not be obvious or immediately apparent from the results alone. Although performance may have fallen short of the desired level, the reasons for this need to be clearly understood so that an appropriate method for effecting changes can be selected. It is sometimes easy to latch on to the most obvious reason, but often the underlying cause is less apparent. Employing some simple investigative techniques from a root cause analysis approach, such as the 'five whys' and fishbone diagrams, can be helpful here. In England, the National Patient Safety Agency's website provides a root cause analysis toolkit as one of its patient safety resources,[10] from which tools can be used to establish the underlying reasons for (or root causes of) the desired performance levels not being reached. It is important to ask not only 'What went wrong?' but also 'Why did it go wrong?' and 'How did it go wrong?' Root cause analysis enables these questions to be clearly answered, thus enabling the underlying cause to be linked to appropriate solutions.

Define and agree goals

In key meetings during which results are presented, a fundamental task is to define and agree clear objectives so that everyone in the room is working towards achieving the same outcomes. Reaching consensus may require compromise, but giving individuals the opportunity to voice their opinions and concerns at this stage can help to prevent blockages and disruptions later on. Aims and objectives need to be written down for all to note, so that everyone shares a common vision.

Develop a tailored strategy

During the process, all possible methods of achieving the change need to be explored before agreement can be reached as to which options are appropriate. A clear decision-making process will need to be in place to assist change. The change process should be tackled as a team in order to enable the sharing of workload and responsibility, with everyone being valued for their contribution. Getting people on board with the need for change is achieved by effective, open, two-way communication and the utilisation of each individual's skills to create a sense of ownership in the task. People are more likely to be committed to the process if they are kept informed and involved. This will build an atmosphere of trust and remove any threat or fear, either perceived or real, which may otherwise be felt in relation to the process of change. When action planning, team members should be set clear tasks and responsibilities, with realistic timescales that should be adhered to as far as possible. At regular stages along the way progress checks need to be made and plans should be set out for ongoing review to sustain change. A clear strategy that includes these tasks will increase the likelihood of the audit achieving its aims. The strategy for change also needs to take into account four key features that will increase the likelihood of success. As far as possible the proposed changes should be:

➤ non-threatening
➤ perceived as being beneficial

➤ compatible with current beliefs and practices
➤ implemented incrementally.[2]

Select the right change

It is crucial that those discussing the results have a good understanding of their meaning and an ability to put them into the context of caregiving and patient management in order to interpret them correctly. If changes are to be made, it is worth spending time at this stage identifying and selecting the right changes that will target the true causes of deficiencies. Clinical staff and stakeholders therefore have a vital role to play here, most importantly because they have a vested interest and are more likely to engage in the process of change if they are involved and enabled to come up with the ideas themselves. It is important that those affected by the changes can see the benefits for them and feel that they really own the changes which are introduced. Clinical staff may see things differently from administrative or managerial staff, as each of these groups will work with a different part or stage of a process or system. Service users will have yet another perspective to bring to the discussions. HQIP has produced a *Guide for Patients in Understanding Clinical Audit Reports*[11] and *Clinical Audit: an introduction for patients*,[12] both of which can be helpful when involving service users in the discussion of results and changes. Everyone needs to be involved in order to ensure that the changes which are selected will work with and improve the whole process from beginning to end, and thereby prevent changes that are made at one stage of a process or pathway from causing new problems at another stage of that process or pathway. Where possible look for 'quick wins', as changes that require little work to implement but which quickly show benefits will win over sceptics and keep supporters on side.

Ensure that you have the power to act

If audit projects are chosen carefully and concern one's own area of service or care delivery, it is more likely that, when it comes to change, those involved will be able to manage and control the implementation of their own changes. It is crucial that the individuals who are discussing and identifying changes have the power to decide what these will be and to implement them. Audits have been found to have fallen short of implementing change because the changes identified were blocked at another level, often where additional financial resource was involved or where not all of the clinical professions affected were involved in the process. Therefore the meeting(s) to present the results and discuss the need for change must include all those who have an influence over the audit and who have a mandate to act. It is worth thinking about who needs to attend, and whether one or more meetings will need to be arranged to present the results in order to capture the views of all stakeholders. Getting the right people at the meeting from the start is critical, and this should include someone who can authorise the need for additional resources if these are deemed necessary. Excluding even one influential stakeholder or clinical professional may mean the difference between success and failure of the changes.

Design the change

Having facilitated a full discussion about the need for change, and having agreed one or more changes that focus on addressing the underlying causes of failure to meet performance levels, attention can now turn to designing the changes. Here again the design can mean the difference between success and failure, and again the best people to involve in the design are those who will be affected by the changes that are agreed. The design needs to be usable, practical and cause minimum disruption to practice, fitting in well with other associated practices and procedures. Wherever possible it is desirable to make use of existing systems, processes and protocols that can be adjusted in line with the changes needed. The use of a reminder system as well as the incorporation of changes into protocols can be effective.[7] Creating new protocols in addition to those already in place can be more problematic, as they tend to generate extra work, and they are more likely to be overlooked in the course of care and service delivery because they create one more thing to remember to do. If a protocol or process has to be replaced completely, time needs to be taken to ensure that everyone affected by this has been properly trained in the use of the new protocol or process and is supported during the transition from old to new.

'Built in' not 'bolted on'

The key is to design 'built-in' changes that work within current systems and processes, rather than to create 'bolted-on' changes that work outside current processes. For example, a practice nurse may undertake an asthma review audit and find that 20% of patients have not had an asthma review within the required time period. She decides that the change she needs to implement is to identify these 20% of patients and send out targeted recall letters to remind and encourage them to attend for a review. This is an appropriate initial change, but only in the short term. It will probably yield quite good results, and upon re-audit the practice nurse may well demonstrate that more patients have had their review following this change. However, it is not a sustainable change, as it is not **built into** what she does routinely to manage asthma reviews. It is a one-off change that is bolted on as an extra task to be done in response to a shortfall in care shown by the results of an audit. However, if the practice nurse was to look at how she could improve the current recall system and build in computer prompts for opportunistic review, the changes would be sustained over time and she would not have to spend extra time identifying individual patients to chase each year. The improved system would do the work for her on an ongoing basis, as an integral part of practice processes.

Be creative

Designing changes should ideally encourage large numbers of ideas to be generated through techniques such as brainstorming in meetings, completion of anonymous questionnaires by staff and service users, or putting suggestion boxes in places where staff and service users can contribute their ideas. All ideas need to be considered on their merits and tested by discussing them with those who will be using them in their day-to-day work. Sometimes the best ideas come from those who are not directly affected by the changes, but nonetheless have an understanding of the systems and processes, due to their support role. For example, ancillary and administrative staff working alongside clinical staff to support clinical caregiving will have a good knowledge of the systems and processes that they see in operation, and may notice where weaknesses in these systems (e.g. bottlenecks) occur, because they 'observe' them from a distance. Providing opportunities for the widest possible range of ideas to be put forward and considered will increase the likelihood of the most effective changes being identified. Individuals should be encouraged to consider and share, by asking them the following questions:

➤ What appeals to them about each idea that has been suggested?

➤ What concerns them about each idea that has been suggested?

➤ What further information do they need to know before they feel that any particular changes can be implemented?

MANAGING MULTIPLE CHANGES

It is sometimes the case that a number of changes are identified as being necessary to ensure that the improvements required can be achieved. In such situations the team may need to decide on its priorities according to the need for and urgency of change introduction. Here it is useful to have some 'quick wins' that can be implemented easily in the short term to get the process started. If some changes can be implemented with minimum disruption, while maximising benefits, evidence will build that audit is worthwhile and can make a difference. Even modest changes that are made regularly can have a significant impact.[7] After this it may be necessary to select other medium-term and finally longer-term changes that may be linked to resource availability. Sometimes further investigation will be needed where changes are on a larger scale and will take more time to achieve. It may be appropriate here to delegate work to individuals or small groups to flesh out the plans. It may also be necessary to arrange pilot studies on different approaches suggested to tackle larger-scale changes. Thorough action planning will help to ensure that the more complex changes are well managed and carefully introduced. Finally, it is worth searching the literature to see whether there are any lessons to be learned from similar audits or studies on the topic concerned with regard to making changes to improve quality.

Consult

Engaging all stakeholders, especially as appropriate, senior clinicians and managers as needed, is crucial to ensure proposed changes secure support. Whenever any changes are identified, it is crucial to take these to all those affected by the changes and talk to them about what is proposed and why. Obtaining feedback about the proposals will help to ensure that nothing is overlooked, and will allow strength of support for and agreement with the changes to be gauged. Consulting widely with others will also help to ensure that the changes chosen are best placed to deliver the desired results when re-audit takes place. Although some suggestions for change may seem appropriate superficially, inclusive consultation may reveal problems with them that would not otherwise have been noted. When discussing the implementation of any changes, some helpful questions to ask of those affected by the audit results include the following:

➤ Do those affected understand the purpose of the changes?
➤ Are the changes going to be beneficial?
➤ Are the changes practical and feasible?
➤ What will be the workload involved?
➤ Who will be involved, both directly and indirectly?
➤ Has the pace of change been considered?

Publicise the change widely

In addition to involving stakeholders in the identification and selection of changes, it is vital to ensure that the changes selected are known about by everyone who is going to be affected, whether directly or indirectly. The audit team must know to whom this applies, and should consider suitable means by which the information can be shared. Use can be made of meeting agendas, newsletters and bulletins, as well as posters and notices displayed as appropriate. Any communications that are written and sent to stakeholders regarding the proposed changes will carry more weight and credibility if they are signed or endorsed by a respected opinion leader.[7] This should be done in a timely manner so that the stakeholders have time to adjust as required to the changes that are being implemented. The rolling out of changes in such a planned way will help to manage the process effectively, increasing the likelihood of sustained improvement.

Agree detailed plans

Once the changes have been agreed, it is important to expand the proposals into a staged and structured process of implementation. This will take the form of an action plan for change, and the more detail the action plan contains, the greater the likelihood of success in achieving and sustaining change. Further advice and detail on action planning can be found in Appendix 3.

Implement change

When the above steps have been followed one by one, culminating in the production of a robust action plan, the changes can be implemented. During this stage it is important that a further mini cycle of change takes place within the main cycle of change that involves the following steps:

➤ Provide support.
➤ Consult with others.
➤ Modify the plans.

Provide support

Even when a thorough job has been done to involve and get the agreement of those affected by the changes, it is important that they continue to be supported when change is implemented. Providing a clear channel for two-way communication is a fundamental part of this, and may be facilitated by a line manager or a member of the audit team. This individual should be known to staff who are implementing changes, and be readily available to answer questions and provide advice to staff as they get used to the changes. It may be necessary to hold short team briefings to ensure that adequate support is provided and everyone is kept informed of the process as it is rolled out. It may also be helpful to provide a forum to enable staff affected by the changes to make comments on how the changes are progressing and to suggest ideas for improving the process and making it easier.

Consult with others

This continues to be important at this implementation stage of the process, because of the knock-on effects that changes can have on other teams or departments, as well as on service users. It is important to provide a forum for consultation as the changes are implemented, to ensure that their impact is assessed fully across relevant parts of the organisation. Inevitably, changing practice in one team or department may have an impact on other teams and departments, and even on other partner organisations. For example, changes that involve an earlier discharge of patients from hospital back into the community may well have an impact on care support services in the community setting. Consulting widely with others will help to keep track of the impact of changes and ensure that they are not having a problematic effect in another area of care or service delivery. However, it is equally important to identify and be aware of any spin-offs that result from the changes implemented and which have beneficial effects that may not have been forecast, such as the ability to retrieve data for a range of requirements.

Modify plans

With the best will in the world, it is not possible to foresee every problem that may occur. Rarely can changes be implemented without the need for any revision or refinement. Until changes are put to the test, any teething problems will not come to light. The change support team needs to be prepared to act quickly when problems arise, so that they can be dealt with efficiently and effectively. It is also important that those affected by the changes and responsible for implementing them understand that teething problems are a normal part of the process. They should be encouraged to report problems to their manager and the support team as soon as possible, and invited to suggest ways in which the problems may be overcome. Keeping people involved is crucial during this rollout phase, to ensure that belief in and commitment to the changes do not dwindle. Most plans will only require minor modifications or adjustments, but sometimes more significant revisions will be necessary. Therefore keeping everyone involved will help to ensure adherence to the process of change, even when it does not go completely according to plan.

Evaluate outcomes

The final stage of the change process is to evaluate the effect of changes made – in other words, to re-audit to complete the audit cycle. This is the topic of the next chapter, which demonstrates the value and importance of closing the audit loop by collecting and analysing data for a second time, after the changes have had ample opportunity to bed in and take effect. The aim of re-audit is to demonstrate the outcomes that follow from robust targeted changes to aspects that are being measured in the audit, with a view to achieving the desired performance levels set at the start of the audit.

REFERENCES

1 Irvine D, Irvine S. *Making Sense of Audit.* Oxford: Radcliffe Medical Press; 1991.
2 Crombie IK, Davies HT, Abraham SC *et al. The Audit Handbook: improving health care through clinical audit.* Chichester: John Wiley & Sons; 1993.
3 Grimshaw J, Eccles M, Thomas R *et al.* Towards evidence-based quality improvement: evidence (and its limitations) of the effectiveness of guideline dissemination and implementation strategies 1966–1998. *Journal of General Internal Medicine* 2006; **21 (Suppl. 2)**: 14–20.
4 Jamtvedt G, Young JM, Kristoffersen DT *et al.* Audit and feedback: effects on professional practice and health care outcomes. *Cochrane Database of Systematic Reviews* 2006; **2**: CD000259.
5 Schofield J, Jenkins J. *How to Implement Local Changes from National Clinical Audit – A Guide for Audit Professionals in Healthcare Organisations.* London: Healthcare Quality Improvement Partnership (HQIP); 2010. http://hqip.dev.bluw-i.com/implementing-local-change-from-national-clinical-audit-projects (accessed 2 August 2010).
6 Gale R, Grant J. *Managing Change in a Medical Context: guidelines for action.* London: Joint Centre for Education in Medicine/British Postgraduate Medical Federation; 1990.
7 National Institute for Health and Clinical Excellence (NICE). *How to Change Practice: understand, identify and overcome barriers to change.* London: NICE; 2007.
8 Pearce M. *Guide on How to Present Clinical Audits for the Public.* London: Healthcare Quality Improvement Partnership (HQIP); 2010. http://hqip.dev.bluw-i.com/assets/3-HQIP-CA-PD-025-Guide-on-how-to-present-clinical-audits-for (accessed 2 August 2010).
9 Ghosh R, ed. *Clinical Audit for Doctors.* Nottingham: Developmedica; 2009.
10 National Patient Safety Agency. *Root Cause Analysis (RCA) Report-Writing Tools and Templates.* London: National Patient Safety Agency; 2008. www.nrls.npsa.nhs.uk/resources/?entryid45=59847&q=0%c2%acroot%c2%ac (accessed 2 August 2010).
11 Pearce M. *Guide for Patients in Understanding Clinical Audit Reports.* London: Healthcare Quality Improvement Partnership (HQIP); 2010. http://hqip.dev.bluw-i.com/assets/2-HQIP-CA-PD-024-Guide-for-patients-in-understanding-clinical-audit-reports-19-April-2010.pdf (accessed 2 August 2010).
12 Pearce M. *Clinical Audit: an introduction for patients.* London: Healthcare Quality Improvement Partnership (HQIP); 2010. http://hqip.dev.bluw-i.com/assets/2-HQIP-CA-PD-024-Guide-for-patients-in-understanding-clinical-audit-reports-19-April-2010.pdf (accessed 2 August 2010).

CHAPTER 5

Stage 4: Sustaining improvement

Stephen Ashmore, Tracy Ruthven and Louise Hazelwood

Key points

- Collection and analysis of data following the implementation of change is a vital part of the audit cycle.
- Further phases of collection of data provide evidence that the changes implemented have had the desired effect and have led to improvements in quality.
- Increasingly, healthcare organisations are expected to provide assurance that new evidence-based healthcare interventions are being implemented, and that poor performance or substandard quality is being addressed and corrected.
- Where further measurement is not deemed necessary, documented reasons are recommended to justify why this has not taken place.
- The timing of the further phases of data collection is important, so that the second data collection provides valid and reliable data that can be compared with those collected in the first data collection.
- A complete audit cycle ideally involves two data collections and a comparison of one with the other, following the implementation of change after the first data collection, in order to determine whether the desired improvements have been made.
- Further cycles may be necessary if performance still fails to attain the levels set at the outset of the audit. At this stage there may be justification for adjusting the desired performance levels in the light of the results obtained.
- Ongoing monitoring arrangements should be agreed and set in place following completion of the audit, in order to ensure that performance is maintained over time and to identify any reduction in quality. These may involve further routine 'snapshot' audits and/or make use of other feedback mechanisms that could indicate performance issues.
- Improvements should be maintained and reinforced over time by ensuring that practical and user-friendly processes are built into systems. A culture that embraces change and encourages feedback will assist with the smooth transition from old to new ways of working.

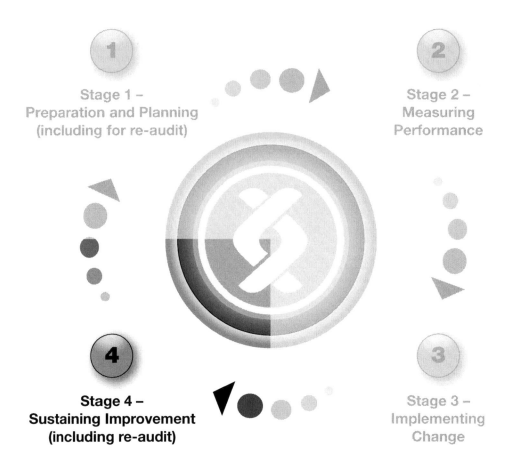

Stage 1 –
Preparation and Planning
(including for re-audit)

Stage 2 –
Measuring
Performance

Stage 4 –
**Sustaining Improvement
(including re-audit)**

Stage 3 –
Implementing
Change

The purpose of this chapter:
- To set out the importance of sustaining improvements over time, and to discuss how this can be achieved.

INTRODUCTION

In traditional clinical audit in its most typical form, the cycle of measurement and change occurs rigidly over time, in stages, rather than in newer or more flexible forms drawn from adapted audit methodologies, which review data continuously and act immediately in response. The processes described below are relevant to both of these approaches, especially for the continuing monitoring of change.

There would be very little point in undertaking clinical audit if change that led to improvements in care and service provision was not sustained. The only way to know this for sure is to review results on a repeated basis, followed by ongoing monitoring arrangements, to provide evidence that this is the case. **The audit cycle**

is not complete if follow-up measurement does not take place, except in circum-stances where a change process following the first round of measurement has not occurred. Where audits have been completed according to the continuous moni-toring approach, evidence of improvements in the way that care is now delivered is often shown.[1-3] In the increasingly demanding world of healthcare provision, in terms of public expectations and professional accountability and regulation, there is a need to demonstrate that quality improvement and monitoring are embedded in the culture of an organisation on an ongoing, routine basis.

However, it is still too often the case that a further period of re-measurement, following the implementation of change, does not occur, and this can be attributed to a range of reasons.[4] In part it may also be due to some emphases within clinical audit in healthcare, which suggests that insufficient importance was attached to the need to complete the audit cycle through re-audit and ongoing monitoring. Indeed, in some of the formative publications on medical or clinical audit that were written in the early 1990s there is very little, if any, coverage of continuous monitoring, or of re-audit as part of the audit cycle. Furthermore, examples of clinical audits have fre-quently been published in leading healthcare journals with no mention of a re-audit or other re-measurement having taken place or been planned. This perhaps sends out a confusing message that ongoing measurement is optional. Lastly, structural reasons lead to audits not being subject to measurement of subsequent improvement (e.g. when they are completed by junior doctors who do not have time to complete a further phase of measurement).[5]

Re-measurement, or collecting data on an ongoing basis, is not the same thing as a complete re-audit. The second phase of measurement is not the same as an entire re-audit process. This distinction needs to be made clear.

However, collection of further sets of data to confirm that changes have been made and improvements have taken place has often been regarded as a **desirable** feature of the audit cycle rather than an **essential** step in the process. In recent years this situation has begun to be redressed, and recent initiatives within the English quality improvement culture have emphasised the need for continuous monitor-ing of improvement (e.g. the revalidation process for doctors,[6] the reports made by provider organisations, which are known as Quality Accounts,[7] and NHS Litigation Authority requirements).

Any systematic approach to changing professional practice should include plans to:
➤ monitor and evaluate the change
➤ maintain and reinforce the change.[8]

MONITORING AND EVALUATING CHANGES
Is a further collection of data necessary?
Except in a few circumstances (e.g. significant organisational change, or where no changes were made after the first round of measurement), there is little justifica-tion for not completing the audit cycle with a further round of measurement or

continuous data collection. In situations where target performance levels have been met or exceeded, as evident from the first data collection and analysis, there may be justification for not completing the audit cycle with further data collection and analysis. However, it is worth considering the reasons for this before the decision is made. These might include the following three scenarios.

Performance levels were set too low

Discussion of the percentages at which initial performance levels were set should take place to decide whether these were not challenging enough in the first place. A recap of how they were agreed aids understanding of the rationale behind the chosen levels. If the performance levels are in line with national levels, the team may still decide that they want to improve upon these. Considering appropriate changes to facilitate this and then continuing to measure in order to determine the effect that this has had on overall performance levels can be rewarding. It is sometimes tempting to rest on one's laurels if performance levels have been achieved, but if effort is put into continuing measurement the potential gains can be significant. **Clinical audit is, after all, about continuous quality improvement and achieving the highest quality for the maximum possible number of service users.**

The chosen audit topic was not a problem area

Sometimes audits are undertaken even though there is not felt to be a problem in the topic area. Care is known to be good, but for a number of reasons the audit is still undertaken. This may be to provide evidence of good care to satisfy certain quality monitoring requirements. The problem with conducting audits to confirm what is already known is the time and resources that they take up, which could have been put to better use examining and improving aspects of care and service provision for which there is evidence of poor or substandard care. In such situations it may be agreed that undertaking extensive further collections of data would be an unnecessary waste of resources. If this does take place, it should be to provide confirmation that the performance levels are being sustained, or that they are a true reflection of ongoing practice performance, rather than simply happening by chance the first time around.

The Hawthorne effect (*see Chapter 2*)

If data have been collected prospectively for the audit, it is important to consider to what extent, if at all, the results have been skewed by changed behaviour during the data collection period. Those whose practice was being audited may have changed their normal practice to that required by the audit standards because they knew that they were being audited. This can lead to falsely high performance levels being achieved that are not a true reflection of normal practice. Where performance levels have been exceeded in an audit of a topic that is known to be a problem, the possibility that the Hawthorne effect may have come into play must be considered before a decision is taken not to continue to collect data.

Comparing like with like

Collecting data for a second time, after changes have been introduced and have had time to take effect, is central to both assessing and maintaining the improvements made during clinical audit. A re-audit should include all criteria where the original analysis demonstrated that acceptable performance levels were not met and changes in practice were implemented. Thus the same procedures for sample selection, data collection and analysis should be used. One should avoid changing or adding to the data collection tool unless it is apparent that there was an issue with completion that was not picked up at the design stage. This should be done carefully so that the second set of data collected can be compared with the data that were collected in the first audit, thus ensuring data validity. Most importantly, the audit criteria, performance levels and thus the standards should not be altered. The aim is to measure the degree of improvement once changes have taken effect, so it is necessary to use the same parameters that were agreed at the outset and which are in line with the original aims and objectives of the audit.

What happens when the evidence changes between cycles

Sometimes new evidence or updated guidelines will emerge between audit cycles that might change the original audit standards. For example, a new target blood pressure level being recommended in a national guideline might affect an audit of diabetes management in primary care that includes a standard on the control of blood pressure. This means that the first data collection is based on a target blood pressure that is not as low as the revised target blood pressure that comes into play before the second data collection. If the new target blood pressure was to be adopted as the standard for the re-audit, in line with the recommended evidence-based guidance, the comparison with the first data collection would not be like for like. It would not be appropriate to compare performance levels if the first data collection was based on achieving a different target blood pressure to the second one.

One way of dealing with this is to collect data to allow measurement of performance levels for both the old and the new target blood pressure levels. Thus in the re-audit the true change in performance level for the percentage meeting the old target blood pressure can be calculated to measure the extent to which the changes have had the desired effect. A calculation can also be made of the percentage of patients who met the new target blood pressure, to give an idea of current performance against updated evidence. This provides the basis for a useful discussion of the issues relating to getting new evidence into routine practice. Indeed a further audit could be set up focusing solely on blood pressure control and agreeing an appropriate revised performance level in the light of the updated guidance.

Timing further periods of data collection

Agreement needs to be reached as to when the time would be right for further collection of data, or the need for continuous collection of data. Some thought will have been given to this in the early planning stage of the audit when the timetable was drawn up to help to project manage the audit. Every audit that makes up part of an audit programme will need to be timetabled in order to effectively manage the workload involved and meet the necessary reporting requirements (e.g. for national audits).

Another factor that needs to be taken into account when timing the second data collection is what else is going on in the department, unit or organisation where the audit is taking place. It is always recommended that formal data collection should be avoided during holiday periods that may affect staffing levels, either of those who will be collecting data or of those who will be overseeing or coordinating the data collection. It is also worth checking what other projects, initiatives or new processes may be affecting the department or unit where the measurement will be taking place (e.g. whether staff appraisals are being conducted, or year-end statistics are being gathered, or an equipment or computer upgrade is taking place that is disrupting normal care delivery). These and other organisational factors need to be taken into account by the audit team to ensure that the second data collection occurs during a normal period when there is nothing else to distract the data collectors or to impede data collection.

However, in addition to this, **the timing of continuing periods of data collection will depend primarily upon the nature of the changes that are being implemented.** These will need time to take effect and to bed into daily practice to have an impact on care and service delivery. Although some changes will be noticeable immediately, others will become apparent more gradually over time as, for example, updated protocols and processes come into play. Some changes will affect daily practice, and others will affect practice on a less frequent basis. Therefore the time that it takes for the changes to have an impact on the service user population to a sufficient extent to be able to re-audit will vary. There will need to be enough data to collect after the changes to ensure that the true effects of the changes can be measured. If data are collected for a second time too soon, the effects of the changes implemented will not be complete. However, if the second data collection is left too long, the audit will lose its momentum and other factors may come into play over and above the changes implemented, so that the true effects of the changes made cannot be measured. For some audits, where practice changes immediately, affecting every patient seen on a daily basis, it may be reasonable to re-audit after 1 to 6 months. For other audits, where the changes take effect more gradually, it may be necessary to leave the re-audit until between 12 and 18 months. However, where the audit takes the form of continuous monitoring and action, these strictures obviously need not apply.

Preparing to collect data for a second time where continuous monitoring is not taking place

Once the timing for the second data collection has been agreed, it is important for the data collectors and all those affected by the data collection to be informed of the time period that has been chosen. It is also helpful to arrange a short meeting with the data collectors to remind them once again about correct completion of the data collection forms. Any questions can be answered and adjustments made as necessary to ensure a smooth passage through the second phase of data collection. For example, in the scenario given earlier where the evidence changed between cycles of measurement, there may be a need to revise the data collection tool to ensure capture of data relating to both the old and the new target blood pressure, and this will need to be explained to the data collectors.

Analysing data for the second time

It will be necessary for the person responsible for data analysis to think about how to present the results in order to show a clear comparison with those from the first data collection. It is important to use the same process for analysis of data, so that the comparison is valid. Graphs that depict the first set of results next to the second set, so that the change in performance levels can be easily seen, are therefore recommended. The graphs should also show clearly the performance levels set for each criterion, so that the degree of change in relation to these can be measured. The aim is to put together a like-for-like comparison that gives a clear and complete picture of performance and the extent of improvement.

PREPARING THE PRESENTATION

The same principles apply here as in the first audit, and the process should be followed again to produce a comprehensive account of the second set of results as compared with the first set. The key point is that the presentation of results from the re-audit should enable the audience to whom the presentation will be made to have a robust discussion about what should happen from this point onwards.

Achievement of performance levels

The results will show one of the following three scenarios:
➤ the performance levels set at the outset of the audit are still not being achieved
➤ some standards fall short, but others meet or exceed the performance levels set at the outset of the audit
➤ all of the performance levels set at the outset of the audit are being achieved.

Standards falling short of performance levels

For standards where the required performance levels have still not been reached, discussion about the need to identify and implement further changes needs to take place. This will depend upon the degree of the shortfall in performance. If it is only a few per cent, there may only be a need to make minor additional changes or adjustments. However, if there is a significant shortfall, a thorough consideration of what more could be changed is needed. It may be that the changes implemented were not ambitious enough or did not correctly target the source of the problem. Often a further discussion of possible changes reveals new ideas that may prove more fruitful. And, of course, it is important to ascertain whether the changes had time to take effect before re-audit took place. If it is found that this was not the case, further change may not be needed, but a further data collection will be required to ensure that performance does indeed reach the desired levels.

Revising the chosen performance levels where these are not reached

If it is agreed that no further change can realistically be implemented, this is now the appropriate time to consider revising the chosen performance levels (unless they have been set at a mandatory level). Discussion of whether the performance levels that have not been reached are in fact realistic and attainable is needed, preferably employing evidence to back up the view that they may be too ambitious or unachievable. If they are to be reviewed, fresh justification for the new lower levels needs to be provided. This is where benchmarking can help to establish what is a reasonable performance level to aim for. Where possible, obtaining the results from other organisations' audits on the same topic will give a better indication of performance levels that are achievable.

Standards meeting or exceeding performance levels

Following the implementation of changes it is likely to be the case that some or hopefully all of the standards have now met or exceeded the set performance levels. It is useful to discuss the degree to which performance levels improved upon re-measurement. If the improvement is small, it may be worth monitoring these standards more closely than in situations where the improvement is large. For example, a standard that achieves a performance level of 70% before the change and a performance level of 90% after the change is different from a standard that achieves a performance level of 70% before the change and a performance level of 73% after the change. Small improvements may be down to chance alone rather than the impact of the changes, and this needs to be borne in mind when the decision as to whether or not to perform a further phase of data collection is taken.

Revising the performance levels where standards are met or exceeded

When standards reach set performance levels, it is worth discussing whether these should be raised higher. Even when national or minimum performance levels are reached, there is a case for increasing these to a new higher level. In some cases, national performance levels may have been reviewed since the second phase of data collection, and the requirement for new, even higher levels has come into play. Alternatively, the organisation itself may have new and higher expectations placed upon it by commissioners of services. As mentioned earlier, clinical audit is about continuous quality improvement, and further incremental increases in performance are desirable for service users if it is felt that this is a realistic possibility. During the discussion of the results, it is worth asking whether further change is considered possible or appropriate for standards that meet or exceed set performance levels. Again, benchmarking against results from other audits can assist with the decision as to whether or not to raise performance levels further.

PERFORMING A FURTHER CYCLE OF AUDIT

For some audits, two data collections will not be sufficient to provide assurance that improvements to the level required have been achieved. This will be either because performance levels were not reached upon re-audit for some or all of the standards, or because they were reached but it was agreed that they should be increased further in the light of new information, as discussed earlier. In any situations where further changes are made, or where performance levels are either raised or lowered, a further data collection and analysis will need to be undertaken at a suitable time point in the future. This extra workload may not have been factored into the audit programme, and thought will need to be given to how and when the further phase of data collection should take place. It may be that this further phase is a smaller undertaking, because it is really only necessary to collect data and perform analysis on those standards affected either by the implementation of further change or by an adjustment to the set performance levels. Following analysis of the third data collection it is of course important to present the results again in a format that can be easily interpreted with a view to moving on to ongoing monitoring arrangements.

Ongoing monitoring arrangements

Once the audit team is satisfied with the performance levels achieved for the audit standards, there is a need to discuss and agree what ongoing monitoring arrangements will be set in place to ensure that the improvements are being maintained. If the right changes have been applied (*see* Chapter 4), improvements in care and service delivery are more likely to be sustained over time. However, **it is prudent to perform checks at agreed intervals (e.g. yearly), to monitor ongoing performance.** Such checks are unlikely to be full audits, as these should not be necessary. A number of methods can be employed to facilitate routine ongoing monitoring that will provide sufficient evidence that improvements are either being sustained or slipping back. Any decline in performance can then be investigated through further more detailed audits. Common monitoring processes include the following:

➤ **Rapid cycle change:** These are short-cycle, small-scale tests of change linked to reflection, and are based on the Plan–Do–See–Act (PDSA) cycles. This method enables clinicians to test out the effectiveness of changes in practice in the short term, thereby enabling changes to be refined and altered as the process continues.

➤ **Snapshot audits:** A small sample of records, say 10%, are audited against the required standards to monitor performance levels. These audits are normally performed yearly to provide assurance that quality is being maintained.

➤ **Computerised data recording:** With certain IT systems it is possible to run regular queries on the data that are captured automatically and continuously. These give instant access to current levels of care (e.g. the system designed for general practice in England to capture clinical performance indicators for the QOF, mentioned in Chapter 2).

➤ **Service user feedback, including complaints:** Relevant information received from users can indicate whether quality problems in previously audited topics are occurring. When such feedback is received it can prompt a more thorough investigation into the area of care or service provision concerned.

➤ **Errors, near misses, and patient safety or adverse incidents:** These are another rich source of data that can act as a signal that quality may be slipping in aspects of care that have been audited and need to be monitored. Again, a cluster of incidents in one area of care will act as a prompt for further action and investigation.

➤ **Significant event audit:** This is a routine process designed to investigate and analyse any out-of-the-ordinary events that occur on a day-to-day basis. It is popular in general practice settings in England. Features from a completed clinical audit can be added to the list of events that are gathered for this form of audit, and provide a means of keeping key topic areas on the quality agenda.

The more systematic the monitoring mechanisms are, the more likely it is that lapses in aspects of quality or declining performance will be detected. Some of these mechanisms depend on an environment that fosters the reporting of errors and adverse incidents. If this is not in place, these less formal mechanisms cannot be relied upon to provide evidence that performance may be slipping, and more systematic methods will need to be implemented.

MAINTAINING AND REINFORCING IMPROVEMENT
Maintaining and reinforcing improvement over time is a complex process. In UK projects in which improvements have been sustained, the following common factors have been identified:[9]

➤ reinforcing or motivating factors built in by the management to support the continual cycle of quality improvement
➤ integration of audit into the organisation's wider quality improvement systems
➤ strong leadership.

In quality improvement initiatives in US hospitals, four interdependent processes have been found to support the lasting impact of changes made, including processes recognisable as clinical audit:

➤ a strategy that recognises audit activity, combined with an achievable plan of quality improvement
➤ a culture that supports the concept of planned audit activity, leading to improvements in quality of which everyone in the organisation is aware and supportive
➤ IT processes that can provide accurate information about the organisation, allowing sensible decisions to be made about where review is needed and whether changes have had the desired effects
➤ appropriate structures to support and implement the changes that are suggested.[10]

Maintaining and reinforcing improvement is as much about the culture of an organisation as it is about the efficiency and effectiveness of the systems and processes that are in place. An organisation, department or team that is committed to continuous quality improvement and believes in the value of clinical audit for achieving this is more likely to encourage and facilitate efforts to maintain high standards of quality achieved through clinical audit projects.

There are a number of practical ways in which improvements can be maintained and reinforced successfully over time, which are summarised below.

Meeting agendas

Whether at team, department or organisational level, change is more likely to be sustained where areas of care and service delivery that were the subject of audits are discussed and revisited at regular intervals in appropriate meetings. Including completed audit follow-up as a standing agenda item provides an opportunity for clinical staff and other stakeholders to raise any issues that may come to light after the completion of an audit. This will help to identify problems quickly so that they can be addressed, and will also provide positive feedback when things continue to go well, thus motivating staff and acknowledging efforts to improve care. Discussion of post-audit evaluation in meeting situations can also serve as an effective reminder of changes made to practice, thus reinforcing the new way of doing things and increasing the likelihood that the changes will become routine practice and be sustained over time.

Clinical audit showcase

Organisations that place quality high on their agenda will provide opportunities for the promotion and sharing of completed audits. Running an event once or twice a year for teams to showcase their audit work can be an effective way to publicise audits and promote their benefits. It delivers a clear message that clinical audit is embedded in the culture of the organisation and that it makes a difference to quality in healthcare. Again, it serves to reinforce the changes that have been implemented, raising awareness of these across the organisation.

Leading by example

A large responsibility for sustaining change lies with clinical and administrative managers and leaders, who can oversee change and keep an eye on daily practice to ensure that lapses back to the old practices do not occur. This involves reminding staff where necessary and motivating the team to adhere to new processes agreed as a result of audit work.

Induction of new staff

Where changes to practice have recently been introduced through audit work, it is important to ensure that new staff arriving (back) in the team or department (e.g. from rotation changes, locums, return from maternity leave, etc.) are inducted into the new processes. There is a risk that old systems and processes may be followed if updated protocols are not visible, accessible and in routine use. Where a team has become an early adopter of new evidence-based practice introduced through audit work, or where updated protocols are now in use, it cannot be assumed that all staff arriving in the department will be as up to date with their own practice or will know what has changed. Therefore it is important to have a system to ensure that new staff are quickly made aware of recent changes to practice, in order to ensure patient safety and maintain quality.

Making changes visible

Following on from the previous point, it is critical that changes to policies, protocols and record completion are visible. Many changes that are agreed from audits include the updating or even rewriting of documentation that supports the delivery of care and services. Too often, however, these important aids to effective practice are not visible or accessible to the staff for whom they are intended. Therefore, if changes made to protocols, etc. are to be sustained, they need to be available and in routine use. Putting them in highly visible places where they will be seen during the course of care delivery, and building reminders into routine recording will serve to ensure that change is sustained over time.

User-friendly systems and processes

A further point to ensure is that the changes are implemented in a usable way that fits in with normal practice and everyday procedures and processes. Changes that are 'built in' rather than 'bolted on' are more likely to sustain improvement over time. Any new or updated policies and protocols that emerge from audit changes need to be usable and user-friendly if they are going to enable the improvements made in practice to be maintained. Therefore it is beneficial if agreed changes are designed to fit in with each team that is affected by them, working in conjunction with existing practices. Again, staff are more likely to maintain the changes introduced if they fit in with their own systems of working.

Trial and error

Often the changes that are agreed following the discussion of audit results are along the right lines and target the specific areas of need, but the finer details of how the changes will be implemented across the organisation may not always cover all eventualities. It is sometimes not until a while after the changes have been implemented that glitches in the way they were introduced become apparent. It is important that the cycle of change goes on for some time if improvements in practice are to be sustained. It is all too easy to revert back to the old ways of working when minor problems arise. However, a supportive environment that encourages the reporting and ironing out of such problems is far more productive than one that dismisses the new changes out of hand. The staff who are affected by the changes are ideally placed to suggest adjustments and alterations to the changes that will work better for them, and this should be encouraged so that quality does not suffer.

A dynamic culture that encourages change and innovation

Organisations that engender a culture of embracing change and new ideas, and which support staff in these endeavours, are best placed to obtain the maximum benefit from audit. Audit is about change and continuous quality improvement, and sustaining change requires a willingness to try out new ways of doing things, getting good ideas quickly into practice and making adjustments along the way to ensure that the desired performance levels are maintained over time.

A more general discussion of why and how change happens, and the underpinning factors that drive change, can be found in Appendix 3 of this volume.

SUMMARY OF THE STAGES OF CLINICAL AUDIT (CHAPTERS 2 TO 5)

The last four chapters have attempted to steer anyone undertaking clinical audit through the key processes necessary to make an audit well managed and effective. These stages are not prescriptive, and must be adapted to fit the setting and systems in place in very different clinical environments. The **essence** is that clinical audit is a cycle, not a single process involving one sweep of measurement. If it is to lead to changes in practice, and then improvements in healthcare outcomes and other effects as a result, clinical audit must make some effort to follow this cycle as closely as possible. This guide has been designed to set out the common pitfalls and problems along the way, and to offer guidance on how these can and should be overcome. It is the strong hope of the authors of this volume that practitioners of audit will read this guidance, apply the process systematically, and as a result the journey of care will become more effective for patients, health service managers and clinicians alike.

REFERENCES

1 Connor SJ, Lienert AR, Brown LA *et al.* Closing the audit loop is necessary to achieve compliance with evidence-based guidelines in the management of acute pancreatitis. *New Zealand Medical Journal* 2008; **121**: 19–25.

2 Gallagher GA, McLintock T, Booth MG. Closing the audit loop – prevention of periop-erative hypothermia: audit and re-audit of perioperative hypothermia. *European Journal of Anaesthesiology* 2003; **20**: 750–52.

3 Martin TN, Irving RJ, Sutherland M *et al.* Improving secondary prevention in coronary bypass patients: closing the audit loop. *Heart* 2005; **91**: 456–9.

4 Guryel E, Acton K, Patel S. Auditing orthopaedic audit. *Annals of the Royal College of Surgeons of England* 2008; **90**: 675–8.

5 Cai A, Greenall J, Ding DC. UK junior doctors' experience of clinical audit in the Foundation Programme. *British Journal of Medical Practitioners* 2009; **2**: 42–5.

6 The General Medical Council website contains details of this process as it develops, and is available at www.gmc-uk.org/doctors/7330.asp (accessed 16 July 2010).

7 Department of Health. *Quality Accounts Toolkit: advisory guidance for providers of NHS services producing Quality Accounts for the year 2009/2010.* London: Department of Health; 2010. www.dh.gov.uk/en/Publicationsandstatistics/Publications/PublicationsPolicyAndGuidance/DH_112359 (accessed 16 July 2010).
8 NHS Centre for Reviews and Dissemination. *Effective Health Care: getting evidence into practice.* York: NHS Centre for Reviews and Dissemination, University of York; 1999.
9 Dunning M, Abi-Aad G, Gilbert D *et al. Experience, Evidence and Everyday Practice: creating systems for delivering health care.* London: King's Fund; 1999.
10 Shortell SM, Bennett CL, Byck GR. Assessing the impact of continuous quality improvement on clinical practice: what it will take to accelerate progress. *Millbank Quarterly* 1998; **76:** 593–624.

Ethics and clinical audit

Nancy Dixon

Key points

- Clinical audit and quality improvement (QI) are ethically driven activities.
- It is a misconception that ethics review is needed for research but not for clinical audit or other QI projects.
- Clinical audits can overlap with quality improvement research, so criteria for making a decision on the nature of the activity are needed.
- Clinical audit and other QI projects can raise ethical issues, and proposals for such projects should be screened in order to flag and handle any ethical issues.
- The findings of clinical audits and quality improvement projects should be screened to ensure that any ethical issues that arise in a project are handled appropriately.
- Healthcare organisations need to have robust structures, policies and processes in place for ethical oversight of clinical audits and QI projects.

The purpose of this appendix

- To set out the ethical issues involved in clinical audit and how these can be managed.

THE ETHICAL OBLIGATION TO UNDERTAKE CLINICAL AUDIT AND QI

The gap between evidence-based practice, actual patient care delivered, and short-comings in patient safety in healthcare organisations is well documented.[1] Doctors, nurses, allied healthcare professionals and healthcare organisations have an ethical obligation to close the gap in implementation of best known practice, and to over-come patient safety shortcomings.[2–4] Disciplined and focused QI efforts can increase the effectiveness and safety of healthcare.[5] If properly conducted, clinical audits and other QI activities can be seen as an ethical imperative in healthcare, something from which both professionals and patients benefit and in which they should cooperate.[5] Failure to undertake clinical audits and other QI projects can be harmful if such lack of participation perpetuates unsafe, unnecessary or ineffective clinical practice.[6]

DIFFERENTIATING RESEARCH AND CLINICAL AUDIT OR QI AS A BASIS FOR ETHICS REVIEW

The importance of identifying research properly

Ethics review of proposed research studies is required because clinical research requires participants in the research to take the risk that they will receive a treatment that is not optimal or which may even be harmful.[7] Participation in research is voluntary, and therefore each participant in a research study is entitled to choose whether or not to be a research subject.[8,9] It is very appropriate that people who volunteer to participate in research are safeguarded through effective ethical review of proposed research projects.

It has become important to attempt to distinguish between research and clinical audit and other QI activities in order to avoid the possibility that clinicians, intentionally or unintentionally, might 'game' the existing system of protection for participants in a research study. By designating a research project as a clinical audit or QI study, clinicians avoid the time-consuming process of review of research proposals, including requirements for informed consent of the participants.[7,10–17]

The problem of reliably differentiating between research and clinical audit or QI

Studies have demonstrated that research ethics committees, researchers, medical directors, quality improvement or clinical governance practitioners, and journal editors are not consistent in reaching decisions as to whether a proposed project represents research or quality improvement.[15,18–21] Clinicians in different countries have experienced misunderstanding by colleagues as well as by authorities as to what constitutes research as opposed to a quality improvement project.[14,22–31]

Concepts that are used to differentiate between research and clinical audit or QI

A number of concepts have been suggested as the basis for differentiating between research and clinical audit or QI, such as purpose, systematic approach, production of generalisable new knowledge, treatment or allocation, intention to publish, and focus on human subjects.[32] These concepts have not been validated as reliably discriminating between research and quality improvement studies. However, as quality improvement studies become increasingly sophisticated, many of these concepts can potentially apply to both research and quality improvement studies.[1,3,4,9,14,24,26,33–40]

No point to differentiating between research and clinical audit or QI as a basis for review

There are three reasons why differentiating between research and clinical audit or QI activities should no longer form the basis for deciding whether an activity requires ethical review.

➤ Distinctions between the two types of activities are blurred and can be ambiguous, unhelpful and arbitrary.[1,11,12,15,19,24,41–47]

➤ There are other ethical issues related to clinical audit and QI activities that are beyond consideration of the design of an individual clinical audit or QI initiative as a project. These issues relate to the healthcare organisation's duty to manage and to act on the findings of audits and QI studies.[4]

➤ Some QI initiatives are truly research on the quality improvement process – that is, 'hybrid' projects.[48–50] Research on the QI process itself or organisational or practice interventions intended to bring about improvements in patient care should be subject to research ethics oversight.

WHAT IS INVOLVED IN ETHICS?

Ethics is the inquiry into situations that have led or which may lead to harms or benefits to others, and into the language that is employed to describe those situations.[51] Ethics is a generic term for various ways of understanding and examining morality. Four principles derived from moral theory are autonomy, beneficence, non-maleficence and justice. An explanation of each of these principles[51] and examples of their application to healthcare can be found in Table A1.1.

TABLE A1.1 Ethics principles and examples of their application

Principle	Meaning	Example of application to healthcare
Autonomy	An obligation to respect the rights of people to make choices concerning their own lives (e.g. by disclosing information to enable people to make decisions, to foster their decision making and not to assume a controlling influence on their decisions); also recognising the right of a person to choose to decline information about choices, and not to make choices on behalf of the person	Providing information to patients about their treatments or procedures in ways that are sufficiently complete and comprehensible about associated benefits and risks of the treatments or procedures so that patients can make informed choices about proposed treatments or procedures Seeking patients' informed consent to treatments or procedures
Beneficence	An obligation to act in ways that benefit others and in ways that prevent harm, including removing circumstances that could lead to harm	Meeting a duty of care to provide patient care that is consistent with known good practice – that is, care that is known to benefit patients

(continued)

Principle	Meaning	Example of application to healthcare
Non-maleficence	An obligation not to harm others and not to impose risks of harm; assuming a standard of due care, that is, taking sufficient and appropriate action to avoid causing harm to a person	Maintaining confidentiality of information about patients, and providing privacy for patients Avoiding the intentional or unintentional imposition of a risk of harm to a patient (e.g. by failing to monitor a patient in accordance with the severity of the patient's condition)
Justice	An obligation to treat others fairly, distribute scarce resources fairly and respect people's rights and morally acceptable laws	Avoiding being selective about patients who receive care or a substantial improvement in care Avoiding wasting resources that could be used to better purpose

ETHICAL ISSUES WITH REGARD TO A CLINICAL AUDIT OR QI PROGRAMME

Five ethical issues related to a clinical audit or QI programme have been identified. These are:

➤ the participation of all healthcare professions in clinical audit and QI activities
➤ assurance that all clinical services are undertaking clinical audits or QI activities
➤ a systematic approach to setting priorities for clinical audits or QI activities
➤ coverage of all patient groups and types of conditions
➤ effective management and conduct of clinical audit and QI activities.

First, it has been acknowledged that all healthcare professionals have a responsibility to provide the best possible care, which could be interpreted as meaning that not to be involved in audit or QI is a breach of a professional code of conduct.[52,53] The duty of care of each healthcare professional to prevent harm coming to others through his or her acts or omissions extends to the duty to participate in clinical audit.[54,55] The inclusion or exclusion of professionals in the clinical audit or QI process raises important ethical issues, not least in terms of representation and the promotion of fair working practices.[36] It is important for audits or QI studies to be conducted in ways that maximise professionals' obligations towards one another, and in doing so, they may improve the quality of clinical audit.[36]

Secondly, all clinical services should have an active clinical audit and QI programme with the aim of achieving improvements in the quality of patient care. Given the concern about informing patients of possible harms, 'perhaps providers who do not monitor quality should be required to inform patients that no systematic improvement efforts are under way and they are thus at risk of receiving suboptimal care'[56] because 'the real risk from QI lay in the absence rather than presence of QI.'[57]

Thirdly, priority setting for clinical audits or QI studies may be influenced by a number of factors, including external requirements and expectations, the resources available to carry out the work, pressure from patients and their representatives, or the perceived ease or difficulty with which work on a particular subject is carried out.[58] There is a perception that clinical audits, for example, have tended to focus on satisfying external pressures rather than on the integrity of self-observation and self-regulation.[36] A system for setting priorities needs to include analysis of benefits and risks to patients in the current system of healthcare delivery and whether or not the proposed audits or QI projects respond to the risk–benefit analysis.[11]

Fourthly, the moral principle of justice and fairness suggests that no patient group should be excluded from the possibility of inclusion in a clinical audit or QI activity. Any criteria that are used to delineate inclusions or exclusions (e.g. patient characteristics, such as gender, race, ethnicity or disease site, or staff characteristics, such as profession or role within the organisation) need to be justified.[59] In addition, the potential burdens or risks as well as the potential benefits of the activities should be distributed fairly across the population of patients who are served by the healthcare organisation.[11]

Finally, if there is an ethical responsibility to undertake clinical audits and QI activities as an ongoing and integral part of the operations of a healthcare organisation, there is also a responsibility to manage and conduct clinical audits and QI projects effectively and well. Unfortunately, clinical audits and QI activities in many organisations are decentralised, fragmented, under-resourced and ad hoc, with little priority setting,[4] and with priorities driven by poorly researched and politically motivated top-down initiatives by central authorities,[16] inadequate structures to ensure the long-term success of the activities, and lack of a reliable structure of management of and accountability for quality.[4] Arrangements for the management of clinical audits and QI projects should include provision at least for oversight of ethical issues, the quality of the design and implementation of the work, information sharing, and resources allocated to the work.[60]

WHEN SHOULD A PROPOSAL FOR A CLINICAL AUDIT OR QI ACTIVITY HAVE AN ETHICS REVIEW?

Situations in proposals that require ethics review

Some key principles can be used to identify a clinical audit or QI activity that should have an ethics review at the proposal stage. These principles relate directly to the moral principles described earlier not being followed.[12,42] They include the following.

➤ Each patient's right to self-determination is respected.[3,11,13,61–64]
➤ There is a benefit to existing or future patients or others that outweighs the potential burdens or risks.[11,13,46,56,57,62–65]
➤ Each patient's privacy and confidentiality are preserved.[11,13,62–64]
➤ The activity is fairly distributed across patient groups.[11,13,63]

In addition, specific circumstances have been identified for which a proposal for a clinical audit or QI activity should have an ethics review (*see* Box A1.1). If it is determined that a clinical audit or QI activity is likely to involve more than minimal burdens or risks to patients or others, or the risks or burdens are uncertain, problematic or controversial, the activity should have an ethics review, and the written permission or informed consent of the participants is needed.[1,11,13,63,66] Risks could include that standards of good practice are not available in the current literature for the project,[67] or that non-compliance with a standard could constitute a 'remediable adverse event.'[67,68]

> **BOX A1.1** Specific circumstances relating to a clinical audit or QI project proposal that require ethics review
>
> **The activity infringes on any patient's rights by:**
> - limiting or restricting patients' rights to make choices about their healthcare.[11,13,61,64]
>
> **The activity places a burden** (the additional time and effort required of patients or others for data collection, taking additional tissue samples, or extra clinic or home visits)[46] **on patients or others by:**[1,11,13,15,16,33,42,46,56,61,63,65,69–74]
> - posing any risk to or burden on a patient beyond those of their routine care
> - involving 'vulnerable' people
> - collecting data directly from any patient or carer, except the use of a minimal number of factually based questions that are not of a sensitive nature, with no patient identification details recorded.[67] If data are being collected directly, the activity should not subject a patient or carer to more than a minimal burden or risk (e.g. by requesting sensitive information or requiring time to provide the information).
>
> If data are being obtained directly from patients, and the process may be intrusive for them (e.g. questionnaires or focus groups that involve patients' personal feelings, that take more than 5 to 10 minutes to complete, or that could involve revealing information about an illegal activity), the activity should be reviewed.[11,13,15,16,36,52,57,61,70,75–78]
>
> **The activity breaches confidentiality or privacy through:**[1,10,11,13,15,16,52,58,61–63,70,72,76,78–81]
> - collecting or disclosing any data that could be used to identify any patient or practitioner
> - using very small sample sizes that would allow identification of individual patients
> - having someone carrying out the activity who does not normally have access to patients' records (e.g. someone who is not part of the clinical care team, who does not have a professional obligation of confidentiality, who is not employed to support QI-related activities, or who is carrying out the work as part of a course of study).
>
> **The activity varies from or disrupts established clinical practice by:**
> - gathering any information about any patient in addition to the data that are normally or routinely collected as part of providing routine care for that patient[70,81]

- providing care that is a clinically significant departure or deviation from current normal (accepted, usual) clinical practice[1,11,16,17,33,46,65,70,81–84]
- causing any disruption to the clinician–patient relationship.[1,11,13,63]

The activity involves a potential conflict of obligation to patients by:
- considering a trade-off between cost and quality to individual patients or to all patients.[4,11,13,16,46,85]

The activity involves any untested intervention, including:
- using any form of selective or untested clinical or systems intervention or testing of a hypothesis[1,2,11,13,15–17,63,76,78,83]
- implementing a new practice that is not already established.[11,13,78]

The activity involves specific allocation or recruitment, including:[1,11,13,17,63,76,78,83]
- allocating treatment or any intervention differently among groups of patients or staff with or without randomisation (e.g. in implementing a change in practice)
- specific recruitment of patients or others to participate.

The activity involves an intention to publish:
- intending at the start of a project to publish or to use any personal health information in the publication.[17,78]

The activity provides no direct benefit to patients, including:
- undertaking an activity for which the patients involved will not directly benefit from the knowledge to be gained.[11,13,33,84]

Ethical issues related to the proposed design and methodology of a clinical audit or QI activity

It has been recognised that poorly conceived clinical audits or QI projects are a waste of everyone's time and are not likely to result in any improvement in care.[86] If a project will be futile, or does not use scientifically valid methods, or will not yield scientifically credible evidence, it should not be undertaken.[2,52,82] What needs to be audited and how a clinical audit is to be conducted may be decided by individual practitioners at a local level, with little consultation with colleagues or other stakeholders. The development of clinical audit activity in this way can raise questions about the validity and ethicality of some studies being undertaken.[78]

Clinical audits and QI projects should be well designed and use measures that are reliable and valid.[11] The activities should be carried out by well-supervised staff who have adequate training in audit or QI methods and access to consultative advice.[11,43] The methods that are used in a clinical audit or QI project need to be as rigorous as those that are used in research if the activity and findings are to be valid, reliable and credible, and clinical audits should be undertaken to the highest professional standard.[61,78,84]

The standards expected of audit in terms of design, data collection, and analysis should be at least as high as for research, if only because audit potentially leads to change more often than research does, and often much greater change. . . . Every study, whether audit or research, should have some prospect of succeeding in its stated aim. The lower the likelihood of an investigation achieving its goal, the less risk or burden that the patient should bear, and generally the more it should be subjected to external ethical scrutiny. Interestingly, one consequence of this rule would be that much current audit and NHS routine data collection would require ethical scrutiny, because they are rarely likely to achieve their stated goals and the costs and risks are often not small.[46]

Ethics-related subjects of a clinical audit or QI activity

If a clinical audit or QI activity is being undertaken on a clinical subject that itself has ethical implications, the design of the clinical audit or QI activity must be consistent with what is agreed to be ethical practice. Examples of subjects of such clinical audits could include end-of-life care, do-not-resuscitate policies, patient understanding of information given as part of the consent process, handling decision making for patients who lack mental capacity, or the care of women experiencing a miscarriage.[87-90]

WHEN SHOULD THE FINDINGS OF A CLINICAL AUDIT OR QI ACTIVITY HAVE AN ETHICS REVIEW?

Of the principles and circumstances considered at the proposal stage, several are applicable following the collection of data for a clinical audit or QI activity. The findings of data collection should be considered from an ethics perspective if they:

➤ pose any risk for patients whose care was reviewed in the clinical audit or for other similar patients (e.g. if care was not provided consistent with good practice)[1,7,11,13,42,46,56,63,65,69-71,73]

➤ identify any patients for whom a life-threatening or quality-of-life-threatening shortcoming in care occurred[91]

➤ disclose any data that could be used to identify any patient or practitioner[11,13,63]

➤ reveal any clinically significant departure from usual clinical care.[1,11,17,46,65,70,81-84]

If a clinical audit or QI activity has unexpectedly revealed that a patient has experienced an adverse event that could have been prevented, the organisation has a responsibility to disclose the event to the patient if the event has had or could have an effect on the patient's health or quality of life. In addition, the organisation has a responsibility to carry out further measurement to verify that the system or process involved in the event has been improved and that the event is unlikely to recur.[67,68]

WHEN SHOULD THE EFFECTIVENESS OF ACTION TAKEN ON A CLINICAL AUDIT OR QI ACTIVITY HAVE AN ETHICS REVIEW?

Having better knowledge of what constitutes good clinical practice is not a guarantee that it will be adopted or that it will actually improve practice in all settings.[92] One contribution of the clinical audit and QI process is that it examines how a local practice environment shapes or influences the implementation of knowledge locally and, through the examination of variation in that local practice, it helps to identify where and how practice might be improved.[92] Although clinical audits and QI projects aim to improve or maintain the quality of patient care, those in charge cannot be certain that the intervention will be effective. There is a risk that the proposed innovation will be ineffective or even harmful.[73] Therefore risk assessment of changes in patient care or service delivery needs to be undertaken in order to pre-empt what could go wrong during the implementation of a change, and identify what to do if it does.[43]

Clinical audits or QI activities that do not address necessary changes to systems fail to meet the ethical responsibilities of healthcare professionals and organisations to improve quality.[57] Minimal changes in clinical practice would rarely require specific ethical consideration. However, moderate changes, such as the introduction of an integrated care pathway, might need ethical review because the change may be ineffective or may place an undue burden on patients or others. Major change should always be subjected to ethical scrutiny.[46]

If the audit or QI project is carried out properly, it measures conformance with clinical practices that are known to be effective. Therefore if the audit or project indicates that such effective practice is not being provided to patients, it would be unethical to continue to provide substandard care and to withhold improvements in practice from patients.[57,78] If action is to be taken on the findings of audit that affect patient care, should there not be ethics checks and balances in place?[78] In addition, lessons learned from the clinical impact and outcomes of successful projects should be disseminated within an organisation in order to promote organisational learning and spread the achievement of improvements.[60]

HOW SHOULD A HEALTHCARE ORGANISATION HANDLE ETHICS AND CLINICAL AUDIT OR QI?

Designation of individual responsibility

An individual who takes the lead for a clinical audit or QI project should inform an appropriate manager that the project is being undertaken,[57] and seek approval of or authorisation for the project. In the absence of such reporting, the individual assuming responsibility for a project may not recognise when an ethics review is required.[42]

Organisational structure for oversight of clinical audit or QI

It may not always be clear who is ultimately accountable for the appropriate conduct of a given clinical audit or QI project, and who has the authority to ensure that applicable ethical standards are followed.[11,13] Therefore healthcare organisations need to ensure that an individual or group, accountable to senior management and the governance of the organisation, is designated as responsible for the ethical conduct of each clinical audit or QI activity.[4,11,13,59,62,69,93]

Given the ethical issues that can arise during the implementation of a patient safety programme, the ethical oversight structure for clinical audit and QI should also include collaboration with the organisation's patient safety activities.[94] Oversight will protect patients from ad hoc or poorly conceived projects. It will also ensure that the organisation has a vigorous and strategic agenda to improve the quality and safety of patient care.[4] Ideally, this agenda should be managed cooperatively by the clinical and management leadership of the organisation, reporting to the board through a committee that oversees clinical audit and QI throughout the organisation.[4]

Management responsibility for all activities that relate to QI and take place within a healthcare organisation is important,[3] because these activities should not be carried out by individuals acting in isolation.[11] Groups or teams carrying out the work should be acting on behalf of the organisation.[11] In order to be effective, the activities must have organisational support, in particular providing authority to act in response to the findings of data collection.[11] Professional and management leaders' roles should include creating the culture of quality and safety improvement throughout the organisation to ensure that when QI is done, it is done right.[57]

> **BOX A1.2** Possible healthcare organisational mechanisms for ethical review of clinical audit and QI activities
>
> **Department heads** assuming responsibility for screening proposals and referring those that require further assessment to a designated individual or group, and also assuming responsibility for the effectiveness of actions taken.[37,57,84]
>
> **The director responsible for clinical audit or QI**, such as a quality improvement director.[57]
>
> **The organisational structure that governs quality management or improvement.**[4,11]
>
> **A committee or group**, accountable to the governance of the healthcare organisation,[37] which could be any of the following:
> - quality improvement or quality improvement review committee[11,12,45,57,62]
> - clinical audit committee[96]
> - ethics (not research ethics) committee[11–13,42,46,70,72–74,97]
> - peer review committee[38,78,84]
> - joint quality improvement and research ethics committee[1,2,5,47,57,98]
> - management ethics committee[60]
> - patient safety committee[71]
> - clinical policy committee[71]
> - special group[12]
> - ad hoc group of ethicists.[84]

The individual or group that oversees ethics in clinical audit and QI activities on behalf of the organisation should be capable of providing an independent review of such activities.[95] That individual or group should define and implement systems for reviewing proposals for clinical audits and QI activities, oversee the findings and ensure that effective actions are implemented in response to the findings. Examples of organisational mechanisms are listed in Box A1.2.

The review mechanism needs to ensure that individuals with a knowledge of QI principles and processes and ethical standards for QI processes are involved.[11,13,57,74] The process which is carried out should be designed to determine that clinical audit or QI activity projects:[3,38]

➤ are well designed and justify the use of resources
➤ ensure patient safety and do not pose more than minimal risk to patients, and if they do, appropriate provision is made for informed consent
➤ ensure that appropriate provision is made for anonymous and confidential data collection
➤ do not overly burden patients or staff
➤ realise benefits to patient care
➤ ensure that those assuming responsibility for the project have the authority to implement actions in response to the findings.[3]

A research ethics committee can be asked to review clinical audit or QI activity proposals routinely or in cases where a possible ethical issue may exist.[1,11,37,66,85,99] It has also been suggested that the chair of a research ethics committee could screen proposals for clinical audits or QI projects, or could expedite projects that involve no more than minimal risk.[6,27] However, there may be several reasons why research ethics committees are not the best solution to overseeing clinical audit and QI.[4,5,8,62,76]

➤ There are significant differences between research and clinical audit or QI[8,42] with regard to the obligations of a healthcare organisation. Research is an optional activity in a healthcare organisation, whereas QI is ethically intrinsic to the provision of care.[2,8] Research falls into the category of an ethically permissible rather than a morally and legally mandatory activity. Society supports research to advance knowledge. However, no particular individual or organisation is obligated to perform research.[2]

   Clinical audit and QI activities, on the other hand, should be part of an overall quality and patient safety improvement strategy that is integrated into the operations of the healthcare organisation.[74] Clinical audits or QI activities should not be viewed as a set of projects, but as the heart of the operations of the healthcare organisation. These projects need to be strategically selected and completed as part of the commitment by the organisation to improve the quality and safety of patient care.[4]

➤ Individuals who take the lead for clinical audit or QI activities should take responsibility for leading changes in practice that are needed to achieve improvements, and they should also assume responsibility for ethical issues related to the work. Research ethics committees were designed to consider the impact of research on research participants; they were not created to assess projects that involve changing practices and systems in the delivery of patient care.[4,8]

➤ Research ethics committees are often overworked and have lengthy backlogs.[4,8,12,13,63] Given the urgency of improvement in the quality and safety of healthcare, it is counterproductive to contemplate delays in the important business of redesigning the quality and safety of patient care.[4]

➤ As currently constituted, research ethics committees may lack the knowledge and expertise necessary to evaluate clinical audits or QI activities.[8,12,42,63]

➤ Many people who are now involved and committed to carrying out QI projects could be discouraged from undertaking such projects in the first place if barriers such as additional paperwork, delays and frustrations associated with research ethics committee review were experienced before the work on improvement could begin.[7,12,13,40] The research ethics committee process could have a 'chilling effect on studies that could substantially improve error-prone systems and that expose subjects to risks no greater than those incurred during routine patient care', and could unintentionally lead to patients being harmed.[19]

➤ In the UK, giving ethical approval for clinical audit or QI projects may put a research ethics committee beyond its indemnity coverage.[84]

Organisational systems for oversight of clinical audit or QI

Healthcare organisations should proactively promote the ethical conduct of clinical audit or QI activities using a systematic approach.[11,72] Systems should provide for screening proposals for clinical audits or QI activities independent of the individual who is leading or carrying out the work, in order to identify any risks or burdens that the project will pose for patients or staff, and provide for an appropriate level of review of any project that involves more than minimal risk or burden beyond those inherent in normal clinical care.[11,76] Examples of organisational systems for ethical oversight of clinical audit and QI activities are listed in Box A1.3.

> **BOX A1.3** Healthcare organisational systems to support ethics oversight of clinical audit and QI activities
>
> **Registering clinical audits or QI activities electronically** with the clinical audit or quality improvement department, where there is one. A web-based interface could allow the individual initiating a project to quickly provide information about the audit or QI activity, which would include answers to a series of questions that would flag whether or not the proposal requires an ethics review and at what level of review. The electronic registration process would enable monitoring and follow-up of findings and the effectiveness of actions taken as part of the audit or QI activity. It would also broaden staff awareness of the standards for the ethical practice of clinical audit or QI.[57,60]
>
> **Promulgating organisational standards, policies and procedures, or guidance for all types of QI projects**, to ensure that patients and staff are protected and clinical

audits and QI projects are carried out consistent with ethics review systems in the organisation.[1,9,13,45,52,57] The standards or policies can provide for efficient screening of proposals for projects for their purpose, level of risk or burden to patients or staff, and the intended process for gathering and handling personal health information.[12,45,71,95]

Examples of standards, policies, procedures or guidance could include the following:

- how data will be collected and analysed to maintain confidentiality and anonymity of the participants in the clinical audit or QI project
- informing patients about clinical audit or QI activity
- making clear when patients have a choice about their participation and when a need for patient permission or consent is needed[64]
- the screening criteria to be used for ethical issues, and the levels and types of review of any such issues
- the action to be taken if an adverse event experienced by a patient is revealed through a clinical audit or QI project.[67,68]

Providing for standards relating to and ethics review of any project that is designed to contain or control costs, particularly if this is the sole purpose of the project, or if the project is initiated by managers of clinical services or represents a potential conflict of interest.[38,57,100]

For example, patients may need to be protected from initiatives that are primarily intended to reduce length of stay without clinical justification, or to substitute therapies when evidence is lacking that intended outcomes can be achieved safely with such reductions.[1,19,100] Management and policy changes in areas such as hours of operation, staffing patterns, acquisition of new equipment or referral for designated treatments or procedures are not subject to review, even if they have a clear potential to affect patient care.[71] Staff shortages may mean that compromises are made which in turn can influence standard setting (e.g. in a clinical audit).[85] It is essential to distinguish between genuine QI and financial, organisational or bureaucratic activities in healthcare that serve interests other than quality, safety and the best interests of patients.[5]

Referring to an expectation of staff participation in clinical audit or QI initiatives in job descriptions and performance appraisals, and following the organisation's ethics policies and systems relating to such projects.[11,57]

Educating staff about the organisation's policies and systems for identifying and handling ethical issues relating to clinical audits or QI activities.[11,13,45,93,101] This includes informing them at the time of hiring that QI is viewed as everyone's responsibility, and how proposed projects are reviewed and carried out in the organisation.[43,59]

Tracking clinical audits or QI projects[11] in order to follow their progress in implementation and their effectiveness.

Monitoring for non-adherence to approved ethical standards[93] or ensuring that failure to conduct a clinical audit or QI project in accordance with approved ethical standards is reported as an incident.[57]

Providing for appropriate review for individuals who wish to publish the results of a clinical audit or QI project.[57,93]

ARRANGING FOR ETHICS OVERSIGHT OF CLINICAL AUDIT AND QI IN PRIMARY CARE

Healthcare professionals working in primary care settings, including family or general practitioner centres, should actively participate in clinical audits and QI projects for the same reasons as any other healthcare practitioners. It is important to ensure that ethical issues relating to clinical audits or QI activities are identified and handled properly in these settings. Many primary care organisations are small, with a less formal accountability structure than that which exists in larger healthcare organisations. It is less clear what method of ethics oversight of clinical audits and QI activities might work best in these care settings.[16]

In the UK, financial incentives for general practitioners have had a significant impact on GP motivation to carry out QI on subjects recognised by the UK government as priorities for improving patient care (e.g. asthma, heart disease and diabetes). It may be important to consider whether a QI programme with substantial financial incentives for practitioners poses ethical questions.[16]

INFORMING AND INVOLVING PATIENTS IN CLINICAL AUDITS OR QI ACTIVITIES

As part of the system of healthcare, patients also have a responsibility to participate in quality improvement.[3,5,9,48] As an ethical matter, the responsibility of patients to cooperate in QI activities is justified by the benefits that each patient receives because of the cooperation of the others in the collective enterprise. It is in the best interest of patients to cooperate with QI activities and even to seek out the healthcare organisations that are most committed to QI.[48]

The patient's responsibility to cooperate is subject to standards of reasonableness, which require that patients have access to general information about QI activities and are kept safe from harms and from violations of their rights. Patients should be given explicit information about the process of clinical audit and quality and safety review and how the work is designed to improve both their health and the health and well-being of other patients.[3,76,82,102,103] The information that is provided for patients should make it clear that clinical audits and QI projects are a regular part of how the organisation fulfils its obligation to patients.[76]

Just as the absence of proper clinical audit is an affront to the rights and interests of patients, patients are entitled to know that the management of their care is subject to audit, and to have the reassurance that all reasonable steps are being taken to ensure that their healthcare is of the highest quality.[55] If a clinical audit or QI project requires the direct involvement of patients, they should be informed that their participation is optional and voluntary. If the project involves significant burdens or risks, the written informed consent of patients is needed.[13]

CONCLUSIONS

As clinical audit becomes more sophisticated as a QI tool, it is no longer appropriate to use a distinction between research and clinical audit or other QI as the basis for deciding whether an ethics review of a proposed study is needed. The distinctions between the activities can be ambiguous, and the activities cannot be distinguished in a reliable or valid way. The principle should be that if any clinical audit or QI activity has ethical implications, it requires review. In addition, if there are ethical issues embedded in a clinical audit or QI project, there are a number of reasons why a research ethics committee is not the best way to provide for a proper review and decision about the project.

There are a number of ethics-related issues relating to clinical audit or QI programmes, and the following all need to be assured:
➤ participation by all healthcare professions in clinical audit and QI activities
➤ coverage of all patient groups and types of conditions
➤ a systematic approach to setting priorities for clinical audits or QI activities
➤ participation in clinical audits or QI activities by all clinical services
➤ effective management and conduct of clinical audit and QI activities.

There are several stages of a clinical audit that may merit an ethics review. Proposals for clinical audits or QI activities should be screened to ensure that any ethical issues in the design of the activity are recognised and handled properly. This must ensure that the proposed design and measures are valid and the data collected are likely to be reliable; and that any ethics-related issues in a clinical audit or QI activity are addressed completely consistently with the healthcare organisation's formal policies on that subject. The findings of data collection and the effectiveness of actions taken should also be screened for ethical issues.

Healthcare organisations need to have mechanisms in place for ethics oversight of clinical audits and QI activities. Individuals undertaking projects should be required to submit proposals for screening. Healthcare organisations need to designate an individual or group to be accountable for ethical oversight of clinical audit and QI activities, and to ensure that there are robust oversight systems in place. Systems should include registration of projects, which includes screening of projects at several stages, defined and disseminated policies, procedures and guidance for staff, staff education about the organisation's processes, and monitoring of compliance with defined policies.

Patients have an ethical responsibility to agree to participate in clinical audits or QI activities if requested, and the risk or burden for patients is minimal. However, they need to be informed about the processes and how they are used in a healthcare organisation to make improvements that benefit the quality and safety of patient care.

Clinical audit and QI programmes are intended to provide the greatest benefit to patients with the least harm, equitable access to participation, and protection of individuals' rights. Ethical oversight of clinical audit and QI by healthcare organisations ensures that these activities protect patients and their rights, and contributes to improved quality and safety of patient care.

REFERENCES

1 Lo B, Groman M. Oversight of quality improvement. *Archives of Internal Medicine* 2003; **163**: 1481–6.

2 Bellin E, Dubler NN. The quality improvement–research divide and the need for external oversight. *American Journal of Public Health* 2001; **91**: 1512–17.

3 Dubler N, Blustein J, Bhalla R *et al.* Information participation: an alternative ethical process for including patients in quality-improvement projects. In: Jennings B, Baily MA, Bottrell M *et al.*, eds. *Health Care Quality Improvement: ethical and regulatory issues.* Garrison, NY: The Hastings Center; 2007. pp. 69–87.

4 O'Kane ME. Do patients need to be protected from quality improvement? In: Jennings B, Baily MA, Bottrell M *et al.*, eds. *Health Care Quality Improvement: ethical and regulatory issues.* Garrison, NY: The Hastings Center; 2007. pp. 89–99.

5 Jennings B, Baily MA, Bottrell M *et al.* Introduction. In: Jennings B, Baily MA, Bottrell M *et al.*, eds. *Health Care Quality Improvement: ethical and regulatory issues.* Garrison, NY: The Hastings Center; 2007. pp. 1–5.

6 Human Research Ethics Committee, Faculty of Health Sciences, University of Cape Town. *Definition of Research and Human Participants: standard operating procedures.* www.health. uct.ac.za/research/humanethics/sop (accessed 5 May 2010).

7 Davidoff F. Publication and the ethics of quality improvement. In: Jennings B, Baily MA, Bottrell M *et al.*, eds. *Health Care Quality Improvement: ethical and regulatory issues.* Garrison, NY: The Hastings Center; 2007. pp. 101–6.

8 Flaming D, Barrett-Smith L, Brown N *et al.* 'Ethics? But it's only quality improvement!' *Healthcare Quarterly* 2009; **12**: 50–5.

9 Lynn J, Baily MA, Bottrell M *et al.* The ethics of using quality improvement methods in health care. *Annals of Internal Medicine* 2007; **146**: 666–73.

10 Brown LH, Shah MN, Menegazzi JJ. Research and quality improvement: drawing lines in the grey zone (editorial). *Prehospital Emergency Care* 2007; **11**: 350–1.

11 Casarett D, Fox E, Tulsky JA. *Recommendations for the Ethical Conduct of Quality Improvement. A report of the National Ethics Committee of the Veterans Health Administration.* Washington, DC: National Center for Ethics in Health Care, Veterans Health Administration; 2002.

12 Hagen B, O'Beirne M, Desai S *et al.* Innovations in the ethical review of health-related quality improvement and research: the Alberta Research Ethics Community Consensus Initiative (ARECCI). *Healthcare Policy* 2007; **2**: 1–14.

13 Layer T. Ethical conduct recommendations for quality improvement projects. *Journal for Healthcare Quality* 2003; **25**: 44–6.

14 Lynn J. When does quality improvement count as research? Human subject protection and theories of knowledge. *Quality and Safety in Health Care* 2004; **13**: 67–70.

15 Reynolds J, Crichton N, Fisher W *et al.* Determining the need for ethical review: a three-stage Delphi study. *Journal of Medical Ethics* 2008; **34**: 889–94.

16 Tapp L, Edwards A, Elwyn G *et al.* Quality improvement in general practice: enabling

general practitioners to judge ethical dilemmas. *Journal of Medical Ethics* 2010; **36:** 184–8.

17 Wise LC. Ethical issues surrounding quality improvement activities. *Journal of Nursing Administration* 2007; **37:** 272–8.

18 Driscoll A, Currey J, Worrall-Carter L *et al.* Ethical dilemmas of a large national multi-centre study in Australia: time for some consistency. *Journal of Clinical Nursing* 2008; **17:** 2212–20.

19 Lindenauer PK, Benjamin EM, Naglieri-Prescod D *et al.* The role of the Institutional Review Board in quality improvement: a survey of quality officers, Institutional Review Board chairs, and journal editors. *American Journal of Medicine* 2002; **113:** 575–9.

20 Maxwell DJ, Kaye KI. Multicentre research: negotiating the ethics approval obstacle course (letter). *Medical Journal of Australia* 2004; **181:** 460.

21 Wilson A, Grimshaw G, Baker R *et al.* Differentiating between audit and research: postal survey of health authorities' views. *British Medical Journal* 1999; **319:** 1235.

22 Candib LM. How turning a QI project into 'research' almost sank a great program. *Hastings Center Report* 2007; **37:** 26–30.

23 Choo V. Thin line between research and audit (commentary). *Lancet* 1998; **352:** 337–8.

24 Doezema D, Hauswald M. Quality improvement or research: a distinction without a difference? *IRB* 2002; **24:** 9–12.

25 Goodyear-Smith F, Arroll B. Audit or research? *New Zealand Medical Journal* 2001; **114:** 499–502.

26 Miller FG, Emanuel EJ. Quality-improvement research and informed consent. *New England Journal of Medicine* 2008; **358:** 765–7.

27 Neff MJ. Institutional Review Board consideration of chart reviews, case reports, and observational studies. *Respiratory Care* 2008; **53:** 1350–3.

28 Palevsky PM, Washington MS, Stevenson JA *et al.* Improving compliance with the dialysis prescription as a strategy to increase the delivered dose of hemodialysis: an ESRD Network 4 quality improvement project. *Advances in Renal Replacement Therapy* 2000; **7 (Suppl. 1):** S21–30.

29 Pronovost P, Needham D, Berenholtz S *et al.* An intervention to decrease catheter-related bloodstream infections in the ICU. *New England Journal of Medicine* 2006; **355:** 2725–32.

30 Savel RH, Goldstein EB, Gropper MA. Critical care checklists, the Keystone Project, and the Office for Human Research Protections: a case for streamlining the approval process in quality-improvement research. *Critical Care Medicine* 2009; **37:** 725–8.

31 Snijders RJ, Noble P, Sebire N *et al.* UK multicentre project on assessment of risk of trisomy 21 by maternal age and fetal nuchal-translucency thickness at 10–14 weeks of gestation. Fetal Medicine Foundation First Trimester Screening Group. *Lancet* 1998; **352:** 343–6.

32 National Research Ethics Service. *Defining Research.* London: National Patient Safety Agency; 2009.

33 Casarett D, Karlawish JHT, Sugarman J. Determining when quality improvement initiatives should be considered research. *Journal of the American Medical Association* 2000; **283:** 2275–80.

34 Godlee F. Improving on improvement (editorial). *British Medical Journal* 2006; **332:**

www.bmj.com/cgi/content/full/332/7549/0-f?maxtoshow=&hits=10&RESULTFORMAT= &fulltext='Improving+on+improvement'&searchid=1&FIRSTINDEX=0&sortspec=date&r esourcetype=HWCIT (accessed 4 May 2010).

35 Harrington L. Quality improvement, research, and the institutional review board. *Journal for Healthcare Quality* 2007; **29**: 4–9.

36 Hughes R. Is audit research? The relationships between clinical audit and social research. *International Journal of Health Care Quality Assurance* 2005; **18**: 289–99.

37 Johnson N, Vermeulen L, Smith KM. A survey of academic medical centers to distinguish between quality improvement and research activities. *Quality Management in Health Care* 2006; **15**: 215–20.

38 Markman M. The role of independent review to ensure ethical quality-improvement activities in oncology: a commentary on the national debate regarding the distinction between quality-improvement initiatives and clinical research. *Cancer* 2007; **110**: 2597–600.

39 McNett M, Lawry K. Research and quality improvement activities: when is institutional review board review needed? *Journal of Neuroscience Nursing* 2009. www.thefreelibrary.com/ Research+and+quality+improvement+activities:+when+is+institutional...-a0214101277 (accessed 5 May 2010).

40 Wise LC. Quality improvement as research: unintended consequences and the slippery slope (letter). *Journal of Nursing Administration* 2006; **36**: 383.

41 Abbasi K, Heath I. Ethics review of research and audit (editorial). *British Medical Journal* 2005; **330**: 431–2.

42 Cave E, Nichols C. Clinical audit and reform of the UK research ethics review system. *Theoretical Medicine and Bioethics* 2007; **28**: 181–203.

43 Gerrish K, Mawson S. Research, audit, practice development and service evaluation: implications for research and clinical governance. *Practice Development in Health Care* 2005; **4**: 33–9.

44 Grifiths P. But who decides when review is needed? (eletter). *British Medical Journal* 2005; 26 February. www.bmj.com/cgi/eletters/330/7489/468#97959 (accessed 4 May 2010).

45 National Health and Medical Research Council, Australian Research Council, Australian Vice-Chancellors' Committee. *National Statement on Ethical Conduct in Human Research.* 2007. www.nhmrc.gov.au/_files_nhmrc/file/publications/synopses/e72-jul09.pdf (accessed 4 May 2010).

46 Wade DT. Ethics, audit, and research: all shades of grey. *British Medical Journal* 2005; **330**: 468–71 (quoted with permission).

47 Weiserbs KF, Lyutic L, Weinberg J. Should quality improvement projects require IRB approval? (letter). *Academic Medicine* 2009; **84**: 153.

48 Baily MA, Bottrell M, Lynn J *et al. The Ethics of Using QI Methods to Improve Health Care Quality and Safety.* Garrison, NY: The Hastings Center; 2006.

49 Lemaire F. Informed consent and studies of a quality improvement program (letter). *Journal of the American Medical Association* 2008; **300**: 1762.

50 Siegel MD, Alfano S. The ethics of quality improvement research. *Critical Care Medicine* 2009; **37**: 791–2.

51 Beauchamp TL, Childress JF. *Principles of Biomedical Ethics.* 4th edn. Oxford: Oxford University Press; 1994.

52 Kinn S. The relationship between clinical audit and ethics. *Journal of Medical Ethics* 1997; **23**: 250–3.

53 Wynia MK, Kurlander JE. Physician ethics and participation in quality improvement: renewing a professional obligation. In: Jennings B, Baily MA, Bottrell M *et al.*, eds. *Health Care Quality Improvement: ethical and regulatory issues*. Garrison, NY: The Hastings Center; 2007. pp. 7–27.

54 General Medical Council. *Good Medical Practice: guidance for doctors*. London: General Medical Council; 2006; updated March 2009. pp. 15, 24. www.gmc-uk.org/static/documents/content/GMC_GMP_0911.pdf (accessed 5 May 2010).

55 Hagger L, Woods S, Barrow P. Autonomy and audit – striking the balance. *Medical Law International* 2004; **6**: 105–16.

56 Cretin S, Keeler EB, Lynn J *et al.* (letter). Should patients in quality-improvement activities have the same protections as participants in research studies? *Journal of the American Medical Association* 2000; **284**: 1786.

57 Bottrell MM. Accountability for the conduct of quality-improvement projects. In: Jennings B, Baily MA, Bottrell M *et al.*, eds. *Health Care Quality Improvement: ethical and regulatory issues*. Garrison, NY: The Hastings Center; 2007. pp. 129–44.

58 Tapp L, Elwyn G, Edwards A *et al.* Quality improvement in primary care: ethical issues explored. *International Journal of Health Care Quality Assurance* 2009; **22**: 8–29.

59 Holm MJ, Selvan M, Smith ML *et al.* Quality improvement or research: defining and supervising QI at the University of Texas MD Anderson Cancer Center. In: Jennings B, Baily MA, Bottrell M *et al.*, eds. *Health Care Quality Improvement: ethical and regulatory issues*. Garrison, NY: The Hastings Center; 2007. pp. 145–68.

60 Paxton R, Whitty P, Zaatar A *et al.* Research, audit and quality improvement. *International Journal of Health Care Quality Assurance* 2006; **19**: 105–11.

61 Carr EC. Talking on the telephone with people who have experienced pain in hospital: clinical audit or research? *Journal of Advanced Nursing* 1999; **29**: 194–200.

62 Diamond LH, Kliger AS, Goldman RS *et al.* Commentary: Quality improvement projects: how do we protect patients' rights? *American Journal of Medical Quality* 2004; **19**: 25–7.

63 Fox E, Tulsky JA. Recommendations for the ethical conduct of quality improvement. *Journal of Clinical Ethics* 2005; **16**: 61–71.

64 Centre for Quality Improvement, Royal College of Psychiatrists. *Ethical Audit at the Centre for Quality Improvement: ensuring that high ethical standards are applied to clinical audit.* www.rcpsych.ac.uk/pdf/Ethical Audit at the CQI.pdf (accessed 4 May 2010).

65 British Medical Journal. *Ethics Approval of Research.* http://resources.bmj.com/bmj/authors/editorial-policies/guidelines (accessed 4 May 2010).

66 Tomlinson SR. Ethics and evidence-based medicine (letter). *Medical Journal of Australia* 2002; **176**: 137.

67 East London NHS Foundation Trust. *Ethics and Confidentiality Guidance for Clinical Audit.* www.eastlondon.nhs.uk/misc/scripts/dl_dms.asp?id=82DED971-4D84-479E-BEB1-8C326169D138 (accessed 5 May 2010).

68 Somers A, Stephenson T. Managing untoward findings from clinical audit – keeping the can of worms under control. *Bulletin of the Royal College of Pathologists* 2004; **126**: 11–14.

69 Morris PE, Dracup K. Quality improvement or research? The ethics of hospital project oversight (editorial). *American Journal of Critical Care* 2007; **16**: 424–6.

70 National Ethics Advisory Committee. *Ethical Guidelines for Observational Studies: observational research, audits and related activities.* Wellington: Ministry of Health; 2006. www.neac. health.govt.nz/moh.nsf/indexcm/neac-resources-publications-ethicalguidelines (accessed 4 May 2010).

71 Nerenz DR, Stoltz PK, Jordan J. Quality improvement and the need for IRB review. *Quality Management in Health Care* 2003; **12**: 159–70.

72 Nelson WA, Gardent PB. Ethics and quality improvement. *Healthcare Executive* 2008; **23**: 40–1.

73 Perneger TV. Why we need ethical oversight of quality improvement projects (editorial). *International Journal for Quality in Health Care* 2004; **16**: 43–4.

74 World Medical Assembly. *WMA Declaration on Guidelines for Continuous Quality Improvement in Health Care.* Adopted by the 49th World Medical Assembly, November 1997, and amended in October 2009. www.wma.net/en/30publications/10policies/g10/index.html (accessed 5 May 2010).

75 Barton A. Monitoring body is needed for audit (letter). *British Medical Journal* 1997; **315**: 1465.

76 Doyal L. Preserving moral quality in research, audit, and quality improvement (commentary). *Quality and Safety in Health Care* 2004; **13**: 11–12.

77 Hill Y, MacGregor J. Is clinical audit under threat? *Nursing Management* 1999/2000; **6**: 6.

78 Rix G, Cutting K. Clinical audit, the case for ethical scrutiny? *International Journal of Health Care Quality Assurance* 1996; **9**: 18–20.

79 Diamond LH. *QIPs vs Research: issues and implications.* Presentation to American College of Medical Informatics Forum and Board of Trustees, 16 November 2004.

80 Royal College of Obstetricians and Gynaecologists. *Confidentiality and Disclosure of Health Information: RCOG Ethics Committee comments on a BMA document.* October 2000. www. rcog.org.uk/womens-health/clinical-guidance/confidentiality-and-disclosure-health-information-rcog-ethics-commit (accessed 10 May 2010).

81 Seddon M, Buchanan J. Quality improvement in New Zealand healthcare. Part 3: achieving effective care through clinical audit. *New Zealand Medical Journal* 2006; **119**: 2108.

82 Boult M, Maddern GJ. Clinical audits: why and for whom. *Australian and New Zealand Journal of Surgery* 2007; **77**: 572–8.

83 Kofke WA, Rie MA. Research ethics and law of healthcare system quality improvement: the conflict of cost containment and quality. *Critical Care Medicine* 2003; **31 (Suppl.)**: 143–52.

84 North West London Hospitals NHS Trust, Harrow Research Ethics Committee, Brent Medical Ethics Committee. *Policy for Review of Audit and Research Projects.* Undated. www. nwlh.nhs.uk/research/assets/docs/ResearchAuditPolicy2.doc (accessed 4 May 2010).

85 Low-Beer TS. Ethics committee review of medical audit: a personal view from the United Kingdom. *Sexually Transmitted Infections* 2001; **77**: 2.

86 Smith R. BMJ's preliminary response to the need for ethics committee approval (letter). *British Medical Journal* 2000; **320**: 713.

87 Cheung D, Sandramouli S. The consent and counselling of patients for cataract surgery: a prospective audit. *Eye* 2005; **19**: 963–71.

88 DeMunter C, Lincoln T. Agreed limitations to treatment plan for children: ethics and audit of the use of a new form for paediatric departments (abstract). *Archives of Disease in Childhood* 2008; **93**: 91–3.

89 Lowe J, Kerridge I. Implementation of guidelines for no-CPR orders by a general medical unit in a teaching hospital. *Australian and New Zealand Journal of Medicine* 1997; **27**: 379–83.

90 Sehdev SS, Wilson A. Hospital care given in the event of a miscarriage: views of women and their partners, and an audit of hospital guidelines. *Journal of Clinical Excellence* 2000; **2**: 161–7.

91 Meenan G, Taylor D. Unexpected outcomes and ethical considerations arising out of an audit of management of paediatric urinary tract infection. *Journal of Clinical Governance* 2001; **9**: 5–9.

92 Redman RW. Knowledge development, quality improvement, and research ethics. *Research and Theory for Nursing Practice* 2007; **21**: 217–19.

93 James BC. Quality-improvement policy at Intermountain Healthcare. In: Jennings B, Baily MA, Bottrell M *et al.*, eds. *Health Care Quality Improvement: ethical and regulatory issues.* Garrison, NY: The Hastings Center; 2007. pp. 169–76.

94 Nelson WA, Neily J, Mills P *et al.* Collaboration of ethics and patient safety programs: opportunities to promote quality care. *HEC Forum* 2008; **20**: 15–27.

95 Grady C. Quality improvement and ethical oversight (editorial). *Annals of Internal Medicine* 2007; **146**: 680–1.

96 Rawlins R. Research discovers the right thing to do; audit ensures that it is done right (letter). *British Medical Journal* 1997; **315**: 1464.

97 Lang NM. Health care quality improvement: a nursing perspective. In: Jennings B, Baily MA, Bottrell M *et al.*, eds. *Health Care Quality Improvement: ethical and regulatory issues.* Garrison, NY: The Hastings Center; 2007. pp. 29–53.

98 Wise L. Quality improvement or research? A report from the trenches (letter). *American Journal of Critical Care* 2008; **17**: 98–9.

99 Koschnitzke L, McCracken SC, Pranulis MF. Ethical considerations for quality assurance versus scientific research. *Western Journal of Nursing Research* 1992; **14**: 392–6.

100 Rie MA, Kofke WA. Nontherapeutic quality improvement: the conflict of organizational ethics and societal rule of law. *Critical Care Medicine* 2007; **35 (Suppl.)**: 66–84.

101 Stirrat GM, Johnston C, Gillon R *et al.* Medical ethics and law for doctors of tomorrow: the 1998 Consensus Statement updated. *Journal of Medical Ethics* 2010; **36**: 55–60.

102 Department of Health. *Confidentiality: NHS code of practice.* London: Department of Health; 2003.

103 Information Commissioner. *Use and Disclosure of Health Data: guidance on the application of the Data Protection Act 1998.* London: Information Commissioner; 2002.

Clinical audit, impact and quality improvement: a discursive review

Christopher Loughlan

The purpose of this appendix
- To discuss the evidence base that clinical audit has with regard to healthcare outcomes and system improvements, and the issues involved in collecting such data.

INTRODUCTION

This chapter considers the **impact** of clinical audit through analysis of three sources of evidence, namely a selected qualitative literature review, a critical analysis of national audit reports, and findings from an online survey of NHS trusts (in England).

In the context of this chapter, the term 'impact' covers a range of effects of clinical audit practice. As the primary purpose of audit is to improve compliance with recommended standards and criteria in the delivery of healthcare, this is defined here as the **outcome** of clinical audit, as distinguished from healthcare outcomes as traditionally defined (e.g. improvements in mortality or morbidity). Impact is defined here as the subsequent results arising from changes to clinical practice and systems identified by clinical audit. These results can include financial savings, efficiencies **and** possible health gains for patients.

The background section opens by looking at the continuing debate about the definition and role of clinical audit in the NHS (in England), and the context of the quality improvement landscape in the health sector. This section also discusses the terms 'outcome' and 'impact' that were used in the review, and the challenges that researchers face in undertaking systematic review of clinical audit. Five areas of impact of clinical audit in this context of the review are noted. The appendix concludes by presenting a number of observations on the future development of clinical audit.

BACKGROUND
A changing landscape of definition and understanding

There is considerable diversity of opinion as to what constitutes clinical audit at the NHS frontline of service provision, with considerable overlap between clinical audit, service evaluation and the requirements of organisational development. Given this basic clarity issue, the estimation of the subsequent results of audit – that is, its outcomes and its impact – is even more challenging.

Quality improvement

The aim of such benchmarking and reflection is to spur quality improvement, not simply to collect data about outcomes. The introductory chapter in this book highlighted the fact that the role of clinical audit as a quality improvement mechanism, although inherent in textbook definitions of the process, was not always clear, with some views that clinical audit was primarily a measurement process, separate from the science of quality improvement. However, a recent report by the National Quality Board (NQB)[1] of the Department of Health in England recommended that clinical teams should measure and benchmark the quality of their services across the three dimensions of quality that were set out in the 2008 Departmental *Next Stage Review*,[2] namely safety, patient experience and effectiveness. The NQB recommended that they should do this by a number of means, highlighting the effective use of **national and local clinical audit programmes**[3] (our emphasis).

Clinical audit that succeeds in supporting quality improvement and change at a local level is more likely to happen if clinicians can trust local data that compare their practice with published standards:

> Clinicians are more likely to engage with improvement in their own specific areas of expertise and can be convinced of the need for change by measuring their own practice against professional standards through audits. Having strong leadership from a lead clinician who undertakes the audit and feeds back results and improvement plans across the service also successfully engages other professionals. All of these factors can help clinicians to trust the evidence for change and know that audits are giving meaningful results.[4]

There is now a wide range of different Quality Improvement Strategies (QIS) for optimising healthcare, some of which are driven by clinicians/patients, while others are driven by managers/policy makers. It remains unclear which of these are most effective, despite concerns having been expressed about the potential for QIS-related patient harm and wastage of resources.[5,6] A recent review of alternative strategies suggested that the most effective approaches include clinician-directed audit and feedback cycles, clinical decision support systems, specialty outreach programmes, chronic disease management programmes, continuing professional education based on interactive small-group case discussions, and patient-mediated clinician reminders.[7] The relationship between clinical audit and other QIS is a complex one, and a range of different understandings were identified by this study.

One area of agreement was that the highest performing healthcare organisations have aligned improvement objectives and operate with a definition of quality that covers both clinical and managerial domains.[8] If clinically led improvement (audit, clinical governance, etc.) is 'treated as a separate entity from managerially led performance improvement, we do so at our peril.'[9] The overviews conducted for this study suggest that the most important factor in relation to quality improvement is the leadership ability to address many simultaneous challenges and to adapt solutions and strategies to the organisation concerned.

OUTCOME AND IMPACT OF CLINICAL AUDIT

There is still a degree of confusion about the way in which the terms 'outcome' and 'impact' are used in the healthcare sector. The following definitions are often used.

Outcomes

Outcomes in healthcare generally are often defined as changes in health status (mortality and morbidity) which result from the provision of health (or other) services.[10,11] In relation to clinical audit, the main objective is to compare current clinical practice with evidence-based nationally recognised guidelines on treatment and/or care, and to make the changes necessary to bring them in line. Following an audit there then normally follows a period of review at individual clinician and clinical team level. The result of this is usually that clinicians agree on what changes to clinical practice need to be implemented in the light of the audit results. These changes are the first level of 'outcome' of a clinical audit, rather than any resulting health gain or other effects, which are normally described as 'health outcomes.' 'Outcomes' in this report, in the context of clinical audit, are therefore taken to be **the extent of (required) documented change against standards, demonstrated quantitatively through the re-audit and report process**.

Impact

Health impact can be defined in healthcare generally as 'the overall effects, direct or indirect, of a policy, strategy, programme or project on the health of a population.'[12]

The following example is cited to highlight the difference between the terms 'outcome' and 'impact' in clinical practice as used in conducting the review. A study of prescription quality through three cycles of clinical audit revealed that significant **outcome** improvements were achieved both in the recording of patient information and in the completeness of regular prescription writing.[13] However, there were no data on the **impact** of such an improvement on health, despite the fact that the actual recording of data on drug allergies **decreased** over the five-year audit cycle review. The authors noted that although the drug allergy trend was a cause for concern, it was very difficult to assess risk. Thus in this particular study we have data on significant improvement in outcomes in relation to prescription quality, but no data on either negative or positive impact as a result of the clinical audit.

In this study we have sought to assess the effect of clinical audit by reviewing how clinical audit has led to changes in practice so as to be more in line with recommended practice or guidelines (the primary outcome), and **as a result there has been a significant impact of some sort**, but one that is broader than simply a health outcome for patients. This area of gain includes benefits in efficiency, productivity and effectiveness.

A subgroup of researchers on the original research panel for this review undertook a preliminary synopsis of the literature on the impact of clinical audit, and grouped this range of impact measures into the following five domains:

➤ length of stay
➤ drug prescribing
➤ unnecessary tests/procedures
➤ enhanced application of a health technology
➤ patient harm.

The general logic of these five impact areas was also confirmed by telephone interviews with clinical audit staff, clinicians involved in clinical audit and educational providers of clinical audit, and is designed to give an indication of where the main gains from audit practice have often been shown to occur. By grouping the findings in this way it is not intended to indicate that these are in some way definitive or especially intended effects, but simply that this is one common set of headings within which to group studies that were suggested by the literature and the surveys conducted. Nonetheless, there were some issues that fall outside these specific areas, and in the case of patient health outcomes, that extend across several areas.

Thus in relation to clinical audit in this study, a good or positive **outcome** can be defined as greater and sustained adherence or compliance with an accepted national standard of treatment or care, whereas **impact** can be defined as the effect of this change in clinical practice, in terms of both better system effects as mentioned above, and in some cases in terms of an effect on health status. However, this distinction can never always be completely clear, as some of the cited evidence will show.

CHALLENGES IN IDENTIFYING THE IMPACT OF CLINICAL AUDIT

There are two important challenges in identifying the impact of clinical audit:
➤ finding reliable data
➤ apportioning causality to clinical audit as a primary discrete intervention in the context of development in a complex setting.

Some of the findings from the review that relate to these two challenges are now discussed.

Data and evidence

A review of paediatric audits concluded that less than 25% of them were re-audited.[14] The difficulty in finding reliable data on the basis of which to make a judgement about the relative merits of clinical audit with regard to impact was confirmed by respondents to the online NHS survey that was conducted as part of the original review. Such comments in part reflect the complexity of measurement of the impact of clinical audit, and the difficulties in measuring change when the context of such change is a multi-factorial clinical service.[15-17] The published literature cautions against the idea that clinical audit can be viewed as a **discrete intervention** in a complex picture of service provision undertaken by a range of individual clinicians within clinical teams.

Causality

The degree to which one can safely apportion causality to clinical audit as being the primary intervention, in the context of multifaceted drivers of change in clinical practice, was picked up by the leads for national clinical audits and by respondents to the online NHS survey. A study of general practice in the UK[18] concluded that clinical audit was frequently used as only one of a complex set of interventions, making precise evaluation difficult.

Other factors that influence impact

The quantitative systematic review by Jamtvedt *et al.*,[19] which largely focused on the degree to which audit led to changes in practice, confirmed that the provision of information alone resulted in little if any change in practice, and highlighted the fact that broader aspects, such as the nature of the information provided (e.g. guidelines, primary research), individual practitioner motivation and the characteristics of the clinical context, were also important. Indeed, a review of diffusion of innovations in service organisations described twelve characteristics of the innovation, seven dimensions of the individual and six domains that were key factors in assimilation by an organisation.[20]

The review by Jamtvedt *et al.* also highlighted the complexity of researching the efficacy of clinical audit, given the other variables that affect change. Within this context, a fundamental requirement in any research into the impact of specific interventions (and analyses of these) is clarity about the definition, nature and description of the intervention involved. There are a number of potential sources of heterogeneity which may help to explain the degree of variation in relation to research and analysis of clinical audit interventions. One aspect, namely **intensity of audit and feedback**, has the following characteristics, and thus variables: the recipient, format and source, and the frequency, duration and content of the feedback. Similarly, the **complexity of targeted behaviour** can be subjectively described as high, moderate or low. Thus there appear to be a significant number of combinations to describe when researching and/or analysing clinical audit as an intervention.

Main findings of the review

This section of the chapter describes the main findings of a review of the evidence for the impact of clinical audit, conducted by the Cambridge Institute for Research, Education and Management (CIREM) on behalf of HQIP in 2010.[21] These findings are presented according to which of the following main methods was used to identify them:

➤ systematic review of published literature
➤ critical appraisal of reports from national clinical audits
➤ online survey of NHS trusts.

For each method, indicative examples are listed for the previously defined areas of impact, where these are available.

FINDINGS FROM A REVIEW OF PUBLISHED LITERATURE

Published studies exist both as single studies and within systematic reviews. These published sources are from the worldwide literature.

The findings from a number of systematic reviews on the effectiveness of clinical audit[18,19] concluded that audit and feedback can be effective in improving professional practice. However, the available evidence says relatively little about the detail of how audit and feedback can be used most efficiently.[22]

An earlier study[23] on perceptions of the impact of clinical indicator data on clinical practice and continuous improvement of quality found that they were rarely used to stimulate quality improvement or shared good practice. Documented action was restricted to checking and auditing the quality of the data rather than direct action to improve delivery of service. Other studies[24,25] have evaluated clinical audit methodologies. When clinical audit was effective, the conclusions were that the effects on clinical practice were small to moderate, and that the relative effectiveness of audit with feedback was greater when baseline adherence to recommended practice was low and when feedback was delivered more intensely.[19]

In practice, many of the primary results from clinical audit activity are changes to the way in which services are organised within the parameters of recommended clinical guidelines, rather than clinical practice changes per se. Nonetheless, these changes can be quite considerable, and make substantial changes to the quality of the way in which clinical services are provided. Such examples bear testimony to the **scope** of clinical audit influence, and include the following:

➤ increasing prescription quality in an inpatient mental health setting[13]
➤ better patient management[26]
➤ workforce development[27]
➤ the economic and clinical implications of implementing national guidance[28,29]
➤ assessment of the effect of guidelines[30]
➤ critical analysis of best care in cases of spinal injury[31]
➤ recommendation for a new care pathway in relation to secondary prevention of fragility fractures[32]
➤ better use of evidence-based smoking cessation management practices[26]
➤ hospital resources (consultant numbers) for patients with acute chronic obstructive pulmonary disease.[33]

Still more relate to productivity (efficiency gains) in terms of getting patients through treatment faster, and a corresponding reduction in waiting-list times.[34,35] This obviously has financial benefits as well.

However, there are many published reports that purport to be of clinical audit but do not satisfy an agreed definition, i.e. measure against a published national or locally agreed standard,[36] or relate to meeting a national target for service provision.[37]

In the next section, examples from the review of published literature on **impact** are offered for each of the five domains of impact of clinical audit given above, to illustrate how clinical audit can have impacts in the area concerned.

Reduction in length of patient stay

Specialist nurses

In a 1997 audit study of the impact of the introduction of a paediatric trained diabetes specialist nurse (PDSN), Cowan and colleagues found that after the nurse had been appointed, the median length of hospital stay for newly diagnosed patients decreased from 5 days to 1 day, with 10 of a total of 24 children not admitted. None of the latter were admitted during the next year. There was no evidence of the PDSN affecting the frequency of readmission or length of stay of children with established insulin dependence within type 1 diabetes. Non-attendance at the outpatient clinic was reduced from a median of 19% to 10%. Patients could be expected to regard the lower length of stay as preferable.

Avoiding unnecessary procedures

One of the greatest threats to waiting-list times is the habitual occupancy of beds by emergency admissions. Nasal bleeding remains one of the most common ENT and OMFS (oral and maxillofacial surgery) emergencies resulting in hospital admission,[38] quoted as approximately 30 per 100 000 adults.[39] Its cause tends only to be identified in 15% of patients, with the remainder being classified as idiopathic. In the majority of cases, apart from nasal packing no other intervention is required. Many cases could therefore ideally be managed at home without further medical interference. Audit studies have shown that continuing admission can be avoided.[38–40] In fact, before the introduction of the NHS, nasal haemorrhage (epistaxis) was largely managed at home, and only the most severe cases were referred for admission.[40] This is obviously a health gain for patients as well.

Self-care as an alternative to inpatient care

A study of the role of surgical audit in improving patient management[41] found that patients with epistaxis could be effectively treated at home by self-care and management. In one NHS organisation the audit identified a saving of over 200 bed days per annum, a specialty saving of around £50 000, the enabling of resource reallocation and more effective management of bed utilisation for other emergency or elective work.

Improvement in drug prescribing

Alternative drugs

A study of antipsychotic prescribing for schizophrenia outpatients over a period of 4.5 years in three mental health services in New Zealand[42] provided evidence of a reduction in drug prescribing. Specific feedback and interventions targeting clozapine use were introduced in two services. Three prescribing variables (antipsychotic mono-therapy, second-generation antipsychotics and clozapine use) were consistent with practice recommendations at the final audit (85.7%, 82.7% and 34.5%, respectively), and had changed in the desired direction for all three services over the 4.5-year period. One service had baseline prescribing variables closest to recommendations, was actively involved in audit, and improved further. The second service, which was also actively involved in audit, had baseline prescribing variables less close to recom-mendations, but improved the most. The service that was not involved in continuing audit and feedback made smaller changes, and second-generation antipsychotic and clozapine use at the endpoint were significantly lower, despite being comparable at baseline to the service which improved the most. This change in prescribing, as well as being a change in clinical practice (an outcome in clinical audit terms), would of course also have positive benefits for the patients involved, although in the study this is not explicitly considered.

Reduction in dosage

Gentamicin is one of the most frequently used antibiotics in neonatal units, and there are many regimes in use based on weight and/or gestational age. Direct costs include prescription and therapeutic drug monitoring (TDM). A retrospective audit (loop 1) identified 48% trough and 51% peak levels outside the desirable range (trough, 2 mg/l; peak, 5–10 mg/l). A prospective re-audit (loop 2) showed improved results (15% and 29%, respectively), which improved further (11% and 26%, respectively) in loop 3. For loops 1, 2 and 3 the mean (±SD) trough levels were 2.16 (±1.04), 1.30 (±0.63) and 1.23 (±0.62), respectively, and peak levels were 5.05 (±1.87), 6.64 (±2.48), and 6.2 (±1.81), respectively. Cost savings occurred, as the number of doses required was reduced by one-third to 50%, depending upon the infant characteristics. Furthermore, in 27% of cases gentamicin was discontin-ued before TDM was necessary. As a result of completing the audit cycle, improved quality of therapeutic care was achieved, with more accurate drug-monitoring targets reached and a reduction in drug costs.[43]

Reduction in unwarranted/unnecessary procedures or tests

Avoiding unnecessary tests

The utilisation of laboratory services has increased during the past few decades in many healthcare jurisdictions around the world.[44–46] Studies have found up to 17-fold variation in the number of tests that physicians order.[47,48] A clinical audit study of a government tertiary hospital immunology laboratory[49] found that unnecessary repeat requesting of tests can represent a large proportion of a laboratory's workload. The numbers of tests for immunoglobulin measurement, common auto-antibodies and tumour markers that were repeated over a 12-month period were analysed. Repeat requests within 12 weeks of a previous request represented almost 17% of the total workload.

It is complicated to assess the economic impact of the elimination of tests that are identified as redundant. Assuming that a system could prevent all such redundant tests from being performed, and assuming no adverse impact on patient care, total costs that could be saved were estimated to be in the region of about US$132250 per annum (around £85000). A recent study reviewed the use of the galactose-1-phosphate uridyltransferase (GALT) assay for newborn screening for improved identification of classic galactosaemia.[50]

As well as these system benefits, the value of these tests to patients is very limited, and they could be expected to appreciate not having to undergo them, so their experience of care would be improved. In practice, these considerations are rarely assessed by clinical audits, yet they offer enormous potential to assess patient perceptions of an improved care experience.

More effective application of a technology

Single-use instruments

In 2001, the Department of Health in England allocated £200 million to modernise NHS decontamination procedures. The introduction of single-use instruments for tonsil surgery cost £25 million per annum.[51] A multi-centre surgical audit cycle study[52] found that although it was difficult to calculate the true cost of re-usable instruments (as costs vary from one hospital to another), the cost of single-use surgical instruments (SUSI) was roughly on a par with that of re-usable instruments, and disposable instruments were as good as, or better than, existing ones.

ENT surgery was the first specialty to implement disposable equipment for routine operations involving lymphoid tissue, but expansion to other surgical specialties is inevitable. The Department of Health is considering the introduction of single-use surgical equipment to other surgical disciplines (e.g. neurosurgery) which deal with tissue that might harbour the prion. If disposable instruments are of a sufficiently high standard, they can be used in other disciplines to avoid cross-infection with highly virulent or life-threatening illnesses such as HIV, and hepatitis B and C. The future of surgery may include wider use of disposable instruments, which will obviate iatrogenic cross-infection, and SUSI will develop to meet the changing demands of surgical practice.

REDUCTION IN PATIENT HARM

All of the following examples have obvious direct benefits for patient health.

Prescription errors

A study of prescriber education in tutorials, ward-based teaching and audit feedback[53] examined prescribing errors in an intensive-care unit. Prescribing audits were conducted three times in each 3-month cycle (once pre-training, once post-training and a final audit after 6 weeks). The audit information was fed back to prescribers with their correct prescribing rates, rates for individual error types and total error rates together with anonymised information about other prescribers' error rates. The percentage of prescriptions with errors decreased over each 3-month cycle.

Achieving therapeutic peak levels

Earlier in the previous decade[54] there were concerns about too many sub-therapeutic peak levels of gentamicin usage in newborns. Gentamicin is one of the most frequently used antibiotics in neonatal units, and there are many regimes in use based on weight and/or gestational age. Direct costs include prescription and therapeutic drug monitoring (TDM). A prospective series of re-audits[55] resulted in revision of the gentamicin regimen. The new regimen achieved therapeutic levels without any added risk of toxicity, and routine peak level determination was stopped, resulting in less trauma and blood sampling for delicate newborns, and the saving of laboratory time. The potential for significant cost savings was also identified, as analysis of gentamicin levels has been reported to represent 75% of the cost of using this relatively inexpensive drug.

FINDINGS FROM A CRITICAL APPRAISAL OF REPORTS FROM NATIONAL CLINICAL AUDITS

Reduction in patient harm

Identification errors

A review of national audits of the blood transfusion service[56] has shown that since 1995 there have been notable improvements in the percentage of patients with identification (from 90% to 98%), in identifications that have surname, first name, date of birth and identification number (from 86% to 98%), in pre-transfusion observations (from 75% to 90%), and in observations within 30 minutes during transfusion (from 59% to 73%).

Serious Hazards of Transfusion (SHOT) is a system[57] that collects data on transfusion incidents in the UK. Recent evidence points to both a reduction in the mortality associated with transfusion, and a downward trend in the most serious type of error (ABO blood group incompatible red cell transfusion).

Being seen by specialist clinicians[58]

In a study that examined the impact of specialty of admitting physician and type of hospital on care and outcome for myocardial infarction,[59] the authors concluded that patients who were cared for by cardiologists had lower levels of comorbidity than other patients. They were more likely to receive proved treatments and angiography, and they had a lower adjusted 90-day mortality.

Changes in drug prescribing

An observational study[60] from the Myocardial Infarction National Audit Project (MINAP) database reported on the early impact of insulin treatment on mortality among hyperglycaemic patients without known diabetes who present with an acute coronary syndrome. The authors concluded that compared with those who received insulin, after adjustment for age, gender, comorbidities and blood glucose concentration on admission, patients who were not treated with insulin had a relative increased risk of death of 56% at 7 days and 51% at 30 days.

A study of the impact of pre-hospital thrombolytic treatment on re-infarction rates found that pre-hospital treatment with tenecteplase was associated with higher re-infarction rates.[61] Longer intervals between pre-hospital treatment and arrival in hospital were associated with high re-infarction rates for both tenecteplase and reteplase. Differences in the use of adjunctive anti-thrombotic therapy in the two treatment environments may underlie the differences in re-infarction rates and bleeding complications observed between pre-hospital and in-hospital thrombolytic treatment.

When considering the contribution of the reports of national clinical audits, it is important to understand the context within which these audits emerged in the UK. The majority of them emerged from clinical interests, sometimes of individuals and small groups, as clinical databases or registers, and then moved into professional societies and Royal Colleges, and finally some went on to recognition via central government funding and became national studies involving clinical audit. Their purpose in their earliest days was as registers or clinical databases to be used for research purposes. Their analysis to show variations in care was conducted as a research exercise, and the degree to which this then led to changes in care was a matter for individual clinicians.

In practice, where such national projects are still conceptualised in this way, as a database that local clinicians use to implement changes in practice at local level, rather than a process which is set up explicitly to drive, lead and influence change from the centre, it is not surprising that their reports do not demonstrate any resulting changes. Those at the national level may not monitor local changes. This approach is an expression of different attitudes to what clinical audit, at the national level, is for – whether it is closer to being research, or acts as an aid to research, or whether it is a change programme involving data collection that is driven centrally.

This situation, in the current financial climate, is changing rapidly and the role of these audits is increasingly likely to be to drive change at the local level through their use in monitoring and regulation and other processes, including (in the case of some audits) the proposed revalidation of individual doctors, and measurement of outcomes. Historically, the vast majority of national clinical audits dealt primarily with variation in outcomes and did not seek to measure the impact of their findings, which their reports did not evidence. This does not mean that these audits have not had a significant impact on local practice. However, the precise nature of the contribution of the national audit to driving changes at the local level, given all the background noise of other activity, is even more difficult to assess than for local audit.

Discussion with members of staff from nominated centres confirmed that some of these reports will increasingly deal with the impact of audit in the future, and the expectation that these audits will monitor and drive changes is now much clearer if they are to continue to receive endorsement and funding from government.

FINDINGS FROM THE SURVEY OF STAFF FROM NHS ORGANISATIONS

When conducting this review of the evidence for the impact of clinical audit, it was apparent that only a small part of all audit practice was captured in the externally published literature, and that there was clearly a large volume of material (examples of effective audits) which was held only at the local level of delivery. The main purpose of the online survey was to gather evidence of impact identified in particular in the 'grey literature' from these sources in NHS organisations in England (i.e. sources that were not externally published). The evidence used in this part of the review represented an opportunistic sample of NHS organisations, but one that was appropriate with regard to identifying evidence of impact at a 'local' level (i.e. individual NHS organisations). The detailed examples of evidence of the impact of clinical audit from the survey of staff in NHS organisations are listed for each of the five domains of impact of clinical audit set out above. The extracts provided in this section are taken from the responses to the online survey.

In describing the following 'impacts' of clinical audit in each defined category, it should be noted that there is considerable crossover of benefit resulting in the implementation of recommendations from any (re)audit. For example, a reduction in length of stay might well be associated with a corresponding reduction in the number of unnecessary tests and procedures, and vice versa.

The type of individual NHS organisation is noted in each example. Respondents to the survey were asked to state their perceptions of the strength of evidence in relation to the described example of impact; this measure is self-reported. It is not possible to make an external judgement on the quality of the evidence presented, so we opted for a self-assessment of the reliability of this evidence.

There are four self-assessed levels of evidence, ranging from 1 (low) to 4 (high):
1 level of evidence not given
2 evidence relating to a wide range of cases
3 objective evidence based on numbers
4 statistically significant improvement in a quantity of interest.

When considering this large volume of 'evidence', several points can be made. Each piece of work was self-assessed and reported by the teams who conducted the audits. No external body assesses the quality of work like this, yet these types of audit are the mainstay of audit practice at the local level. In seeking to consider the extent to which these 'grey literature' sources evidence the impact of clinical audit, reviewers will no doubt query the scientific rigour involved and their reliability as 'evidence.' This is the circular problem that underpins any evaluation of the impact of clinical audit – only studies that have research standards get published, and by their very nature, clinical audit processes are not research, **or have not been researched**. It might be argued that such sources are inevitably and unfairly discounted as evidence of effectiveness because they are being assessed against standards that they cannot be expected to meet. However, on their own terms they attempt to measure a higher level of effect and are a form of evidence that is too easily discounted. This is the rationale behind the intention to review them here.

The examples given below should be read within this context.

Reduction in patient stay

Audit of compliance with guidelines on management of coagulopathy has shown improvements in compliance over successive re-audits and led to a reduction in blood transfusion and reduced length of stay on ICU.

(Level 4; tertiary, research and teaching NHS trust)

Following a lower limb trauma audit in 2005, a new structure was put in place with semi-elective operating list and dedicated surgeon – resulting in better transfer times and few cancellations. Following re-audit in 2007, a new Outlier Services team was set up to include consultant surgeon and anaesthetist, dedicated nurse practitioner and admin support. Data from 2009 indicate high patient turnover with improved patient experience and reduced lengths of stay.

(Level 1; specialist reconstructive surgery NHS trust)

Post-surgical management of deep vein thrombosis. Initial audit indicated shortcomings in pathway knowledge. Education including posters and discussion at audit presentation. Re-audit undertaken. Results indicated all recommendations from initial audit were in place. Patients were being referred appropriately to anticoagulation specialist nurses and having appropriate investigations and reduced admission and length of stay.

(Level 2; NHS trust, general hospital services)

Change in drug prescribing

Broad-spectrum antibiotic prescribing in general practice. Improvement (reduction) in prescribing levels as a result of data feedback, information from Medical Director and Medicines Management and peer review.

(Level 3; primary care trust)

In the 2008 inpatient ward audit, only 29% of case notes were using the correct discharge checklist. By 2009 this had reached 100%, facilitating better discharge planning, effective discharge, proper supply of medication and identification of most appropriate follow-up.

(Level 3; partnership NHS foundation trust)

Reduction in unwarranted/unnecessary procedures or tests

An audit of transfusion practice regarding the appropriate use of red cells resulted in a reduction of red cell units transfused by 11.7%, and a reduction (from 40% to 2.5%) in the number of inappropriate transfusions. The impact of this was improved resource stewardship (through reduced number of transfusion requests and reduced actual transfusions) as well as a reduction in the number of patients being exposed to unnecessary risk (by inappropriate transfusion).

(Level 3; NHS foundation trust)

Audit of Choose and Book service has resulted in some practices reviewing all referrals, and has reduced the incidence of inappropriate referrals.

(Level 3; commissioning primary care trust)

An audit of intra-operative assessment of axillary sentinel lymph nodes using an RT-PCR-based assay for mammaglobin (MG) and cytokeratin 19 (1131) demonstrated improved patient outcomes by reducing the necessity for a second surgical operation. The audit demonstrated that this technique was safe, acceptable and accurate.

(Level 4; NHS trust)

In addition to the significant improvement in productivity, the following example also highlights an impact measure in the form of a reduction in the number of unnecessary tests in oncology.

A repeat audit of chest X-rays suspicious of lung cancer has shown a reduction in the mean referral times from 15 days to 4.88 days, and a dramatic reduction in those abnormal chest X-rays not copied to the Respiratory Department as a fail-safe measure.

(Level 2; acute and mental health trust)

More effective application of a technology
Adult parenteral nutrition (PN)

Clinical audit recommendations were that PN bags have higher nitrogen content to improve the nutritional status of adult patients (particularly in the elderly). Nursing and pharmacy staff discussed this with commercial suppliers and as a result the hospital now procures new bags that meet a higher specification.

(No declared level; acute foundation trust)

Software application

As a result of one of the audits taking place on a learning disability ward, new software has been purchased and adapted to allow for the development of Easy-Read care plans (pictorial representations of the care plan). This has promoted inclusion and accessibility, as it allows those with learning difficulties to be involved (despite difficulties) with agreeing, updating and reviewing their care plan.

(Level 2; mental health NHS trust)

Reduction in patient (or staff) harm

An audit of 30-day mortality following systemic anti-cancer therapy has been rolled out across the trust since 2007. All deaths within 30 days are followed up to identify which of them may be therapy related, with a view to identifying themes and pathway issues that will inform future decision making. Individual cases are increasingly discussed at morbidity and mortality meetings. Regimens contributing significantly to mortality are being reviewed. A disease-specific protocol has been revised to provide routine antibiotic prophylaxis for patients over 70 years old. Further audits have taken place – for example, in the management of neutropenic sepsis.

(Level 1; Cancer Centre)

Transrectal ultrasound-guided biopsies had a 20% infection rate. A change in the antibiotic regime resulted in a 2% infection rate. Repeat audit showed that this improvement was maintained.

(Level 4; NHS trust)

A recent re-audit considered whether blood tests performed either by a GP or a psychiatrist have potential for some people on lithium medication not to receive necessary blood tests, with potentially serious results. Evidence of a need for clear communication between primary and secondary services was a finding. We are looking at to what extent this improvement in defining responsibilities between GPs and psychiatrists led to improved blood testing and physical health monitoring thus improving outcomes for the service users.

(Level 3; mental health trust)

Clinical audit of manual handling followed an incident. An action was an enhanced training programme. Following the implementation of the course, there was a reduction in associated incidents.

(Level 2; community NHS trust)

OTHER DIMENSIONS OF IMPACT

In addition to the above five areas of impact which were identified initially, two further dimensions of **outcome** were suggested in the qualitative review (by clinical
audit staff and policy leads), which may be sources of **potential** impact. Both of these
dimensions reflect wider and perhaps more lasting changes that result from clinical
audit (both nationally organised and locally conducted) at the local level. The further dimensions encompass **strategic outcomes** (i.e. influencing change in others
towards an agreed or shared goal) and **cultural change** (i.e. change in the 'ways of
working' or in general acceptance of the ways in which clinical practice should be
undertaken, where new clinical practice is accepted as the norm or standard clinical
practice).

Strategic impacts

The third National Audit of Cardiac Rehabilitation (NACR) revealed a number of positive outcomes (e.g. a significant reduction in waiting times for cardiac rehabilitation,
and an improvement in the range of professions available to patients, particularly
dietitians, pharmacists, psychologists and occupational therapists). Furthermore,
the annual report documented reduced waiting times and improved weekly exercise
trends. Positive outcomes for health-related quality of life reinforce the message that
cardiac rehabilitation outcomes are transferable into daily life. One of the longer-
term benefits of cardiac rehabilitation is that physical activity remains high, which
aligns well with effective rehabilitation, sound risk factor management and overall
prevention of disease. Thus in addition to longer-term impacts, the audit programme
in cardiac rehabilitation could have a strategic effect (i.e. the NACR findings may start
to influence national decision making and contribute to a change in thinking of the
British Association of Cardiac Rehabilitation (BACR) about staffing).[62]

Cultural change

Positive cultural change can be defined as a significant alteration in thinking and
perception towards specific treatment activity stimulated by clinical audit acting as a
meaningful, valuable process to bring about quality improvement in healthcare.

A recent report on thoracic surgery highlighted several differences in approach
that reflected varying philosophical approaches to some difficult diseases. For
example, there are considerable differences in the **open and close** rate for lung and
gastrointestinal cancer surgery between units.[63] In other words, some patients are
being subjected to exploratory operations to see whether anything can be done sur-
gically. The open and close rate represents the proportion of patients who undergo
an exploratory operation and for whom nothing can be done. Some surgeons argue
that such operations can be avoided by good pre-operative screening, while others
argue that these operations are for cancer and it is better to seek every opportunity
rather than to eliminate all hope prematurely.

Clinical audit in this context of care has helped to bring about a fundamental
shift in culture to one of greater 'openness' in relation to the **acceptance** of the need

for and justification of transparency in key clinical performance data and metrics. Clinicians now have a better understanding (and consequently less 'fear') of variation in individual clinical outcomes.

CONCLUSIONS

The review confirmed that there is still some confusion about the definition of clinical audit in the NHS. Discussions with clinical audit specialists and a review of online findings from a survey of NHS organisations revealed that many practitioners presented service development and organisational development as examples of clinical audit. This state of affairs causes real problems when undertaking formal evaluation of the impact of audit and indeed strategic development at local, regional and national levels.

The qualitative review of the published literature revealed that the vast majority of papers were focused on clinical audit 'outcomes' in terms of improved adherence to guidelines, and the process of clinical audit, rather than further impact as defined here, although there were some examples of impact from the international literature. However, where published papers purported to be about impact, the main metrics were on short-term clinical measures. The review also found that there is limited assessment of impact in the reports of national clinical audits in England, which probably fails to reflect the degree to which this occurs, instead reflecting the historic orientation of audit towards process compliance and, in certain cases, the quasi-research nature of some national audit.

The online survey of NHS organisations found examples in each of the five main areas of impact. However, the level of evidence of these examples inevitably varies from one organisation to another.

As part of the broader qualitative review that was conducted, discussions with clinical audit specialists and clinicians revealed two further dimensions of impact, namely strategic and cultural dimensions. These discussions also highlighted the need for further studies on the economic impact of clinical audit, especially given the pressures on health service funding at the present time.

It is clear from the review that clinical audit **can** have a range of impacts on the health of patients and on the wider healthcare system. It is also clear that despite the extensive use of data and measurements within clinical audit, the evidence for the impact of clinical audit is often of a qualitative nature, or not sufficiently robust for publication, and therefore there is a tendency for this evidence (especially from individual NHS organisations) to remain unpublished and to add to the already large source of 'grey literature' in the NHS. It remains difficult to get studies of audit (as opposed to research) published, simply because they are not research. Nonetheless, these sources may contain evidence that is of real value. As yet, there is no uniform or comprehensive system for capturing and disseminating the intelligence from a large part of clinical audit practice, which might have a considerable impact on the experience and effectiveness of care.

Moreover, this analysis of the evidence of impact demonstrates three fundamental components of effective clinical audit that are required for any effect to be obtained, namely that:

➤ there have been repeated cycles of audit
➤ the audit was conducted using proper methodology
➤ there was intention from the outset to record primary outcomes – i.e. adherence to practice – and resulting impacts.

Clinical audit is designed to measure compliance with standards of proven clinical practice and to record the required and documented changes in clinical practice shown by re-audit. However, many audits do not reach the re-audit stage, and still fewer follow through to repeat cycles of audit. The potential to measure and/or research such change and to evaluate clinical audit is therefore severely restricted by this failure to follow simple guidelines for best practice.

However, despite this failure to follow best practice, there are still many examples of good practice, as the review has identified. Thus if standard methodology and processes are followed and there is a commitment to follow through to repeat cycles of audit, significant change in clinical practice and meaningful impact **can** be achieved, although this is by no means common practice in the NHS in England at the present time.

By seeking to establish a concept of 'impact' of audit that goes beyond patient health outcomes to look at improvements in system-wide productivity and effectiveness, this review also identified economic and financial impacts of clinical audit practice. Because audit effectively streamlines care, it has the potential to reduce costs and make efficiencies, while at the same time the primary purpose is still to improve patient care. The examples given above identify an approach that clinical audit needs to incorporate more systematically into its practice.

REFERENCES

1 The National Quality Board (NQB) is a multi-stakeholder board established by the Department of Health in England to champion quality and ensure alignment of quality throughout the NHS. The Board is a key aspect of the work to deliver high-quality care for patients. Further information can be found at www.dh.gov.uk/en/Healthcare/ Highqualitycareforall/NationalQualityBoard/index.htm (accessed 9 June 2010).

2 Department of Health. *High Quality Care for All: NHS Next Stage Review final report.* London: Department of Health; 2008.

3 Department of Health. *Review of Early Warning Systems in the NHS: acute and community services.* London: Department of Health; 2010.

4 Health Foundation. *Engaging Clinicians in Quality Improvement.* London: Health Foundation; 2009 (quoted with permission).

5 Scott I. What are the most effective strategies for improving quality and safety of health care? *Internal Medicine Journal* 2009; **39**: 389–400.

6 Department of Health. *Implementing the Next Stage Review Visions: the quality and productivity challenge.* London: Department of Health; 2009. www.dh.gov.uk/prod_consum_dh/

groups/dh_digitalassets/documents/digitalasset/dh_104255.pdf (accessed 3 August 2010).

7 Pay-for-performance schemes directed to clinician groups and organisational process redesign were modestly effective. Other manager/policy-maker-driven QIS, including continuous quality improvement programmes, risk and safety management systems, public scorecards and performance reports, external accreditation, and clinical governance arrangements have not been adequately evaluated with regard to effectiveness. QIS are heterogeneous, and methodological flaws in much of the evaluative literature limit the validity of the results and their ability to be generalised.

8 National Audit Office. *A Safer Place for Patients: learning to improve patient safety.* www.nao.org.uk/publications/0506/a_safer_place_for_patients.aspx (accessed 9 June 2010).

9 Øvretveit J. *Does Improving Quality Save Money? A review of evidence of which improvements to quality reduce costs to health service providers.* London: Health Foundation; 2009.

10 European Observatory on Health Systems and Policies. Available at www.euro.who.int/observatory/Glossary (accessed 9 June 2010).

11 See, for example, www.ohe.org/page/commission.cfm (accessed 9 June 2010).

12 World Health Organization. *Gothenburg Consensus Paper, December 1999.* Copenhagen: WHO Regional Office for Europe; 1999. www.euro.who.int/document/PAE/Gothenburgpaper.pdf (accessed 9 June 2010) (quoted with permission).

13 Ved P, Coupe T. Improving prescription quality in an in-patient mental health unit: three cycles of clinical audit. *Psychiatric Bulletin* 2007; **31**: 293–4.

14 John C, Mathew DE, Gnanalingham MG. An audit of paediatric audits. *Archives of Disease in Childhood* 2004; **89**: 1128–9.

15 Dickinson E, Deighan M. Collaboration and communication – the millennium agenda for clinical improvement? *International Journal for Quality in Health Care* 1999; **11**: 279–81.

16 Balogh R, Bond S. Completing the audit cycle: the outcomes of audits in mental health services. *International Journal for Quality in Health Care* 2001; **13**: 135–42.

17 Prasad K, Reddy K. Auditing the audit cycle: an open-ended evaluation. *Journal of Clinical Governance* 2004; **9**: 110–14.

18 Holden JD. Systematic review of published multi-practice audits from British general practice. *Journal of Evaluation in Clinical Practice* 2004; **10**: 247–72.

19 Jamtvedt G, Young JM, Kristoffersen DT *et al.* Audit and feedback: effects on professional practice and health care outcomes. *Cochrane Database of Systematic Reviews* 2006; Issue 2: CD000259.

20 Greenhalgh T, Robert G, MacFarlane F *et al.* Diffusion of innovations in service organisations: systematic review and recommendations. *Milbank Quarterly* 2004; **82**: 581–629.

21 Loughlan C, Burgess R. *Challenges in Evaluation of Quality Improvement Methodologies: the example of clinical audit.* London: HQIP; 2011. In press.

22 Foy R, Eccles MP, Jamtvedt G *et al.* What do we know about how to do audit and feedback? Pitfalls in applying evidence from a systematic review. *BMC Health Services Research* 2005; **5**: 50.

23 Mannion R, Goddard M. Impact of published clinical outcomes data: case study in NHS hospital trusts. *British Medical Journal* 2001; **4**: 260–3.

24   Johnston G, Crombie I, Alder E *et al*. Reviewing audit: barriers and facilitating factors for effective clinical audit. *Quality in Health Care* 2000; **9**: 23–36.

25   Hearnshaw HM, Harker RM, Cheater FM *et al*. Are audits wasting resources by measuring the wrong things? A survey of methods used to select audit review criteria. *Quality and Safety in Health Care* 2003; **12**: 24–8.

26   McKay-Brown L, Bishop B, Balmford J *et al*. The impact of a GP clinical audit on the provision of smoking cessation advice. *Asia Pacific Family Medicine* 2008; **7**: 4.

27   Martin S, Purkayastha S, Massey R *et al*. The surgical care practitioner: a feasible alternative. Results of a prospective 4-year audit at St Mary's Hospital Trust, London. *Annals of the Royal College of Surgeons of England* 2007; **89**: 30–5.

28   Mounsey JP, Ray SG, Griffith MJ *et al*. Impact of internal audit on pacemaker prescription and the immediate costs of pacing in the northern region: towards implementation of the recommendations of the British Pacing and Electrophysiology Group. *British Heart Journal* 1994; **71**: 395–8.

29   Shravat BP, Huseyin TS, Hynes KA. NICE guideline for the management of head injury: an audit demonstrating its impact on a district general hospital, with a cost analysis for England and Wales. *Emergency Medicine Journal* 2006; **23**: 109–13.

30   Thyagarajan S, Sharma V, Austin S *et al*. An audit of corneal abrasion management following the introduction of local guidelines in an accident and emergency department. *Emergency Medicine Journal* 2006; **23**: 526–9.

31   McGregor AH, Dicken B, Jamrozik K. National audit of post-operative management in spinal surgery. *BMC Musculoskeletal Disorders* 2006; **7**: 47.

32   Prasad N, Sunderamoorthy D, Martin J *et al*. Secondary prevention of fragility fractures: are we following the guidelines? Closing the audit loop. *Annals of the Royal College of Surgeons of England* 2006; **88**: 470–4.

33   Price LC, Lowe D, Hosker HS *et al*. UK National COPD Audit 2003: impact of hospital resources and organisation of care on patient outcome following admission for acute COPD exacerbation. *Thorax* 2006; **61**: 837–42.

34   Khunti K, Carr M. Impact of an audiology clinic in one general practice. *British Journal of General Practice* 1997; **47**: 643–4.

35   Chivers KC, Basnyat P, Taffinder N. The impact of national guidelines on the waiting list for colonoscopy: a quantitative clinical audit. *Colorectal Disease* 2010; **12**: 632–9.

36   el-Boghdadly S, al-Yousef Z, Bedah K. Pancreatic injury: an audit and a practical approach. *Annals of the Royal College of Surgeons of England* 2000; **82**: 258–62.

37   Khawaja AR, Allan SM. Audit of referral practice to a fast-access breast clinic before the guaranteed 2-week wait. *Annals of the Royal College of Surgeons of England* 2001; **83**: 58–60.

38   Viehweg TL, Roberson JB, Hudson JW. Epistaxis: diagnosis and treatment. *Journal of Oral and Maxillofacial Surgery* 2006; **64**: 11–18.

39   Juselius H. Epistaxis. A clinical study of 1,724 patients. *Journal of Laryngology and Otology* 1974; **88**: 317–27.

40   Chaiyasate S, Roongrotwattanasiri K, Fooanan S *et al*. Epistaxis in Chiang Mai University Hospital. *Journal of the Medical Association of Thailand* 2005; **88**: 1282–6.

41 Upile T, Jerjes W, Sipaul F *et al.* The role of surgical audit in improving patient management; nasal haemorrhage: an audit study. *BMC Surgery* 2007; **7**: 19.

42 Wheeler A, Humberstone V, Robinson E *et al.* Impact of audit and feedback on antipsychotic prescribing in schizophrenia. *Journal of Evaluation in Clinical Practice* 2009; **15**: 441–50.

43 Bhatt J, Nye C, Kirkbride V. Quality and cost improvement in neonatal prescribing through clinical audit. *Clinical Governance* 2004; **9**: 232–6.

44 Danzon PM, Manning WG, Marquis MS. Factors affecting laboratory test use and prices. *Health Care Financing Review* 1984; **5**: 23–32.

45 Fowkes FG, Catford JC, Logan RF. Containing the use of laboratory tests. *British Medical Journal* 1985; **290**: 488–90.

46 Showstack JA, Schroeder SA, Matsumoto MF. Changes in the use of medical technologies, 1972–1977: a study of 10 inpatient diagnoses. *New England Journal of Medicine* 1982; **306**: 706–12.

47 Epstein AM, McNeil BJ. Physician characteristics and organizational factors influencing use of ambulatory tests. *Medical Decision Making* 1985; **5**: 401–15.

48 Schroeder SA, Kenders K, Cooper JK *et al.* Use of laboratory tests and pharmaceuticals. Variation among physicians and effect of cost audit on subsequent use. *Journal of the American Medical Association* 1973; **225**: 969–73.

49 Kwok J, Jones B. Unnecessary repeat requesting of tests: an audit in a government hospital immunology laboratory. *Journal of Clinical Pathology* 2005; **58**: 457–62.

50 Freer DE, Ficicioglu C, Finegold D. Newborn screening for galactosemia: a review of 5 years of data and audit of a revised reporting approach. *Clinical Chemistry* 2010; **56**: 437–44.

51 Department of Health. *£200 Million for NHS Equipment to Protect Patients against Possible Variant CJD Risk.* London: Department of Health; 2001.

52 O'Flynn P, Silva S, Kothari P *et al.* A multicentre audit of single-use surgical instruments (SUSI) for tonsillectomy and adenoidectomy. *Annals of the Royal College of Surgeons of England* 2007; **89**: 616–23.

53 Thomas AN, Boxall EM, Laha SK *et al.* An educational and audit tool to reduce prescribing error in intensive care. *Quality and Safety in Health Care* 2008; **17**: 360–3.

54 See, for example, 'Safety concerns over baby antibiotic use rise amid errors.' *The Times*, 15 February 2010.

55 Bajaj M, Palmer K. Gentamicin usage in newborns: an audit. *Archives of Disease in Childhood* 2003; **88**: 645.

56 The audits before 1995 were run with smaller numbers of hospitals participating, and the trends before 1995 are less interpretable. The rate for no observations being recorded during transfusion appears to have remained stable (at around 1 in 8 patients) throughout the time period covered by these audits.

57 SHOT is based at the Manchester Blood Transfusion Centre and is affiliated to the Royal College of Pathologists. Ownership of the scheme and data generated from it resides with the Steering Group, which has representation from a number of Royal Colleges and professional bodies. Available at www.shotuk.org/home.htm (accessed 9 June 2010).

58 The Myocardial Infarction National Audit Project (MINAP) provides data to cardiac

networks to support service improvement. MINAP is the first national audit to release annual reports showing hospital performance against National Service Framework (NSF) targets in the public domain. Sustained improvement of performance against NSF targets for thrombolysis and use of secondary prevention medication has been demonstrated since the end of 2000. Available at www.rcplondon.ac.uk/clinical-standards/organisation/partnership/Pages/MINAP-.aspx (accessed 9 June 2010).

59 Birkhead J, Clive-Weston C, Lowe D. Impact of specialty of admitting physician and type of hospital on care and outcome for myocardial infarction in England and Wales during 2004–5: observational study. *British Medical Journal* 2006; **332:** 1306–11.

60 Weston C, Walker L, Birkhead J. Early impact of insulin treatment on mortality for hyperglycaemic patients without known diabetes who present with an acute coronary syndrome. *Heart* 2007; **93:** 1542–6.

61 Horne S, Weston C, Quinn T *et al.* The impact of pre-hospital thrombolytic treatment on re-infarction rates: analysis of the Myocardial Infarction National Audit Project (MINAP). *Heart* 2009; **95:** 559–63.

62 Investment in and findings from clinical audit have undoubtedly created a higher profile for cardiac rehabilitation, and have influenced the establishment of a national Priority Project for Cardiac Rehabilitation by NHS Improvement.

63 Society for Cardio-Thoracic Surgery in Great Britain and Ireland. *First National Thoracic Surgery Activity and Outcomes Report 2008.* London: Society for Cardiothoracic Surgery in Great Britain and Ireland; 2008.

Four principles of change management

Kate Godfrey

The purpose of this appendix

- To give an overview of the theory of change management in healthcare settings, and how change can be implemented.

INTRODUCTION

There is no magic bullet or 'one size fits all' solution to implementing change, including that arising from clinical audits. Changing clinical practice involves people, and people can be enthusiastic or stubborn, imaginative or lacklustre. Most individuals are capable of all of these traits, depending on external factors such as how heavy their workload is or how secure they are within their role. For a change to be effective, the people involved must be informed of why a change is needed and feel empowered to contribute to the decisions about how the change should be implemented. The aim of this appendix is to set out four key principles to managing change that will help to make the transition from current practice to best practice smoother and less cumbersome.

BARRIERS TO CHANGE

Prior to introducing any form of change, whether it is within a single clinical team or involves the whole organisation, it is necessary to identify any potential barriers or challenges, so that they can be planned for and, wherever possible, prevented.[1]

Identifying potential barriers

Practical or situational barriers to change are usually caused by disparities between best practice and current clinical circumstances. This may be because service provision needs to be significantly altered, or a need for further education is identified, or the change requires a higher level of investment of resources.

Change may also be difficult to achieve because of people's reluctance to leave what is perceived to be a 'comfort zone.' Change is all about people, either as part of an organisation or as individuals. Models of organisational culture have been described by Handy.[2] The model that fits most healthcare structures is 'role culture', where jobs within the organisation are structured in such a way that there are clear cut-off points for decision making, and where departments tend to be set up around specialist functions. It is important to remember that each department will also have its own subculture (e.g. Accident and Emergency departments, intensive-care units), and that each profession is also a distinct subculture.

Individuals react in complex and diverse ways.[3] Their feelings are influenced by factors such as personality, background, experience, prejudices, influential status and their own personal preferences. It is useful to know the individuals you will be dealing with, as people always have reasons for behaving in the way that they do, and these need to be explored before change can be introduced.

The effect that change has on self-esteem has often been likened to that of a bereavement process.[3-5] For example, the various stages of the process include disbelief, anger and acceptance. Not everyone will go through all of the stages, and those that do will not do so in a synchronised fashion, but knowledge of the possible effects that change can have on people enables one to anticipate and act accordingly when situations do arise.

Force field analysis

Force field analysis was originally developed by an American social psychologist named Kurt Lewin[6] (1890–1947). It is a widely used tool that enables the user to identify the drivers for change and the forces against it by investigating the balance of power; identifying the most important people (stakeholders) and groups involved or affected by the proposed change, identifying opponents and allies, and identifying how to influence the target group through action planning.

TABLE A3.1 Force field analysis template

Score	Forces for change	Plan	Forces against change	Score
1–5	Driving force 1	Desired change	Restraining force 1	1–5
1–5	Driving force 2		Restraining force 2	1–5
1–5	Driving force 3		Restraining force 3	1–5
1–5	Driving force 4		Restraining force 4	1–5

This method allows you to visualise both the driving forces and the restraining forces through the use of a diagram. The latter should consist of three sections. First, describe your plan or proposal for change in the middle section, and then list all of the forces for change in one column, and all of the forces against change in the third column. A score should then be applied to each force, from 1 (weak) to 5 (strong), thereby enabling you to prioritise which barriers should be tackled first, and how. It is far better to try to reduce the strength of the forces that are in favour of maintaining the status quo than it is to increase the drivers for change. People are usually uncooperative if they perceive that change is being forced upon them.

STAKEHOLDERS

A project stakeholder may be defined as anyone who is actively involved in the project, or whose interests may be affected by the proposed change. They are the people on whom the success or failure of the project rests. Each stakeholder should be given a specific role when implementing change.[7]

Change sponsor

This is an individual who has both the authority and the enthusiasm to lead the changes. Their role does not necessarily involve the day-to-day management of the process, but they need to be visibly supportive of it and regularly evaluate the progress that has been made. The change sponsor must ensure that the required resources are available and be accountable for the successful implementation of the change. For example, they should:

➤ approve the action plan
➤ be a 'champion' of the shared vision
➤ monitor and communicate progress to all interested parties.

Change manager

This role needs to be filled by someone who has the skills and expertise to manage and organise implementation of the change. They need to have good social skills in order to be able to influence and negotiate with any recalcitrants while at the same time maintaining enthusiasm in other members of the team. Responsibilities should include:

➤ designing the action plan and ensuring that it is agreed by the change team and approved by the sponsor
➤ ensuring that there is a clear communication strategy and contingency plans
➤ monitoring and reporting progress
➤ liaising up and down the organisational structure.

Change agents

These individuals need to be passionate about the change process, and must therefore be given time and support to adjust to the changes before being required to gain commitment from their staff/departments. They are the key to implementing change effectively. Their responsibilities include:

➤ ensuring that all of those who are implementing the change are fully informed
➤ obtaining commitment to the process from their staff
➤ monitoring and reporting on progress to the change manager and their staff

➤ identifying sources of resistance and bottlenecks
➤ disseminating lessons learned.

Change champions

These are also known as early adopters. They should be healthcare professionals who want the change implementation to be a success and who strongly believe that it will improve patient care. Change champions do not need to have management responsibilities, but they need to be respected by their peers and other members of staff whose clinical practice is affected by the change. Change champions often act as catalysts for others when they:

➤ speak positively about the change
➤ demonstrate how it can be done
➤ make clear what the benefits have been for them and/or their patients
➤ support colleagues informally.

Change team

This is the group of staff responsible for implementing the change. It is crucial that this team contains the optimum mix of people and that it is given the right amount of time and the necessary conditions to succeed. The change team must have the confidence of management and staff alike. They should:

➤ be representative of all areas affected by the change
➤ clearly demonstrate their commitment to the process
➤ support the change manager
➤ identify any training needs.

PLANNING THE CHANGE

Any change in practice or culture needs to be carefully planned with the stakeholders. The potential barriers need to be taken into account, and a clear and comprehensive plan of action should be shared with all relevant parties.

Creating a shared vision

A shared vision is much more than just a list of corporate style objectives. It needs to be something that can inspire and enthuse people to pull together in order to accomplish something worthwhile. Staff should be able to identify what their role would be in bringing the vision to life, and to feel that their values and ideas are being incorporated.

The vision should be agreed by all members of the change team, who in turn should ensure that the message is communicated to all staff involved in the change. When issues arise or there are unexpected delays in implementing the change, the shared vision should be used as a vehicle to get people back on track.

Writing an effective action plan

The action plan needs to be a 'live document' that can be updated as tasks are completed or altered when unexpected issues arise, so that these can be incorporated into the plan. The action plan needs to be SMART (Specific, Measurable, Agreed to, Realistic and Time phased). An effective action plan should have eight discrete headings as follows.

The recommendation

This column should include the requirements for change that were identified after the analysis of the original data collection. Recommendations should be:
➤ based on the conclusions of the audit
➤ clear and concise
➤ explicitly related to the action required.

Objective

An action plan objective needs to be a concrete statement that describes what the project is trying to achieve. The objective should be written in a way that can be evaluated at the conclusion of a project to see whether it was achieved.

Action required

This section covers the actual activities that are required to meet the recommendation. It is vital that it is worded simply and clearly so that it is obvious to all involved exactly what measures need to be taken in order to achieve the objective.

Timescales

In order to ensure that the change management process takes place as smoothly and quickly as is appropriate, realistic timescales need to be agreed by the whole change team. If too much time is allocated, the actions required will not remain on everyone's radar and may be seen as less important than they really are, and not completed effectively as a consequence. However, if not enough time is allocated to a specific action and the project runs over time, this can be perceived as a failure and lead to early adopters feeling disillusioned, and recalcitrants feeling that their original concerns were justified.

Constraints/barriers

These need to be identified clearly so that they can be prevented or circumnavigated. The force field analysis will have identified some of the constraints/barriers, but those in the role of change agents will also be able to identify areas of concern and bottlenecks in the system before and during the implementation of the changes required.

Responsible individuals

This column needs to include the names and/or job titles of key individuals who are accountable for ensuring that specific actions are put into place within the allotted timescale. The word 'all' should never be used here, as this usually leads to an abdication of responsibility, with everyone hoping that someone else will take the lead, and as a result no one does so. At most, two individuals should be made respons-ible, and at best, one should be.

Outcome measure

The outcome measure needs to refer directly to the objective and the recommenda-tion. It needs to signify what the end result should be, and to show the anticipated result of what successful implementation would achieve. This can then be used to evaluate how effectively the change has been implemented.

Monitoring

This column identifies who will be monitoring each specific action. In most cases this will be done either in the change team meetings or by the change manager.

MANAGING THE TRANSITION

Any change process involves three core phases.[8] First, the old ways of working have to end. Secondly, there is a period of uncertainty and upheaval. Finally, if everything has gone to plan, there is a new beginning when the changes in practice have been adopted and accepted as the mainstream.

The old ways

It is important that people talk about the practices that have to end.[7] In many cases people are so busy discussing what is about to begin that there is barely any acknowl-edgment of this. No one can develop a new way of working until they have let go of the old one. As was mentioned earlier, going through a transition can be similar to bereavement, and it is best to deal with this up front and realistically in order to help people to gain closure on the past. They will then move on more readily and take advantage of what the future has to offer.

The interim period

In between the old and familiar ways of doing things and embracing the new ways of working there is usually a period of high activity. This can be a dangerous time when new systems don't work well and people become disheartened. It is vital that staff are reassured that it is usual to go through a chaotic interim period before new practices are embedded, and that it is normal to feel discouraged and confused from time to time. Temporary sources of support should be made available through members of the change team. In addition, communication channels should be established that enable staff to be involved in decisions that affect them.

However, it is useful to remember that the upheaval that makes this interim period potentially difficult also has a detrimental effect on efforts to resist new ideas and behaviours. This means that this period can also be a time of consider-able creativity.

New beginnings

As the changes in practice start to become embedded, the process still needs to be encouraged, supported and reinforced. Many changes in practice have been known to fail because support for the project was withdrawn too early, there was no clear ending of the project or there was no celebration of its success.

How to revive a stalled transition

Through careful monitoring of the action plan, it will become evident if the project starts to falter. If this happens, you need to do a reality check and apply corrective measures as swiftly as possible.[9] This process involves the following three stages.

Conduct a status review

This involves asking two key questions:
1 Is there still a need for change?
2 If the objectives of the change were to be achieved, what would clinical practice look like?

If it is decided that the change is no longer relevant, it is important that a review takes place to identify lessons for the future. Sweeping failure under the carpet fuels the conviction that trying to change is pointless, and can encourage a culture of blame rather than a culture of change.

Two further questions are also important to help to ensure that the mistakes are not repeated:
3 Why didn't we recognise the signs that the change effort was not on track?
4 Why didn't we do anything about it?

Apply corrective measures

Actions that may be necessary to reinvigorate the process include:
➤ restructuring the change team/reviewing the membership
➤ obtaining more visible involvement from senior management
➤ responding more readily to staff concerns
➤ a greater investment in resources (time, staff or financial)
➤ increasing the profile and use of change champions
➤ better targeted staff development.

Reviving a stalled effort will raise questions in people's minds about how the project is being managed. They will need to be reassured that the reasoning behind the change remains sound, and that their involvement is highly valued.

Monitor the results

It is likely that there will be only one opportunity to revive the project and therefore effect the change required. Another failure will almost certainly condemn the initiative to an irredeemable breakdown. This is why it is so important to put in place effective monitoring processes at the beginning of the project, to help to ensure that early signs of faltering can be detected and responded to immediately.

CLOSING THE PROJECT

How do you know when a process of change is complete? Most often the change just becomes accepted practice and other change projects take its place. However, there are a number of methods that can help to indicate whether the project has reached its conclusion. The best way is to go back to the shared vision and original aims and objectives, and assess the extent to which they have been met. If the objectives have not been met, look at other ways that changes can be made which may be more acceptable to those involved in the process. You should also ask whether the right people have been given the right roles, or whether there are others who would be more suitable. If you decide that the original objectives have been met, write a final report (and circulate it widely) to indicate a formal end to the project. This ensures that everyone knows not only that the project has come to an end but also, more importantly, that it has been a success. All of those involved should be commended for their hard work and reminded that, by making the changes required, they have improved the way in which patients are cared for.

REFERENCES

1 National Institute for Health and Clinical Excellence (NICE). *How to Change Practice: understand, identify and overcome barriers to change.* London: NICE; 2007.

2 Handy C. *Understanding Organisations.* 4th edn. London: Penguin; 1993.

3 NHS Institute for Innovation and Improvement. *Improvement Leaders' Guide: managing the human dimensions of change: personal and organisational change.* Coventry: NHS Institute for Innovation and Improvement; 2005.

4 Royal Pharmaceutical Society of Great Britain. *Beyond the Baseline: the role of clinical governance facilitators working with community pharmacists.* London: Royal Pharmaceutical Society of Great Britain; 2003.

5 Kubler-Ross E, Kessler D. *On Grief and Grieving: finding the meaning of grief through the five stages of loss.* London: Simon and Schuster; 2005.

6 Greenwood D, Levin M. *Introduction to Action Research: social research for change.* London: Sage; 1999.

7 Available at www.jiscinfonet.ac.uk/infokits/change-management (accessed 25 May 2010).

8 Weick KE, Quinn RE. Organisational change and development. *Annual Review of Psychology* 1999; **50**: 361–86.

9 NHS Institute for Innovation and Improvement. *Reviving a Stalled Effort.* www.institute.nhs.uk/quality_and_service_improvement_tools (accessed 21 May 2010).

Criteria and indicators for best practice in clinical audit

Healthcare Quality Improvement Partnership (HQIP)

The purpose of this appendix
- To set out the criteria by which to assess the quality of a clinical audit, and standards against which audits can be measured.

INTRODUCTION

During 2009, the Healthcare Quality Improvement Partnership (HQIP) consulted among healthcare professionals active in audit, both nationally and locally, across the UK on what they considered to be the essential criteria for good-quality audit. The result was this document, which was published in September 2009. It is adapted and reproduced here in full, with permission from HQIP. Copies of the document in a print-designed format can be downloaded from HQIP's website at www.hqip. org.uk/criteria-of-best-practice-in-clinical-audit, and the document can be adapted for use in any country (with permission and acknowledgement).

DEFINITION OF CLINICAL AUDIT

Clinical audit is a quality improvement process that seeks to improve patient care and outcomes through systematic review of care against explicit criteria. Where indicated, changes are implemented at an individual, team or service level, and further monitoring is used to confirm improvement in healthcare delivery.

(National Institute for Clinical Excellence, 2002)[1]

PURPOSE

The purpose of this guidance is to define the markers or indicators of good-quality clinical audit, at both national and local level, conducted both by individuals and (more commonly) by teams, taking into account the views of those active in audit at all levels – clinicians, managers and audit specialists.

The **purpose** of this activity was to set an agreed, definitive, widely consulted consensus standard for audit quality, which could then be used to assess the quality of audits in other processes. These include revalidation of individual professionals, the allocation of funding for audit, the offer of support (e.g. from audit departments) for audits proposed by provider teams, the accreditation or kite marking of audits and audit departments, the performance management of audit teams, the commissioning of services, and the regulation and performance management of healthcare.

The **aims of the process** were to be inclusive, by engaging people (including patients) from a range of disciplines, roles and locations, as well as having experience in the use of audit. The aim was to draw from the history and experience of audit over the last 40 years, starting work from accepted and agreed definitions instead of re-inventing terminology. We sought to be thorough and extensive, consulting widely and repeatedly at greater levels of detail, which allowed participants to reflect on their original views after others had made comments, and then to re-contribute.

PROCESS

This list of criteria against which to assess the quality of any clinical audit was derived from the following drafting consultation processes:

1 the identification of a large number of pre-existing but recent definitional lists of quality indicators for audit from the international literature
2 compiled from these, a synthesis document that incorporated the common elements and which was used as the basis for consultation
3 a series of focus groups that were conducted after an open invitation with those who run national audits and work locally on audit, including methodologists, clinicians, managers and audit staff, with representatives from professional bodies of several disciplines. These were held across England and involved 65 participants
4 further focus groups consisting of patients with experience of involvement in audit of a range of conditions
5 two workshops with attendees at the HQIP national conference of local audit practitioners (a further 60 participants)
6 wide email consultation with HQIP's list of contacts, which reflects the groups listed above (a total of 250 participants)
7 further consultation with the National Clinical Audit Advisory Group (*see* p. 186)
8 revalidation workshops that have discussed these criteria as a tool in the revalidation process, including members of the Academy of Medical Royal Colleges (the association of medical Royal Colleges in the UK)
9 a final email consultation with all of the above with the updated version.

OUTPUTS

These processes led to the identification of the following key headings, with definitional expansion in each case with regard to what the heading means, derived from the views expressed in focus group work and the broader consultation.

The consistent consensus view was that audit must have four stages of activity if it is to be considered a high-quality audit:

➤ Stage 1: Preparation and planning
➤ Stage 2: Measuring performance
➤ Stage 3: Implementing change
➤ Stage 4: Sustaining improvement.

Quality in audit is then further defined by detailed indicators or markers under each heading, as set out below.

These stages, and the definitional markers of quality within them, are common to both national and local audit work, although some of the emphasis will necessarily be different.

FOLLOWING THE CRITERIA

The 'criteria' given here are not criteria as used in their technical sense within clinical audit, but rather the term refers to the markers or attributes of a high-quality clinical audit as agreed by practitioners.

Of course audits vary greatly in style, size and orientation. Given this diversity, not every criterion or indicator will apply to every clinical audit project that is undertaken by every specialty, nor will they be relevant for consideration of audit products in all of the processes outlined above. The list given here represents a 'gold standard' that would apply to an ideal clinical audit project. In circumstances where a criterion or indicator cannot be applied, the reason should be followed and omissions made with exception and explanation.

The criteria have been designed to apply in principle to all types of audit (outcome, process and input, at the local, regional and national level, and by all professional disciplines), although inevitably some criteria are more applicable to one setting than to another, or will need to be adapted to specific settings.

TABLE A4.1 Criteria for best practice in clinical audit

Criteria	Key indicators	Remarks
Stage 1: Preparation and planning		
1 The topic for the audit is a priority	1.1 The audit topic reflects a local service, specialty or national priority which merits evaluation and where care could be improved or refined through audit	Some topics will be maintenance audits
	1.2 The key stakeholders, both clinical and non-clinical, agree that the audit topic is a priority	Stakeholders may include providers, commissioners, non-clinical managers, trust boards (or equivalents), clinicians, staff, patients/ service users and national organisations representing both clinicians and patients/service users
2 The audit measures against standards for quality of care	2.1 The audit standards are based upon the best available evidence	For example, NICE guidelines (or the equivalent), National Service Frameworks, national guidelines, etc. A literature source to identify suitable standards may be appropriate
		If there is no other evidence, the standards should be developed through an appropriate process (e.g. a properly designed consensus exercise). Some outcomes audits will have a role in defining or refining standards
	2.2 The audit standards are referenced back to their source, and an explanation of this link is provided	
	2.3 The audit standards are agreed and signed off by the clinical audit team and by those clinicians, clinical governance teams and patients to whose practice they relate	

(continued)

	Criteria	Key indicators	Remarks
2	**The audit measures (*cont.*)**	2.4 The audit standards are expressed in a form that enables measurement	For example, the standards are expressed as criteria that are 'SMART-compatible' (i.e. **S**pecific, **M**easurable, **A**chievable, **R**elevant and **T**heoretically sound) ('T' can also refer to **T**imely, which is appropriate as well, but needs to be in keeping with a scientific process)
3	**The organisation enables the conduct of the audit**	3.1 A written plan describes the structures and processes necessary to support the audit	This includes a statement about who provides the leadership, the composition of the audit project team, the frequency of meetings, how commitment from the key clinical and non-clinical stakeholders will be secured, and a communications plan that includes the production of a comprehensive audit report to disseminate the findings
		3.2 Staff have time to participate fully in the audit	As far as possible, audit work should be embedded in the routine work of clinicians. If clinicians will be required to give time over and above normal practice, this must be identified at the outset of the audit, and all relevant clinicians should be given protected time in which to participate
		3.3 The organisation provides the administrative and other practical support necessary to conduct the audit	When necessary this should be provided by experienced clinical audit support staff
		3.4 Any training necessary to conduct the audit is identified and provided	Managers need to accept reasonable training requirements to support effective delivery of audit programmes
		3.5 Any financial costs associated with running the audit are identified and met	

	Criteria	Key indicators	Remarks
4	**The audit engages with clinical and non-clinical stakeholders**	4.1 Where possible, the audit should review the practice of all clinical disciplines in the service unit or team whose work is relevant to the audit topic area	Most healthcare practice takes place in teams that include a variety of disciplines, and the audit should cover the whole team rather than the practice of individual disciplines within the team
		4.2 Those clinicians with senior responsibility for the area of healthcare that is being audited show commitment to the audit and provide the necessary leadership	This commitment should be at board level and, if appropriate, should involve commissioning organisations as well as providers
		4.3 There is ownership of the audit findings at the most senior management level. Responsibility to enact change resulting from an audit is accepted by those with power to implement change	
		4.4 The roles of stakeholders, and their accountability, are defined clearly from the outset and are included in the audit plan	
		4.5 All relevant stakeholders are involved from the beginning of the audit cycle through to completion	
		4.6 Active communication with stakeholders is maintained throughout the audit process	

(continued)

	Criteria	Key indicators	Remarks
5	**Patients or their representatives are involved in the audit if appropriate**	5.1 The patient group to whom the audit standards apply is clearly defined	
		5.2 The audit standards take full account of patient priorities and patient-defined outcomes	For example, the audit incorporates patient-reported outcome measures (PROMS)
		5.3 Patients/carers are recognised as key stakeholders in the audit process	If appropriate and feasible, patient representatives and relevant patient organisations are involved in audit governance, treated as stakeholders, and where appropriate, in all stages of the audit cycle are treated as equal members of the audit team
		5.4 Patients who are members of the audit team are fully informed about what is expected from them in terms of participation, commitment and workload	Not all patients and/or patient organisations will be members of the audit team, but as relevant stakeholders they should still be kept informed and engaged
		5.5 If required, patients who are members of the audit team are given basic audit training to enable them to contribute effectively to the audit process	
		5.6 Patients are kept informed throughout the audit process about timescales, progress, results and actions	All communications should use plain English, avoiding the use of jargon and acronyms

Criteria	Key indicators	Remarks
Stage 2: Measuring performance		
6 The audit method is described in a written protocol	6.1 The timetable for the audit is described, including timescales for completion and re-audit, where necessary	
	6.2 The protocol describes the methodology and data collection process in detail	
	6.3 Systematic consideration is given to ethics, data confidentiality and consent issues, and Caldicott principles are applied	Audits should not require approval from a research ethics committee, but still have ethical issues to address (e.g. maintaining confidentiality and obtaining process consent)
	6.4 The methods used in the audit are recorded so that re-audit can be undertaken later in the audit cycle	
7 The target sample should be appropriate, in order to generate meaningful results	7.1 If a sample of the population is to be audited, the method for sampling is that which is best suited to measuring performance against the standards and, as best as possible, scientifically reliable	Those planning the audit should consider seeking statistical advice about how to ensure that the sample is adequately significant, representative, clinically relevant, unbiased, etc.
	7.2 The sample size is sufficient to generate meaningful results	Those planning the audit should consider seeking statistical advice about sample size relevant to a given topic

(continued)

	Criteria	Key indicators	Remarks
7	**The target sample** *(cont.)*	7.3 When necessary, the sample allows for adjustment for case mix	Those planning the audit should consider seeking statistical advice about case-mix adjustment
8	**The data collection process is robust**	8.1 The audit utilises pre-existing data sets where possible	Those planning the audit should consult with appropriate advisers to identify any relevant data sets, but these should be used with caution, depending on their reliability
		8.2 The data collection tool(s) and process have been validated	This might include undertaking simple statistical tests on the data collection tools to examine their reliability and accuracy in practice, or using data collection tools that have already been proven for this type of audit
		8.3 The data collection process aims to ensure complete capture of data	This should demonstrate full case ascertainment and full completion of each case within the audit. Any excluded data should be explained
9	**The data are analysed and the results reported in a way that maximises the impact of the audit**	9.1 Data are analysed, and feedback of the results is given, so that the momentum of the audit is maintained in line with the agreed timetable	
		9.2 The results of the audit are presented in the most appropriate manner for each potential audience, to ensure that the audit results stimulate and support action planning	For example, the use of accessible graphics
		9.3 The results are communicated effectively to all key stakeholders, including patients	Through presentations at meetings, in written reports, posters, etc., in such a form as to be easily understood

Criteria	Key indicators	Remarks
Stage 3: Implementing change		
10 An action plan is developed and implemented to take forward any recommendations made	10.1 The audit results are channelled into a plan that sets out the areas where attention is needed and where there is good compliance, recommends the actions required to address the identified issues, and sets out how these will be carried through	Recommended actions should be targeted at service, team, managerial or organisational level, where possible. Local teams will need to devise their own action plans in relation to the results of national audits
	10.2 The action plan has the agreement of all or the majority of the stakeholders involved in the audit process, including managers who may have to commit resources to the changes, and patients whose care they will affect	Any barriers to implementing change are identified in the plan and action is taken to address them. A suitable risk management strategy will need to be incorporated into the plan
	10.3 The plan identifies who is responsible for taking which actions and by when, and when the achievement of actions will be reviewed	
	10.4 The plan identifies any financial or other resource implications associated with the recommended actions	Managers need to be involved from the start to ensure that any resource requirements are anticipated
	10.5 The results and the following action plan are communicated and distributed widely and effectively, including to managers and patients	There should be a clear pathway through which the audit results are reviewed by the immediate clinical team and their patients, and by the senior management team responsible

(continued)

Criteria	Key indicators	Remarks
10 An action plan *(cont.)*	10.6	Timetables for implementation need to be set
	Implementation of the action is closely monitored and progress is regularly communicated to stakeholders. Those with responsibility oversee and drive the implementation of the action plan and its subsequent follow-up	

Stage 4: Achieving and sustaining improvement

Criteria	Key indicators	Remarks
11 The audit is a cyclical process which demonstrates that improvement has been achieved and sustained	11.1	Re-audit can measure continuing compliance with the audit standards, confirm that recommendations arising from the initial audit have been implemented, or measure whether good practice has been maintained.
	The topic is re-audited to complete the audit cycle where necessary	In some cases, re-audit may not be necessary or possible (e.g. if all standards are met in the first audit, or there has been a significant structural change)
	11.2	
	Where recommended action has not been achieved in full, the topic is re-audited at agreed intervals	
	11.3	Audits that demonstrate both compliance and non-compliance should be widely shared and made widely available
	The results of re-audit are recorded and disseminated appropriately, including to patients	

REFERENCE

1 National Institute for Health and Clinical Excellence. *Principles for Best Practice in Clinical Audit.* Oxford: Radcliffe Medical Press; 2002.

Clinical audit: a guide for NHS boards and partners

John Bullivant and Andrew Corbett-Nolan

> **The purpose of this appendix**
> - To set out for governing bodies of healthcare organisations why they take responsibility for clinical audit, how it can be a useful process for them, and how they can maximise the value of clinical audit programmes.

INTRODUCTION

This summary is adapted from *Clinical Audit: a simple guide for NHS boards and partners*, which was written and published in 2010 by John Bullivant and Andrew Corbett-Nolan from the Good Governance Institute in partnership with HQIP. It is reproduced here with the permission of HQIP and GGI.[1]

This summary from the guide is targeted at managing organisations in England, with suggestions as to how they should oversee clinical audit programmes, but much of what is described here is relevant to the way in which **any** healthcare organisation can monitor clinical quality as a whole within the context of clinical or integrated governance.

THE CONTEXT

Clinical audit has been endorsed by the Department of Health in England in successive strategic documents as a significant way in which the quality of clinical care can be measured and improved. Originally, clinical audit was developed as a process by which clinicians reviewed their own practice. However, clinical audit is now recognised as an effective mechanism for improving the quality of care that patients receive within the context of organisational strategic governance at board level. It offers a crucial component of the drive to improve quality. Boards have not always done enough in the past to measure quality, but now they must do so, and clinical audit provides a mechanism for this.

THE VALUE OF DIFFERENT PROCESSES

There are a variety of related processes which also have a role in the measurement and improvement of quality, such as confidential or significant event inquiries, patient surveys, research, peer review and internal audit. None of these replace clinical audit, and systematic clinical audit is the main way of assessing compliance of ongoing clinical care against evidence-based standards.

Clinical audit needs to be a strategic priority for boards as part of their clinical governance function. It is effectively the review of clinical performance against agreed standards, and the refining of clinical practice as a result. It is one of the key compliance tools at a board's disposal, and has an important role within the assurance framework. Clinical audit needs to be carefully compared with, and is complementary to, internal audit. However, they are two different processes.

THE ROLE OF THE MANAGING BODY IN DRIVING QUALITY IMPROVEMENT

Boards or comparable managing bodies have a role in driving quality assurance, compliance, internal audit and 'closing the loop.' They need to ensure that the recommendations of reviews and clinical audits are enacted by seeking assurance that improvements in care have been made. Ideally this should be part of an overall quality framework and should be reported in the trust's publicly reported 'Quality Accounts' – the reporting system that NHS trusts in England have been required to use since April 2010 to identify what they are doing with regard to quality.[2]

Trusts will be regulated and performance managed against their participation in clinical audit and the findings of audit.

Boards will want assurance that there is a clinical audit strategy in place which meets their strategic priorities, and which also:
➤ meets national commitments and expectations
➤ prioritises local concerns
➤ integrates financial and clinical audit
➤ delivers a return on investment
➤ ensures that improvements are implemented and sustained.

In England, a primary care trust or PCT (the body with responsibility for commissioning health services for a local area until 2013, when this responsibility will be transferred to general practitioner consortia) has specific responsibilities in relation to clinical audit that should be managed through the Professional Executive Committee (PEC) or an equivalent committee of GPs and other clinicians.

Boards should use clinical audit to confirm that current practice compares favourably with evidence of good practice, and to ensure that where this is not the case, changes are made that improve the delivery of care.

THE SPECIFIC CONTRIBUTION OF CLINICAL AUDIT

Clinical audit can:

➤ provide evidence of current practice against national guidelines or NHS standards
➤ provide information about the structures and processes of a healthcare service and patient outcomes
➤ assess how closely local practice resembles recommended practice
➤ answer the question 'Are we actually doing what we think we are doing?'
➤ provide evidence about the quality of care in a service to establish confidence among all of its stakeholders (staff, patients, carers, managers and the public).

BOARD OVERSIGHT OF CLINICAL AUDIT PROGRAMMES

Boards will want to be assured that clinical audits are:

➤ **material** (i.e. that they are prioritised to focus on key issues, and that the value outweighs the cost)
➤ **professionally undertaken and completed** (i.e. clinical audits are undertaken and completed to professional standards, including the quality of data being analysed)
➤ **producing results** that are shared and acted upon
➤ **followed by improvements** that are sustained.

There are clear questions that boards should ask about any clinical audit programme in their trust. In order to advance clinical audit, roles and responsibilities need to be clearly established. The board's role is to ensure that clinical audit is strategic, happens regularly, is clinically effective and cost-effective, and is linked to the Quality, Innovation, Productivity and Prevention (QIPP) agenda.[3]

> **BOX A5.1** Clinical audit – 10 simple rules for NHS boards
>
> 1 Ensure that clinical audit strategy is allied to broader interests and targets that the board needs to address.
> 2 Develop a programme of work which gives direction and focus with regard to how and which clinical audit activity will be supported in the organisation.
> 3 Develop appropriate processes for instigating clinical audit as a direct result of adverse clinical events, critical incidents and breaches in patient safety.
> 4 Check the clinical audit programme for relevance to board strategic interests and concerns. Ensure that the results are turned into action plans, followed through and re-audit completed.

5 Ensure that there is a lead clinician who manages clinical audit within the trust, with partners/suppliers outside, and who is clearly accountable at board level.

6 Ensure that patient involvement is considered in all elements of clinical audit, including priority setting, means of engagement, sharing of results and plans for sustainable improvement.

7 Build clinical audit into planning, performance management and reporting.

8 Ensure with others that clinical audit crosses care boundaries and encompasses the whole patient pathway.

9 Agree the criteria for prioritisation of clinical audits, balancing national and local interests and the need to address specific local risks, strategic interests and concerns.

10 Check whether clinical audit results provide evidence of complaints, and if so, develop a system whereby complaints act as a stimulus to review and improvement.

REFERENCES

1 Bullivant J, Corbett-Nolan A. *Clinical Audit: a simple guide for NHS boards and partners.* London: HQIP; 2010. http://hqip.org.uk/assets/Uploads/NewFolder/HQIP-Clinical-Audit-Simple-Guide-online1.pdf (accessed 3 August 2010).

2 Department of Health. *Quality Accounts Toolkit: advisory guidance for providers of NHS services producing Quality Accounts for the year 2009/2010.* London: Department of Health; 2010. www.dh.gov.uk/en/Publicationsandstatistics/Publications/PublicationsPolicyAndGuidance/DH_112359 (accessed 16 July 2010).

3 Department of Health. *Implementing the Next Stage Review visions: the quality and productivity challenge.* London: Department of Health; 2009.

Patient and public engagement (PPE) in clinical audit

HQIP

The purpose of this appendix

- To set out why engagement of patients in clinical audit governance and practice is desirable, and how this can be achieved.

This appendix is adapted from HQIP's guidance, which was published in 2010[1] and is reproduced here with permission.

INTRODUCTION

HQIP, as an organisation set up by a consortium of professional and patient groups, has several key aims in relation to patient involvement that are expressed in the way it works as an organisation and the models of clinical quality improvement that it recommends. For example:

➤ patients and professionals in the NHS need to work together to improve quality

➤ patients or their representatives should play a role in advising on the products or guidance that it develops as an organisation

➤ patients need to be involved and engaged in the selection of initiatives to improve quality, in the governance of these initiatives (e.g. clinical audit), in the collection of data for the audit, and as part of the dissemination of the products to ensure, as consumers, that they are provided with reassurance and possible choice of healthcare provider, where such a choice is realistic or possible.

THE HQIP PATIENT NETWORK

The HQIP Patient Network, which is comprised of service users with an interest in and experience of clinical audit, was set up in early 2009. It identified, and therefore recommended, that guidance was needed to support patient engagement in clinical audit. Patients were consulted throughout the development of this document via the use of focus groups and email consultations, and they identified much of the content of this work.

THE PURPOSE OF THIS GUIDANCE

Sometimes also known as **patient and public involvement (PPI)**, a fuller concept, **patient and public engagement (PPE)**, has developed, partly from grounding in services for people with mental health or substance misuse problems, so that now nearly all of healthcare understands the importance and value of PPE. This appendix seeks to interpret the principles of PPE specifically in relation to clinical audit.

This document sets out guidance covering:

➤ **why** PPE is a legal requirement and also a genuine benefit to clinical audit
➤ **how** to involve and engage patients, adapting recent standards and indicators published by the NHS Centre for Involvement (NCI) and integrating them with HQIP's patient involvement criteria as detailed in Section 5 of the *Criteria and Indicators for Best Practice in Clinical Audit* (*see* Appendix 4 in this volume).

SCOPE OF THE DOCUMENT

This guidance has been produced by HQIP, after wide consultation, to encourage and facilitate patient and public engagement in clinical audit. The document:

➤ is aimed at those who run, manage, design or are involved in clinical audits nationally, regionally or locally, whether they are managers, clinicians or audit specialist support staff
➤ focuses on the engagement of patient and public representatives, including those who are currently receiving or have previously received care that has been subject to a clinical audit, or those who volunteer to participate in clinical audit practice
➤ covers how information about clinical audit, including the results, should be communicated to patients and the public, to enhance their knowledge and aid their decision making about services
➤ represents the views of patients about how they want to be involved in and informed about clinical audit.

WHY SHOULD PATIENTS BE INVOLVED IN CLINICAL AUDIT?
Background to PPE

Internationally, PPE is increasingly seen to enhance all healthcare, including clinical audit, by serving as a marker of services that are oriented, planned and delivered in terms of patient interests.[2] The involvement of patients provides a different perspective from that of clinicians. Within clinical audit it is a way of showing that what is being measured matters to patients, and that their views are taken into account. Historically, clinical audit has been an area dominated by clinical interests, but there is now a new need to ensure that this is balanced by effective PPE.

The Department of Health in England has published a range of guidance and legislation to promote PPE within health and social care as a whole, and strives to ensure that it is incorporated into the way in which the NHS makes decisions and improves services.[3]

Models of involvement

Historically, Sherry Arnstein's ladder of participation has been used to describe a hierarchy of ways in which a patient/service user may wish to become involved, and illustrates what level of involvement an organisation has reached.[4]

The ladder has been frequently adapted, but often the models show **information** (informing patients of the services available, expectations and the results of a clinical audit) as the lowest level of engagement.

Consultation is often mistaken for a high level of involvement, but is commonly interpreted as merely sending out a survey. It is placed in the middle of the ladder and is considered to represent a lower level than actual engaging with or partnering the patient.

The highest level of engagement is described as **partnership**. This refers to working together to develop a clinical audit from the beginning, participating throughout the process and with potential for some audits being **patient led**.[5]

The benefits of PPE in clinical audit

The evidence for the value of PPE generally for both patient and healthcare professions has been summarised in the academic literature.[2,6] These benefits are also likely to be achieved through participation in audit.

Experts

Those who have lived with or cared for someone with a particular illness are 'experts' in the condition. The patient has a subjective and most valid viewpoint based on actual experience about where quality could, and should, be improved.

Different perspectives

Patients' direct experience of care gives them a different perspective about ways to improve the quality of a service. Patients and clinicians will make different choices about the various elements of care that are reflected in standards and which are measured by a clinical audit. This can lead to improvements which are more responsive to patient needs.[7]

Creating a desired service/successful clinical audit that is more attuned to patient interest

By becoming involved in a PPE programme, patients can influence and participate in the development of services that are better focused on their needs. Through participation and engagement, a patient can enhance clinical audit by assisting with the developing action plans that address the concerns they will have raised, thereby giving the staff a clearer picture of what changes are needed within a service, and helping to ensure that services are being provided in the way that people want.

Informed choices

Clinical audit results can provide patients and the public with more knowledge about the quality of care in a particular healthcare setting, enabling them to make more informed choices, where this is possible, about where they obtain treatment. As part of good PPE in clinical audit, the communication of audit results should be undertaken in a way that ensures it is accessible and understandable to the public (i.e. written in clear simple language with clearly understandable conclusions and data). Public reporting will raise public confidence in the NHS as it boosts trust and satisfaction, and PPE in clinical audit will give patients a deeper insight into the care that is provided. Provider organisations should beware of suppressing clinical audit results that are negative or critical about care.

Many clinicians, and some managers, are concerned about audit data being used to inform patient choice. They may feel that the primary purpose of audit is internal review of compliance with clinical standards. Their concerns would be that audit data can be difficult to understand, and very often require a degree of interpretation and context to clarify the meaning. For example, straight 'like-for-like' comparisons may be problematic, as issues of case mix may mask variation in clinical competence and lead to uninformed expressions of choice rather than informed ones. Furthermore, some clinicians are unclear about how the 'choice argument' is applied.

HQIP shares and understands these arguments. Inevitably there must be a balance. In practice many patients neither want nor need to exercise choice – they want to be able to receive good services everywhere – and in this context choice is a diversion from the pursuit of universal high standards. Nonetheless, patients have a right to see whether a unit or individual practitioner is competent, rather than just having to assume that they are. Those who participate in clinical audit should share their audit results, even if they need to have appropriate caveats in order to make accurate comparison.

Improving health

Strong social support networks have been shown to benefit health, and increased confidence and self-esteem are directly related to health and well-being. Being involved in improving the quality of care can bring health benefits to patients through the satisfaction of having influenced their care, being listened to, and from the social interaction and engagement that this offers.

Engaging new people

Finding new people to comment on or become involved in informing care is sometimes a challenge. For example, in England local NHS patient involvement networks (LINks) provide the connection that trusts need to access interested and enthusiastic patients and members of the public who may want to become involved in clinical audit. National organisations can do the same. For example, the Myocardial Infarction National Audit Project (MINAP) made links with patients through the British Heart Foundation.

There may also be opportunities to reach out to people who want to comment and give their views, but who do not necessarily want to be extensively involved (e.g. through the use of electronic media). The various websites that exist to channel patients with a view about the care that they receive, such as Patient Opinion (www. patientopinion.org.uk), provide opportunities to widen the pool of individuals who might become engaged.

Responsiveness to local needs

Communication with LINks, or other local patient forums and organisations, provides a way of listening to local people and developing clinical audits that are responsive to local needs. Patients and the public feel a greater ownership of local health services if they are consulted and listened to. Furthermore, LINks can help to access other people who are often 'seldom heard'. This will contribute to a more cohesive local society and active citizenship.

Developing improved quality of care

Patients and service users have a legitimate role in determining what constitutes high quality and in contributing ideas for improvement. PPE gives clinical audit insight into the preferences of patients with regard to suitable indicators of the quality of care provided. It assists in the identification of what is needed to maintain and improve care in the future.

A study drawing on reviews conducted between 1998 and 2006 has evaluated the efficacy of patient-focused interventions. The evidence in this study suggested that carefully designed interventions can have positive effects on patient satisfaction and outcomes.[8]

Measuring outcomes and experience

When considering the quality of care from patients' perspectives, there are two main aspects, namely its effectiveness (outcome) and its humanity (experience). We all want to receive effective care in a humane way.

Traditionally, the outcome of care, if measured at all, has been based on clinicians' assessments. Given that most care aims to reduce patients' symptoms and disability and improve their quality of life, it makes sense to ask patients directly. Recently, **patient-reported outcome measures (PROMs)** have started to be used in audits. Indeed, their use has been mandatory in the NHS for patients undergoing one of four elective operations since April 2009. The National Elective Surgery PROMs

Programme is a major initiative in England, with potentially around 250 000 patients involved. The use of PROMs is now being encouraged in all national clinical audits that consider the outcome of care. Involvement of patients in this way can complement clinicians' reports of outcomes.

Patients' experiences of the humanity of their care (e.g. dignity and respect, receiving the information requested, waiting times, cleanliness of facilities) are just as important as outcomes, and can be collected from them by means of questionnaires. **Patient-reported experience measures (PREMs)** can be used to assess the extent to which the care that was offered and provided met criteria of good quality. As with any survey, questionnaires need to be reliable and valid.

THE CLINICAL AUDIT CYCLE

HQIP's *Criteria and Indicators for Best Practice in Clinical Audit* (reproduced as Appendix 4 in this volume) was compiled after extensive consultation with clinical staff, patients and audit professionals, and represents the 'gold standard' that can be applied to a good clinical audit project or process. It highlights four main stages of the clinical audit cycle, which are summarised below.

Stage 1: Preparation and planning (including for re-audit)
➤ Organisational arrangements
➤ Stakeholder engagement
➤ Patient engagement

Stage 2: Measuring performance
➤ Clinical audit methodology
➤ Data collection process
➤ Data analysis and reporting

Stage 3: Implementing change
➤ Action plan development (including action to take forward any recommendations made)

Stage 4: Achieving and sustaining improvement (including re-audit where necessary)
➤ Re-audit
➤ Continuous improvement

This framework identifies patients and carers as key stakeholders in the clinical audit process, and recommends 'that if appropriate and feasible, patients, patient representatives and relevant patient organisations should be involved at all stages of the audit cycle as equal members of the audit team.'

HOW TO INVOLVE AND ENGAGE PATIENTS AND THE PUBLIC IN CLINICAL AUDIT

HQIP's *Criteria and Indicators for Best Practice in Clinical Audit* refers to patient representation and participation as a key element in achieving good-quality clinical audit.

The suggestions on how to involve patients (and carers as appropriate) are anchored around the draft set of six organisational standards of the former NHS Centre for Involvement (NCI),[9] which identify what NHS organisations need to do to ensure meaningful PPE in clinical practice, and are adapted for this guidance to make them specifically applicable to clinical audit.

This framework can be used as a helpful structure to support and aid PPE in clinical audit, with suggestions given as to how the standards may be achieved. HQIP has adapted the standards and included additional criteria in order to give more in-depth guidance for specific engagement in clinical audit.

Standard 1

People

➤ Roles and responsibilities for PPE are clearly defined, visible and effective throughout the organisation, including leadership at all levels.
➤ Patients involved in clinical audit know what their role is and what they are being asked to do. This needs to be widely understood and agreed, or patient engagement will be tokenistic and unfocused, and patients will not feel valued and their skills and experience will not be utilised effectively.

Criteria

➤ PPE in an organisation is managed and led. Staff and clinicians who lead clinical audit projects are trained and informed about the benefits of PPE. Systems and policies are in place, and steps are taken to engage patients and carers in clinical audit.
➤ Patients who are members of a clinical audit management or delivery team are fully informed about what is expected of them in terms of participation, commitment and workload.
➤ The patient group to whom the clinical audit standards apply is clearly defined.
➤ If required, patients who are members of the clinical audit team are given basic training to enable them to contribute effectively to the process.

How?

➤ The organisation has named individuals responsible for defined PPE in clinical audit.
➤ All staff and volunteers within an organisation, or working on clinical audit, know their responsibility for PPE.
➤ Patients and carers with formal PPE links to the organisation have clearly defined role descriptions covering the scope of their engagement in clinical audit.

➤ There are policies in place to support PPE activity, including:
  — a reimbursement policy and a reward and recognition policy
  — a communications policy
  — a policy on information governance related to patient engagement
  — a policy or policies outlining governance arrangements for PPE
  — a policy or policies outlining health and safety arrangements for PPE
  — a policy on support available to involved users.
➤ There is a training programme in place to support PPE, including:
  — PPE in induction training of staff
  — the need to involve patients
  — training of patients and public volunteers.

Standard 2
PPE strategy and vision
➤ There is an explicit strategic framework that makes clear the organisation's commitment to PPE.
➤ The rationale and purpose behind PPE are understood by those responsible for management, and its value is shared by those with responsibility. This shared vision is expressed within a strategic framework.

Criteria
➤ PPE is owned at board or senior management level.
➤ There is an explicit link between the organisation's clinical audit strategy and its PPE strategy.

How?
➤ The organisation has a defined set of objectives for PPE activity, which cover clinical audit.
➤ There is a publicly available document, approved by the board or management group, that sets out the organisation's vision for PPE, and makes it clear that this covers clinical audit.

Standard 3
PPE structures
➤ Structures are in place at all levels of the organisation that facilitate dialogue and communication with patients, carers, the wider community and the public.

Criteria
➤ A major effort is made to ensure that the patient is engaged systematically, especially in communication or dissemination strategies.
➤ Patients are kept informed and supported throughout the clinical audit process with regard to timescales, progress, results and actions. All communication should use simple language that is free from jargon and acronyms.

How?

➤ An organisation's clinical audit programme, and the results of this, should be proactively communicated to patients and the public via appropriate communication channels (e.g. mailings, meetings, LINks groups, ward notice boards, websites, newsletters or local media). This should include clinical audit results that are critical as well as those which are positive.

➤ The value and potential impact of any national or local clinical audit are effectively communicated to patients who will be directly affected. A greater understanding of the process and their role within it is more likely to increase patients' and carers' support.

➤ Progress updates and clinical audit results are shared with patients in an accessible format. If too many clinical audit data are presented, clinicians, managers and patients alike will find them difficult to understand. Efforts should be made to communicate them more easily.

➤ National clinical audits should be proactive in assisting local provider organisations and commissioning bodies with their patient communications by supplying relevant clinical audit data and results as required. National clinical audits must make every effort to ensure that their data are usable, as this helps to prompt change, and that they are timely with regard to patient interests.

Standard 4

PPE processes

➤ Processes are in place at all levels of the organisation that enable patients, carers, the wider community and the public to effectively influence the planning, delivery, development, review and decision making about changing and improving healthcare services.

Criteria

➤ Patient engagement is integral to an organisation. Such engagement has a direct impact at all levels in the organisation and in relation to such processes as clinical audit, at an early stage.

➤ The organisation takes steps to ensure PPE in the setting of clinical audit priorities and in the development of the annual clinical audit programme.

➤ Patients are involved in helping to plan and enact changes arising from clinical audit, and to monitor results.

➤ Where the public is part of the clinical audit team, systems must be in place so that the Caldicott guidelines[10] are not breached (i.e. access to other patient data must be restricted).

➤ Clinical audit standards take full account of patient priorities and patient-defined outcomes. Where possible the audit incorporates PROMs.

How?

➤ The local organisation or national clinical audit is able to demonstrate that it evaluates both the experience and outcomes of PPE activity and their impact on staff, patients and the public.

➤ The results of the clinical audit and action plans are openly shared and communicated with patients and the public.

➤ Patients are involved in both the conduct of clinical audits and their governance.

➤ Patient groups are advised of the healthcare organisation's clinical audit programme and supplied with results on a routine basis.

➤ Any reporting framework for regulatory purposes (e.g. Quality Accounts in England[11]) should show organisational participation in clinical audit and how patients have been involved.

➤ Patients are involved in standard selection for clinical audit, or were involved in the development of national standards which are used. Any national standards that are set should be reviewed for their relevance to patient interests and added to as necessary with validated patient-relevant standards. For example, in the UK, NICE guidelines are developed with extensive patient involvement.[12]

Standard 5

Partnership working

➤ The organisation has clearly defined structures and processes in place that enable effective dialogue with partner organisations at national, local and regional levels.

Criteria

➤ Patients/carers are recognised as key stakeholders in the clinical audit process and, if appropriate, patient representatives and relevant patient organisations are involved in all stages of the clinical audit cycle as equal members of the clinical audit team.

How?

➤ The organisation has defined pathways mapping how it works with relevant patient groups and other health and social care partners, including:
  — LINks
  — voluntary and community organisations at the local or national level
  — disease/condition-specific interest groups, locally and nationally
  — hard-to-reach and 'seldom heard' individuals, groups or communities
  — overview and scrutiny committees
  — strategic health authorities (SHAs)
  — other healthcare organisations
  — social care providers

— advocacy and support agencies and organisations

— independent organisations.

➤ Patients who may be affected by changes in practice resulting from clinical audits of services that they use should be consulted, advised and involved in those audits.

➤ Patients should be encouraged to request clinical audit results.

➤ Carers and other relatives need to be involved in clinical audits, alongside the patient, in cases where the patient cannot contribute fully.

➤ Informal and ad hoc systems of engaging the public in clinical audit and other PPE processes, such as online capture, can have a role in any engagement strategy.

Standard 6

PPE monitoring and evaluation of effectiveness

➤ Systems are in place that monitor PPE activity and evaluate effectiveness and impact, and which influence future PPE planning.

➤ It is very easy to assume that PPE is worth doing, and that the very existence of engagement processes is sufficient. However, they need to be constantly reviewed with regard to their effectiveness and value.

Criteria

➤ PPE activity needs to be monitored, evaluated and reported.

How?

➤ The organisation accurately maps and records all PPE activity on a continuous basis, and this is reported and managed at board/senior management level.

➤ PPE is fully documented in all clinical audit reports.

SUMMARY

The involvement and engagement of patients in clinical audit is vital, and is a marker of high-quality audit.

In essence, the engagement of patients and public in clinical audit, both nationally and locally, needs to involve:

➤ engagement in governance and strategic direction of clinical audit

➤ consultation with regard to standards (and outcomes, where appropriate) to be audited

➤ active participation in collection and analysis of clinical audit data

➤ engaging the public in communication activity about clinical audit, partly as patients or potential patients of treatment, and also through involvement in governance.

In order to achieve this, patient engagement needs to be part of the whole conception of the clinical audit, from beginning to end, and it needs to be an integral part of the fabric of the whole project.

The information in these guidelines is open to adaptation, and the suggestions are not intended as absolute instructions, but HQIP hopes that they will provide organisations with enough information to ensure that there is PPE within their own clinical audits.

HQIP will continue to develop and publish further guidelines on various aspects of patient engagement, and these will be posted on the HQIP website.

REFERENCES

 1 Healthcare Quality Improvement Partnership (HQIP). *Patient and Public Engagement (PPE): PPE in clinical audit.* London: HQIP; 2010. www.hqip.org.uk/patient-and-public-engagement (accessed 3 August 2010).
 2 Crawford MJ, Rutter D, Manley C *et al. Systematic review of involving patients in the planning and development of health care. British Medical Journal* 2002; **325:** 1263.
 3 This guidance and much other relevant material are available at www.library.nhs.uk/PPI/SearchResults.aspx?tabID=289&catID=8684 (accessed 25 May 2010).
 4 Arnstein SR. A ladder of citizen participation. *Journal of the American Institute of Planners* 1969; **35:** 216–24.
 5 Hanley B, Bradburn J, Barnes M *et al. Involving the Public in NHS, Public Health and Social Care Research: briefing notes for researchers.* 2nd edn. Eastleigh: INVOLVE; 2003.
 6 Coulter A, Ellins J. Effectiveness of strategies for informing, educating, and involving patients. *British Medical Journal* 2007; **335:** 24–7.
 7 Howell E, Graham C, Hoffman A *et al.* Comparison of patients' assessments of the quality of stroke care with audit findings, *Quality and Safety in Health Care* 2007; **16:** 450–5.
 8 National Institute for Health and Clinical Excellence (NICE). *Community Engagement to Improve Health.* London: NICE; 2008. www.nice.org.uk/PH009 (accessed 25 May 2010).
 9 These standards have not been published, and remained in draft form when the NHS Centre for Involvement was closed in 2009. They have been adapted for use in the HQIP document. The draft version can be accessed within this report from the NCI, available at www.nhscentreforinvolvement.nhs.uk/docs/OD%20report%20-%20Peterborough%20Community%20Services.pdf (accessed 25 May 2010).
10 The Caldicott Committee, Department of Health. *Report on the Review of Patient-Identifiable Information.* London: Department of Health; 1997.
11 Department of Health. *The National Health Service (Quality Accounts) Regulations 2010.* London: Department of Health; 2010. www.opsi.gov.uk/si/si2010/uksi_20100279_en_18.NHS (accessed 16 July 2010).
12 National Institute for Health and Clinical Excellence (NICE). *Policy Statement on Patient Engagement.* www.nice.org.uk/getinvolved/patientandpublicinvolvement/patient_and_public_involvement.jsp (accessed 25 May 2010).

Further sources of help and information

We offer here a selection of other points of contact that provide a useful body of information about clinical audit, and best practice in conducting it. This list is not designed to be definitive, but to suggest a number of sources which, in the opinion of the authors of this book, offer a range of high-quality material that complements the guidance available on the HQIP website and in this book.

Similarly, we do not provide a lengthy list of further reading. The various chapters of this book provide a large number of references which can be followed up by anyone seeking further information on specific topics.

HQIP

The HQIP website (www.hqip.org.uk) provides the most complete and easy-to-use compendium of resources on clinical audit worldwide, as well as links to other sources of help. Rather than providing an extensive list of other websites here, we would encourage any reader who wishes to learn more about clinical audit to use this site as a point of navigation to other sources.

The website contains access to a large number of downloadable reference guides to various aspects of clinical audit, including its organisation, with material aimed both at clinicians and at those who support clinical audit and work in it full-time. Many of these reference guides have been cited throughout this volume, but a large number of others are included as well.

Among these resources we would draw attention to two other simple 'how to' guides on clinical audit practice, aimed at specific groups, which are complementary to this volume. For doctors, especially physicians, *Local Clinical Audit: Handbook for Physicians* by Jonathan Potter, Claire Fuller and Martin Ferris, and published jointly by the Royal College of Physicians and HQIP in 2010, is particularly valuable (it can be found at www.hqip.org.uk/assets/Dev-Team-Uploads/Local-clinical-audit-handbook-for-physicians-August-2010-v3.pdf).

For those who are helping to manage audits conducted by junior doctors, Nancy Dixon's handbook, *A Guide to Involving Junior Doctors in Clinical Audit* (www.hqip.org.uk/assets/5-HQIP-CA-PD-026-Guide-to-Involving-Junior-Doctors-in-Clinical-Audit-19-April-2010.pdf), is also very useful. Finally, for anyone involved in clinical audit, an older resource that still contains valuable insights is the *Clinical Audit Handbook*, by Graham Copeland (www.hqip.org.uk/assets/Downloads/Practical-Clinical-Audit-Handbook-CGSupport.pdf).

In addition to the above, we would recommend the following:

➤ Ghosh R, ed. *Clinical Audit for Doctors.* Nottingham: Developmedica; 2009.
➤ Chambers R. *Clinical Audit in Primary Care: demonstrating quality and outcomes.* Oxford: Radcliffe Publishing; 2005.

OTHER ORGANISATIONS

Nearly all of the UK Royal Colleges' websites contain references to work on clinical audit, but for some of them membership-dependent log-in is required. Listed below is a selection of sources that are free to access, together with other organisations that are active in the field.

National Clinical Audit Advisory Group (NCAAG)

This group offers advice to the Department of Health in England on clinical audit matters, and as such it works closely with HQIP.
www.dh.gov.uk/ab/NCAAG/DH_099788

National Institute for Health and Clinical Excellence (NICE)

www.nice.org.uk/usingguidance/implementationtools/auditadvice/audit_advice.jsp

Royal College of Physicians

www.rcplondon.ac.uk/clinical-standards/organisation/Pages/Clinical-Audit.aspx

Royal College of Psychiatrists

www.rcpsych.ac.uk/quality/quality,accreditationaudit.aspx

Clinical Audit Support Centre (authors of Chapters 2 to 5 of this book)

www.clinicalauditsupport.com

Healthcare Quality Quest (author of Appendix 1 of this book, and various resources on the HQIP site)

www.hqq.co.uk

Quality Improvement Scotland

www.clinicalgovernance.scot.nhs.uk/section2/audit.asp

NHS Information Centre

This organisation manages national audits in the UK and also communicates other health data on behalf of the NHS.
www.ic.nhs.uk/ncasp

The Health Foundation

A charitable body with a strong interest in clinically-led quality improvement, including clinical audit.
www.health.org.uk

JOURNALS

The following journals specifically address clinical audit:

Journal of Clinical Audit
www.dovepress.com/clinical-audit-journal

The Online Journal of Clinical Audits
www.clinicalaudits.com/index.php/ojca

Journals that occasionally cover clinical audit (selected) include the following:

Journal of Evaluation in Clinical Practice
www.blackwellpublishing.com/journal.asp?ref=1356-1294

International Journal of Health Care Quality Assurance
http://info.emeraldinsight.com/products/journals/journals.htm?PHPSESSID=aa4o
sinjehsohi2e8jg0vo1bj4&id=ijhcqa

International Journal of Quality in Health Care
www.oxfordjournals.org/our_journals/intqhc/about.html

List of abbreviations

BACR	British Association of Cardiac Rehabilitation
BRI	Bristol Royal Infirmary
BTS	British Thoracic Society
CASC	Clinical Audit Support Centre
CHI	Commission for Healthcare Audit and Improvement
CIREM	Cambridge Institute for Research, Education and Management
CPD	Continuing professional development
ENT	Ear, nose and throat
GALT	Galactose-1-phosphate uridyltransferase
GP	General practitioner
HIV	Human immunodeficiency virus
HQIP	Healthcare Quality Improvement Partnership
HQQ	Healthcare Quality Quest
LINks	Local Involvement Networks
MINAP	Myocardial Infarction National Audit Project
NACR	National Audit of Cardiac Rehabilitation
NCAAG	National Clinical Audit Advisory Group
NCAPOP	National Clinical Audit and Patient Outcomes Programme
NCI	NHS Centre for Involvement
NHS	National Health Service
NICE	National Institute for Health and Clinical Excellence
NMC	Nursing and Midwifery Council
NQB	National Quality Board
OMFS	Oral and maxillo-facial surgery
PCT	Primary care trust
PDSA	Plan–Do–Study–Act
PDSN	Paediatric trained diabetes specialist nurse
PEC	Professional Executive Committee
PN	Parenteral nutrition
PPE	Patient and public engagement
PPI	Patient and public involvement

QI	Quality improvement
QIPP	Quality, Innovation, Prevention and Productivity
QIS	Quality Improvement Strategies
QOF	Quality and Outcomes Framework
RCT	Randomised controlled trial
RTP-CR	Reverse transcription polymerase chain reaction
SEA	Significant event auditing
SHOT	Serious Hazards of Transfusion
SIGN	Scottish Intercollegiate Guidelines Network
SMART	Specific, Measurable, Achievable, Relevant and Timely
SUSI	Single-use surgical instruments
TDM	Therapeutic drug monitoring

Index